"THERE ARE DRAGONS IN THE WOODS BEYOND THE POND. . . . This is not mere fancy; these are green dragons, wildflowers of the Arum family, which includes the jack-in-the-pulpit, wild calla, and arrow arum. They are untold riches, unexpected as diamonds on the ground, and I watched their development from sprout to oddly shaped leaf to even odder flower with a growing interest. These green dragons—like gryphons, like unicorns—are comparatively rare (much more so than their cousin, the jack). They're subtle, hidden from ordinary view by their choice of color; in the spring woods, flowers of camouflage green go unnoticed among drifts of bright yellow, lavender, red and pink. These other plants—the mustards, the sweet williams, the roses—spend a fortune on advertising; the solitary green hood of the dragon hides beneath the understory, waiting private and self-contained for discovery."

"Cathy Johnson shares with us the delightful story of her elegant, eloquent space in the woods."
            —Ann Zwinger, author of *The Mysterious Lands*

CATHY JOHNSON is a Missouri native and lifelong naturalist. A professional writer and accomplished artist, she is the author of several books, including *On Becoming Lost*, and a columnist for *The Artist* and *Country Living*, where her art has also been extensively published. She lives in Excelsior Springs, Missouri.

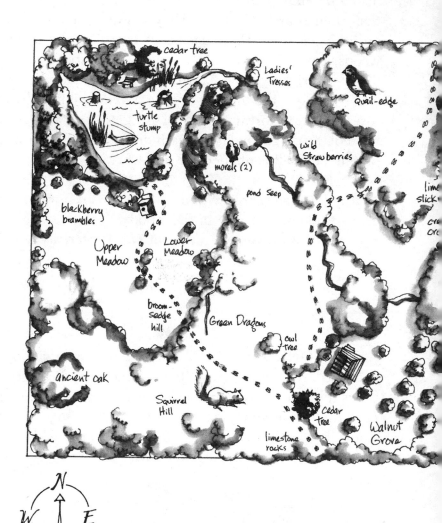

A NATURALIST'S CABIN

Constructing a Dream

Cathy Johnson

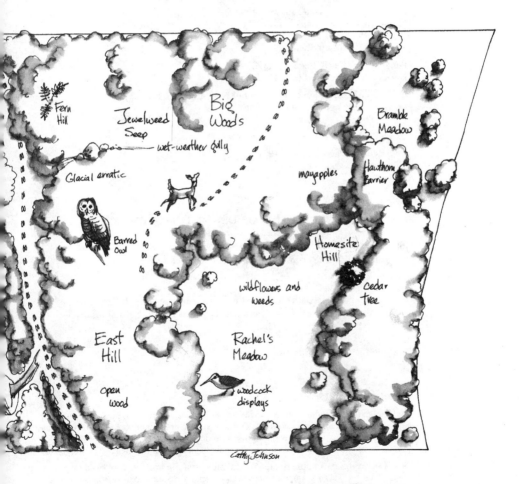

Fern Hill

Jewelweed Seep

Big Woods

Bramble Meadow

wet-weather gully

Glacial erratic

mayapples

Hawthorn Barrier

Barred Owl

Homesite Hill

wildflowers and weeds

Cedar Tree

East Hill

Rachel's Meadow

open wood

woodcock displays

Cathy Johnson

A PLUME BOOK

PLUME
Published by the Penguin Group
Penguin Books USA Inc., 375 Hudson Street,
New York, New York 10014, U.S.A.
Penguin Books Ltd, 27 Wrights Lane,
London W8 5TZ, England
Penguin Books Australia Ltd, Ringwood,
Victoria, Australia
Penguin Books Canada Ltd, 2801 John Street,
Markham, Ontario, Canada L3R 1B4
Penguin Books (N.Z.) Ltd, 182-190 Wairau Road,
Auckland 10, New Zealand

Penguin Books Ltd, Registered Offices:
Harmondsworth, Middlesex, England

First published by Plume, an imprint of New American Library,
a division of Penguin Books USA Inc.

First Printing, July, 1991
10 9 8 7 6 5 4 3 2 1

 Registered Trademark — Marca Registrada

LIBRARY OF CONGRESS CATALOGING IN PUBLICATION DATA:

Johnson, Cathy (Cathy A.)
   A naturalist's cabin : constructing a dream / Cathy Johnson.
   p.   cm.
   ISBN 0-452-26648-3
   1. Johnson, Cathy (Cathy A.) 2. Naturalists — Missouri — Biography.
3. Log cabins — Missouri — Design and construction. 4. Natural history —
Missouri. I. Title.
QA31.J68A3 1991
508'.092 — dc20
[B]   91-2215
                                                                              CIP

Printed in the United States of America

BOOKS ARE AVAILABLE AT QUANTITY DISCOUNTS WHEN USED TO PROMOTE PRODUCTS OR SERVICES.
FOR INFORMATION PLEASE WRITE TO PREMIUM MARKETING DIVISION, PENGUIN BOOKS USA INC.
375 HUDSON STREET, NEW YORK, NEW YORK 10014

For Harris, who cares

Contents

Foreword

Cathy Johnson writes, "There is an enchantment in tiny cabins all out of proportion to their sizes." Both she and I can attest to this and to the love they engender for the land, be it in Missouri or the Adirondacks. Having found and purchased 18 acres of Missouri wildland, Cathy builds a 16-by-14 "shed" in the midst of a whispering walnut grove. This golden-sided, glass-bright retreat becomes her base camp, her studio, her office, her source of endless enchantment. Her goal to sketch and observe wildlife closely and daily come through here. Her sensitive pen-and-ink sketches, which span the book, show this commitment well met.

This is a remarkably honest book, full of feeling and description. The wheel of seasons that passes under Ms. Johnson's scrutiny is as finely and fastidiously wrought as a filigree created by a silversmith.

While the charming cabin is hardly a wilderness structure or full-time residence, the author manages to make you feel you're in the outback of Montana. She shuttles between a conventional Victorian town home and helpful husband four miles away, and succumbs to the umbilical cords of electricity and phone service. Nevertheless, the land teems with wildlife and her book is filled with factual, colorful vignettes on botany, zoology, and geology.

Cathy also provides a perfectly practical how-to manual, which other would-be cabin dwellers may learn from. She explains not only the construction of her cabin but also the psychological stages she went through to reach completion. The occasional conservation message emerges with her accounting, though the reader might wish for more.

There's a good, solid cozy feel to this book that made me want to curl up by a crackling wood stove with it on a winter day. Whenever you decide to read *A Naturalist's Cabin*, it's a delight.

— ANNE LaBASTILLE

Acknowledgements

This book, like the cabin, was the result of the efforts of many people. Greg Young, our carpenter, made it happen; without him the book would have had an entirely different slant. Charlie Swafford helped me to finish the details. Rob Maples of Owen Lumber helped me find information on the lumber and processes that went into cabin building — and made sure that things arrived at the building site in good time.

Dr. Richard Gentile, professor of geology at the University of Missouri/Kansas City, was endlessly helpful, as were the men and women of the Missouri Department of Conservation and the Missouri Native Plant Society.

Pete Rucker, one of our veterinarians, answered my questions and allowed me to sketch and photograph the wildlife that finds its way to him for rehabilitation.

Gordon Hardy is as fine an editor as you'd ever want to work with, steering these pages into a better, more readable direction; and my friend and fellow writer Patti DeLano read the book for content and form, offering suggestions that inevitably found their way into the finished work.

Wendy McDougal is responsible for my finding the place at all; she can't be thanked too often for that. Brief parts of this manuscript appeared in different form in Country Living magazine; they appear with permission, and my thanks are due to my friends there.

And last but never least, my husband, Harris, supported the dream from the beginning — or shortly thereafter. He held down the fort at home, acting as coordinator and command post facilitator throughout the building process.

Introduction

There are times when an idea gets inside your brain and takes up permanent residence. Nothing will shake it, nothing long takes its place as a focal point. It was that way with building a cabin in these Missouri woods, for me. At first I wanted only the land, a place to study and wander and inhale an air not immediately expelled by other lungs. But once the idea of a cabin in the walnut grove presented itself there was no getting around it. Like one's beloved in the first flush of love, nothing else much mattered.

This idea—so sudden, so unshakeable—had been a long time building, I'll admit. I had dreamed of a tiny cabin of my own since childhood. I had inhabited dozens of them in my life, for lesser or greater periods. Not one was a negative experience but each of them a containment of a kind of mysterious possibility. There was an enchantment in these tiny houses all out of proportion to their size.

In the most serendipitous of lives, a lifelong dream becomes suddenly, inexplicably attainable. It appears like Brigadoon, where nothing was before and now, for reasons not yet quite understood, it is not only the chimera of dream but a distinct and tangible possibility. And more: it is fact.

So it was with this dream of mine, a dream I share with family and with friends and strangers—and with virtually everyone else who hears of my unexpected luck, it would seem. Who hasn't imagined a getaway, a little place of one's own—a place to live deliberately or otherwise? Thoreau did it; so did John Burroughs and Henry Beston and a dozen others I could name. Why not me? (And for that matter, why not you?) I could build it myself, with help. Regardless of gender or age, I've always felt capable of tackling anything that really needed doing, anything I wanted badly enough; that made it easier. Finances would have been a problem otherwise, but the work of my own hands was free, and everything else fell, somehow, together. And "I should not talk so much about myself," as Henry David Thoreau said in *Walden*, "if there were anybody else whom I knew so well." My feelings for the land and the cabin are my own, but I share the basic longing and a certain sense of experience, I hope, with others.

I inhabit this microcosm of landscape on a part-time basis only—my cabin is a base camp for learning, a studio, an office. I go to work and play like a child. This place, tucked far back from the road in the middle of eighteen acres, is a source of endless enlightenment; I am never bored—there is always something here among the trees.

Perhaps it would seem parochial to concentrate so fully on such a small area. Eighteen acres is, after all, only one drop in a very large bucket—a molecule, an atom. Maybe a quark. But as Ed Abbey said in speaking of the nature books of Joseph Wood Krutch, "in any careful work, the results of regional investigations have planetary significance"—and each day as I ramble here alone, I find the planetary in the particular. What I learn here is as true of this northwest quadrant of Missouri as it is of temperate-zone mixed-habitats anywhere. And if you take into account the fact that my plot of Missouri was an inland sea near the equator when all the continents were but one great supercontinent—Pangea—-the focus is less "regional" still.

The weathered limestone slopes overlain with spice-scented bergamot flowers that nonetheless fail to hide the bald spot of poor soil are like dry, rocky slopes everywhere. In the valley, deep black loam—the result of centuries of alluvial deposits and the carbon that indicates life in abundance—are like rich deposits of loam the world over. Limestone outcroppings underlie these hills like a bony infrastructure, interrupted only by millions of years of erosion by ancestral streams. They pop up again in Iowa and Oklahoma—and in the U.S.S.R. If a geologist were to inspect a limestone rock from my particular exposure of the Bethany Falls and Winterset members, they would seem little different from similar rocks from Russia—same invertebrate fossils, same pale gray or iron-tinted brown coloring, same chemical makeup—calcite is calcite, no matter where you find it. Glacial erratics season the stew as they do wherever ice sheets advanced half a million years ago; Missouri is no different from the hills of Finland.

My woods share plant life with other, similar woods of this general latitude. At the edges, where forest bows to old meadows, the same birds and mammals search for dinner—give or take a shrew or two. White-tailed deer, so common on my place, range over 90 percent of America, behaving much the same as they do here. Black-eyed Susans, or *Rudbeckia,* make my meadows a reflection of the native Americans' "month the yellow flowers bloom." Once as parochial as Catholic schoolchildren and found only in the Midwest, these peripatetic wildflowers have spread eastward. They are now listed as Maryland's state flower—not bad for an immigrant.

My place *is* microcosm. Rain falls, sun rises, night brings changing of the guard as it does the world over. The general is visible within the particular, the whole is indeed found in the sum of its parts. I see it all from the cabin's bay windows and from the game trails that wind through the woods.

PART I: DISCOVERY

Wild Garlic bed
by the pond —
smells wonderful.

1. *Finding Home*

It was the pond that stopped me. All that long, dry summer my mind was held captive by the thought of water, any water at all—moving, still, forming each dawn on the thick velvet mullein plants, falling like rare benediction from a parched and cracking sky.

Here in the Midwest, many ponds had dried to nothing. Wildfires were everywhere, set by lightning or burning trash or the careless cigarette flicked from a car window. Acres of wood and wildlands were under this dark threat. Farms and small towns in the path of wildfire scrambled to plow firebreaks or waited through the long hot night, hoping for a change in wind direction or the natural dying of the fire; there was not enough water left in many communities to fight the flames, and farm wells scraped bottom for enough for the morning coffee. A pall of smoke hung like an eclipse over the hot afternoon sun.

Livestock was desperate for water; there were fish kills all over the Midwest. The smell of death was sickeningly familiar, and water—any water at all—was the promise of life.

Here was that promise, spelled out in the calligraphy of long reflections on gentle, windblown waves, answer to a question I had not asked in years. It caught the pale rose tint of the sunset in its bowl, blushed, and returned the compliment. Life ringed it thirstily, crowding its shore—rich, green, squirming life, a soft, welcome contrast to the hot dry whisper of the weeds, the hiss-and-bang percussion of leaves falling from the trees before their time. Prints were everywhere around the pond's damp edge. Even the mud daubers left their tiny feather-stitched prints in the soft black muck; I could follow their comings and goings like a tracker and see where they rolled a ball of adobe for their minuscule constructions.

I couldn't break away from the little pond; each time I told myself it was

3

time to go, something inside argued: just a bit longer, just a little while longer. I wanted a relationship, not a flirtation; I wanted permanence. It was not so farfetched as it might have seemed, no heat-induced hallucination. My sudden longing, so intense I felt it in the back of my throat, was a definite possibility; half-hidden in the weeds I had pushed through to get here was a red-and-blue for sale sign. Not only was this small pond lovely, it was available.

I tried reason. I tried calm. I tried to be the devil's advocate, reminding myself of the years when Harris and I lived on our ramshackle farm and our discouraging and comical failures at country living. All the while, I prowled the pond's cool banks and watched the willow trail languid leaves in the water. All the while, I listened to the scolding of the red-winged blackbirds and tried to take it personally.

"Why do you need this all of a sudden? You just saw it. What's the big emergency?" Indeed—except that it fit so perfectly everything I had ever wanted, everything I had dreamed of since childhood.

There were chorus frogs at the edges of the water; map turtles and sliders bobbed like transient islands, pawing at the surface with bowlegged strokes, their carapaces smooth and polished. Deep brown clubs of cattail ringed the water; cottonwood trees made a glistening screen between pond and meadow beyond, their leaves flashing semaphores in the least breeze.

Limestone slump block and
ferns by the creek.

The devil's advocate in me was losing; the more I looked, the more I discovered, the more I lost my grip on the practical and slipped backwards into delight.

The land surrounding the pond was a naturalist's playground, with any number of habitat types—deep woods of varied age and community; old, overgrown meadows calicoed with flowers; edges attractive to deer and owl and bluebirds. Squirrels chattered in the huge oak tree by the fence, raining down acorns with each bound through the tough, resilient limbs. There was the tiny creek, the grove of slender walnut trees reaching upward as gracefully as the tall sedges beside the road, limestone bluffs and slicks. I wanted to explore it all.

The soil in the meadow beyond the pond was thin and rocky; the woods were mostly second growth, with only a few giants—and those twisted or partly rotten. I liked that. This wasn't about making a living from the land, not about *good* land at all—not in the farmer's or economist's sense. I remembered Aldo Leopold's definition of this fine point:

> There is much confusion between land and country. Land is the place where corn, gullies and mortgages grow. Country is the personality of the land, the collective harmony of its soil, life and weather. Country knows no mortgages, no alphabetical agencies, no tobacco road; it is calmly aloof to these petty exigencies of its alleged owners....Poor land may be rich country, and vice versa. Only economists mistake physical opulence for riches. Country may be rich despite a conspicuous poverty of physical endowment, and its quality may not be apparent at first glance, nor at all times.

This was country. I saw the beauty and the poverty at once and was enchanted. No wonder the real estate agent's sign leaned crazily, caked with the dust of months of neglect; those looking for land had seen only its shortcomings.

I had expected this land—this country—to be like the rest of the plots along the road, two or five or seven acres, small but private, easily bought, almost as easily paid for. But when I investigated, I found it was nearly eighteen acres, running from the pond at the western boundary to the next road over. It was big. Not by wilderness standards, of course, not even by most rural standards, but held up and measured against my idea of possibility, it was big—really big.

Still, the timing could not have been better, no matter what its size. After years of living off advances from free-lance work, dancing one step ahead of financial disaster, at last I was due my first decent royalty check—not huge, but enough.

Now all that was necessary was to convince Harris; no easy task.

Of course, I could have dug in my heels, called up all the Missouri stubbornness at my command, and gone ahead. I had earned the money, worked for over two years to get it; it was mine to do with as I saw fit. But that's not the way I needed to buy this land. It was a place of peace; to begin a lifetime of exploration in contention and confrontation seemed all wrong. After over twenty years of marriage, I wanted consensus. I wanted him to want the place, too. I wanted him to love it.

"We did that already, remember?" he asked with a trace of panic in his voice.

"I know—but this is different." I sounded like a child. I felt like one, too. From the first moment I spied the place, I wanted to cry, "Mine! Mine!"

I could understand his apprehension. In the sixties, infused with equal parts idealism, disillusionment, and naïveté, we bought twenty acres with a tiny, ancient house and barns. We fed chickens, milked goats, buried our mistakes. We tilled the soil, lived with an outhouse, heated with wood. We contended with icy gravel roads, blow-downs, and cold so deep that the cats' water froze on the kitchen floor. We barely survived droughts and tornados and blizzards.

The land chewed us up—along with our idealistic dreams—and spit us out, spent and beaten. It took seven years (somewhat longer, I imagine, than the old-timers around us had booked on), but at last we gave it up. The bad finally buried the good, and we ran to a safe, warm little Victorian at the edge of town, a house where the snowplow clanks by in the small hours like a friendly armored tank, the water never freezes in the pipes, and the garden is the size of a handkerchief.

The idea of buying land in the country again scared the socks off my husband.

There was something seriously missing in my life, though; some part of me had been bound too tightly with the tourniquet of civilization, and it threatened to atrophy. I loved my home and the comfort it afforded but couldn't wait to get out of it—away, anywhere. I felt hemmed in, constrained, as though my flesh were rubbed raw by forced contact. There was not air enough to breathe. Simply for the peace the night hours afforded, I took to a good case of insomnia. It was wonderful—except that exhaustion is the coin you pay for this sort of privacy.

My unrest was exacerbated by my husband's early retirement. Ironically, the very thing that freed us from that long, crowded commute also brought its share of changes. Harris is the most loving of men and a constant delight —but he was also a constant. His retirement was an adjustment for us both. When I needed silence to write, that's just when something would come up to require conversation. When we took walks together, we talked; there was no chance to observe or absorb; taking time to stop and sketch felt suddenly inconsiderate.

I needed this land and the peace it promised. I intended to have it. But —I wanted him to want it, too. We had always talked about finding "a place," a bit of country to walk in without need for the kind of hearty, shallow conviviality of the busy public park. A shack would do; a hole in the ground would do. I had dreamed of a tiny place in the woods for as long as I could remember. I'd even tried to buy a place in the Ozarks when I was seventeen (couldn't be done by an unemployed minor, no matter how little per acre the land was then).

It was on the road to my friend Wendy's that I first spied the pond and its red-and-blue for sale sign.

I could hardly wait to show Harris. He hadn't seen the place; my descriptions had been intriguing, a whiff of something more—and disquieting. He remembered last time.

And now, this morning, the dew hung heavy in the meadow grass, soaking us to the knees. It was early, in that rare coolness before August clamps the lid back down on the steam cooker—the only time it is bearable to move. Deptford pinks bloomed on their dried, brown stems, each a single, hot pink flower etched with a delicate dotted pattern near its lighter center. The dry remains of earlier flowers, skeletons of that endless summer, stood eighteen inches tall, but close to the ground each plant had sent out a final bright, brave flag; somewhere, the flowers had found moisture enough for that gallant declaration.

Wood Sage
Teucrium
canadense

An old tractor road led back into the woods, its edges gold with broom sedge. That deserted path and the pond were the only discernible signs of humanity. It was different land from our farm—there were trees, ridges and waves and ranks of them. The hills beyond the road were a tangle of oak and walnut, ash and hedge and hickory. Dark cedars punctuated the edge of the forest. Willows and sycamores lined the seasonal creek, a tiny, rocky, fall-and-spring stream, dry now and deserted.

The tractor road made a Y at the creek, the left branch crossing limestone slickrock domes beside the rocky streambed and fading back into the woods. The right branch widened into a walnut grove, tall and blued with humidity. Beneath the slender trees the ground was blanketed with the crayon-box yellow of brown-eyed Susans on their multiple stems. The edges of the grove were dotted with the cool hues of tall bellflower and wood sage; the effect was magic.

There was a deer in the grove, regarding us calmly across the expanse of flower; I felt an intake of breath (his, mine) and the deer bounded away—but only a few feet. He stopped again to gaze at us across the sable eyes of the flowers, then snorted loudly and sprang away through the brush, tail exploding white against the dimness.

It was the deer that got to Harris. The deer, and the silent blue grove, and the tall, reaching walnut trees moving gently, imperceptibly against the

wind. We agreed to $14,000 for the land; the asking price was $18,000. I had wanted to offer more, in a panic that we would lose out, but Harris had reservations about practicality and possibility. Now he wanted the place too, almost as badly as I did, but he was anxious; he wanted to be able to keep it.

I was sure they would turn us down. We talked and discussed and argued and dreamed and discussed some more, trying to think of all the possibilities, trying to reach agreement that would satisfy both our anxieties—his that we might not be able to keep it, mine that we would lose it before it was ever ours. But in the end we agreed. As a concession to my anxiety, we agreed to go up another thousand if it was rejected, but it was a thousand that would seriously strain our ability to pay.

The offer was accepted; it stood, as it was. With my royalty, I could pay an amazing $10,000 down; we would afford the payments on the balance—somehow.

The land was ours, by gentleman's agreement, but another week went by before we were able to legally close, a week of red tape and frustrations. We were in an agony of impatience; what could be taking so long? Had they changed their minds? But at last everything was in order, the lengthy litany of paperwork signed and notarized, agreements finalized, checks written. After fits and starts and obstructions, we closed at last. Our friends were amazed at our rapid transformation to landowners; we couldn't imagine how it took so long.

We drove to the county seat to stake our paper claim and learned we could buy an aerial photo with a map overlaid to tell us what it was we had; I pored over it in the evenings, trying to make sense of boundaries and property lines. The land was in three separate pieces, bought by the previous owner with a bad case of own-it-as-far-as-the-eye-can-see. As each bit became available—or affordable—he snapped it up, from the lovely little pond on the west to the single lot in the mobile-home enclave to the east.

The surveyor, I'm told, had had a bit of a problem with the bottle; hence the interesting legal description that seemed to tell me we had a dogleg in our southern border. The fence was old and fallen here or there—I took the boundary on faith. Did it matter that there were five feet more in one spot than another?

This land snugs up to 300 acres I have known for twenty years; we passed its long meadows and wooded hills each time we drove to town from our farm. Snaking back into the acreage is the little limestone creek that passes through the short dimension of our new property, here hidden in deep woods and rimmed with limestone bluffs that wear ornate coats of moss and walking fern. The local kids told of caves back in this reach of wildness; I never found them, but I did find my own Brigadoon.

We discovered a big limestone waterfall the first week. It was lovely, hidden away on these adjacent acres, dwarfing the tiny, eighteen-inch drop on my own place. Like everything else in this part of Missouri, it was dry. No water had flowed there in months. But I could see that it had and would again; it was water that formed the rocky precipice, wearing away the soft stone, undermining it until it dropped away, undercut, and the edge of the falls retreated uphill through the thick bed of stone. There was an unusual coolness in the heat of the drought; it was quiet, protected from the wind overhead by the bristle of trees and the twin walls of stone. Wendy and I walked here and then, through a circuitous route, back to my place—we knew we were home by the golden glow of black-eyed Susans in the walnut grove across the creek.

But the next time I tried to find the falls—alone, now, and wandering down the creek—it had disappeared. Every side creek that veered off to the right yielded nothing. It simply wasn't there.

I told Wendy I had lost it, jokingly calling the place Brigadoon, that storied place that appears only once every hundred years, but she told me how to find my way. It wasn't lost, just hidden, screened by a slight rise and a thick barrier of head-high pokeweed; there was no rocky inlet from there to the creek to lead me to it. The name has stuck, and we visit the rocky, hidden beauty of Brigadoon whenever the weeds are not head high and daunting.

And now it was Sunday and I was alone with the dry creek, the voiceless waterfall, the whisper of drying leaves in the walnut grove. I couldn't help but wonder what I did to deserve the conversation of cicadas and this deep-throated rustling in the trees, but I knew the answer already: not a thing. It was pure gift.

There were signs of other human life within our new borders, subtle ones of use and transient occupancy. I found a square nail on the slickrocks by the creek. The Boy Scouts had left a latrine hole in the woods by the walnut grove; their trash midden surfaced as the old boards that covered it rotted away, and I carried out rusting tin cans and soda bottles. In the woods, there was another, odder midden, far from any use I could discern; a cache of baby-food jars and one tiny, white beaded moccasin—a baby's souvenir of the West. How these came to be here, away from any house or road, I couldn't imagine, but the moccasin is on my desk to remind me that this is not entirely wilderness.

There are cut stumps in the woods; my neighbors told me that someone pulled into the grove to steal walnut trees—worth good money in this area —but were caught and prosecuted before they could do much damage.

There are older tales, as well. Somewhere back beyond our place are the remains of a log cabin, a moonshiner's still, and a camp. I have yet to find the fallen remains, but Wendy says they are there. During Prohibition, many of these secluded hollows had their moonshine stills, and this was certainly backwoods sixty years ago. Our road didn't exist, nor did the one to the trailer enclave on the hill. The old state highway was narrow and unpaved; the track to this little money-making operation must have been hidden indeed. I wish my father were still alive; I'd ask him if he knew it.

During the Great Depression, many people did whatever they had to, to keep their families fed. My father took a variety of measures, from picking up the fallen wheat grains between the floorboards of railroad cars and hunting rabbits with a stick (there was no money for bullets), to hauling bootleg "likker" in the trunk of his car. They survived, my older sister tells me, but barely. Perhaps he knew this place, visiting it in the dark on his rounds, and I wondered if there were a family history in common with the place I had chosen. I felt at home here and imagined I could smell the bootlegger's fire in the woods on moonlit nights and the sharp tang of grain alcohol.

2. *The Pond*

There was a flash of white that caught my eye, anomalous in the lush *millifiore* mosaic of autumn colors. It caught my eye like a white flag of surrender. A big white bird sat half obscured by the tall grass beside the pond, still, on guard, the head on that long neck outstretched, checking out who these intruders might be.

We were just coming home from a business trip to southern Missouri, and after five days away I had a powerful thirst to see my new land; it was my birthday, and no matter how far I had driven, this visit was my gift to myself. The bird was a delightful surprise that might have been tied up in ribbons and delivered with a card for all the pleasure it brought.

It was a domestic goose, like the cantankerous old honker we had on the farm; distrustful, awkward as a tank on the land as it bustled off complaining, but the absolute of grace once launched on the water. It made almost no wake; a pencil line traced its trajectory, arrowing after it.

Bruce, our farm goose, was almost pure pet, following me to pick berries and thrusting his serpentine neck under my arm in an avian embrace. He waddled after me, his honking a piercing bid for attention. He coexisted most happily with our goats; they were as crusty as he, and their personalities complemented rather than clashed. When I'd go to milk the nannies, my cockeyed livestock ganged up on me, dancing around me on hind legs, threatening to butt, coming down a full foot from my knees as though to see if I would flinch, while Bruce ran in and out of the melee, honking wildly. And when I took the ladies off to be bred, Bruce missed them like the friends they were.

This new goose was no pet; it must have grown up in a crowd. It feared me, hissing rancor as it sidled away to the water, launching itself beyond my reach. I could see the big orange toes spread to catch maximum thrust at

13

each stroke, pushing itself through the water like a disgruntled paddle wheeler; it moved with a speed that seemed impossible for its size.

I might only have gone every few days or so, thinking myself too busy to be so self-indulgent, and missing the day-to-day changes that this place supplies in plenty. But the visitor needed to be fed, and regularly. I left out yellow heaps of cracked corn; unless I replenished them daily, they were gone before I returned. When it rained, the corn became sodden, and if not quickly replaced with fresh, it molded. I came the four miles each day to see that the goose was well supplied, that he was all right, that he was here. It was a delightful duty, the perfect reason to escape; I reveled in each day on the new property, wondering again what I did to deserve it.

Still, I worried; what would happen when winter locked the goose's escape route in ice? The dogs and coyotes and foxes that left their prints in the soft mud were not benign, as I was, but deadly dangerous. They'd corner him and leave nothing but his white down floating on the pond like the remains of a burst feather pillow. I worried about his welfare in the coming cold; would it be possible to capture him somehow, take him to someone who has facilities to care for these big birds? My concern grew for this cranky domestic bird in this fenceless, unprotected place. He had become, of his own, a feature of the place; I looked for him first, each time I pulled up on the road above the pond.

But as mysteriously as the goose appeared, he vanished, three months to the day after his advent. There was no sign of struggle, no blood, no pile of feathers to mark his demise. He was just gone, as if he remembered one day where he belonged and walked home. Perhaps his real owners—his original owners—spotted him there on our pond and returned for him.

I drew him the afternoon before he disappeared, on a clear, chill New Year's Day. The colors were rich, fully saturated as though with strong, transparent dyes: the high, clear sky, nearly turquoise overhead; the maroon and gray and blue of damp limbs and last autumn's sumac beyond the dam; a tawny fringe of broom sedge. The pond reflected it all, deepening the colors to a stained-glass richness. The paper-white of that big goose stood out as though willing himself the focal point of my drawing.

Sketching was pure pleasure in the transient warmth of a January thaw. Sitting protected in the lee of the wind, I could have been no more comfortable at home in my chair. The goose posed quietly in the tall, dry grasses beside the pond, the first time we had simply sat in proximity to one another.

I missed him when he was gone. I walked the meadow beyond the pond to find a clue to his fate. I wound my way through the upright bars of little saplings and bramble canes at the edge of the woods, watching for a sign of white feathers and finding instead a sense of place. His being there had tied me more closely to the land; his going reinforced the tie as the search led me, nose down and wandering, to discover places I didn't know existed, things I didn't know I owned.

Our pond is an artificial thing. Most are, unless carved out by a departing glacier. Maybe a lake will appear when moving water slowly dissolves away a bowl for itself in the limestone bedrock and a sinkhole develops, filling drop by rivulet with rain. A river abandons a section of its ancestral bed, leaving behind an oxbow and a new biosystem. Beavers make their own habitat, damming streams to create lakes and ponds. But here in the Midwest, most bodies of water are man-made, for our pleasure or need—as water for our stock, a place to fish, convenient in time of fire or drought. That was the case with our small pond.

Nature can't abide our add-ons, not without making them over in her own image. What begins as raw and empty is soon seeded by the wind, and aquatic plants appear as though for an intentional water garden. The ponds are stocked by birds if no one else volunteers for the job, transporting fish or their sticky, gelatinous eggs from points unknown; the new fish airlifted in on a bird's legs or inadvertently dropped in flight from a butterfingered bill will feed future avian generations. Frogs and salamanders, dragonflies and mosquitoes find this new biosystem and make themselves a home.

Moisture-tolerant plants seed these ponds; their exotic shapes thrive in the transitional zone that is neither adamantly land nor water but which trades territory back and forth with equanimity as the water level rises and lowers. What plants you find depends on which zone you are looking at—in the water itself, half in and half out, or nearby. Among the plants that like the wading zone are arrowhead—"duck potatoes," or *Sagittaria latifolia*—and the cattail plant, aquatic supermarket of the wetland, providing food for wildlife and for us. The clublike cattail, *Typha latifolia,* bears both male and female parts, the narrow golden spike of male flowers crowning the dark, smooth cigar shape. Sedges and bur reed and pickerelweed stand wet-footed beside them, adapting to changing water levels through eons of evolution. Flecks of duckweed resemble bits of green-dyed grain floating on the veneer of water; bladderwort, quillwort, and water celery flourish just beneath the surface, dying off if the level drops too low.

The food chain holds, all the way down to the pea green algae that rises in the water twice a year as the pond turns over. Eutrophic seasonal oxygen deficiency provides a graphic show-and-tell to just how prolific this simple plant form is. Long green peninsulas and islands of algae reach nearly to midpond, pushed far beyond its normal limits.

Spring to fall, the red-wing blackbirds on our pond leave off their musical "ok-a-leees" to scold me, swooping low over my head and displaying their impressive red-and-gold epaulets when I crowd the invisible territorial lines they've drawn to surround the nests, moats I cannot see; I sense them instead by the agitation of the birds. At any season the nests—occupied or long deserted—hang like hammocks in the cattail leaves.

An eastern red cedar, dense as night, screens the upper arm of the pond from the road, and when I sit beside it no passing car would know I was there. The smell of juniper is strong on the air, an incense that takes me back to the pleasant closeness of my grandmother's cedar closet. Willows grow beside the dam, and on it, and behind it; in the early spring, tender twigs blush with gold. Sometime after the pond was built, the cottonwoods accepted the general invitation; they like moisture. Across the dam, a stand of them glitters in the sun as the polished surfaces of their leaves catch and reflect the light. When the water is high they stand up to their ankles without complaint.

Burr and red and white oaks crowd the water's edge, and I listen to the scutter and plop of half-formed acorns falling from the big oaks that remain from the time when this was woods, not shoreline; the squirrels mine these trees like forty-niners. The pond that mirrors them looks as though it has been there always, a part of the landscape, a fully functioning biosphere.

In fact, this small pond began as a rock and clay hole scraped into the wounded, resistant earth, unmistakably unnatural. The dam was painted in broad strokes with the sienna color of iron-rich clay; excess dirt was skinned

clear across the meadow beyond and piled at the edge of the woods; like all new ponds, the bare earth of pond hole and dam looked as though it had been raped and left for dead. It was an eyesore.

It didn't stay that way. Within months, ringed in vegetation and singing with life, it winked in conspiracy with the sky, the source of all its comeliness.

How the rough little hole ever held water is beyond me, dug as it was from these angular slivers of weathered rock. If I had asked the water district to evaluate the place for a possible homesite—with attendant rural septic tank and leach field—they'd have turned me down flat. There would be sewage everywhere. This stuff is not good for the slow percolation of wastewater; it runs right through. But beneath these leaky plates is good Missouri clay; we found the fine-grained, gummy stuff when we banged our way through the pebbles and small rocks to sink a post—not such a bad dam-building material. The pond holds its water in all seasons, even through the drought. Perhaps the natural processes of eutrophication and decay kicked in to epoxy shut what leaks remained. At any rate, now the water stays where it belongs—for the most part.

It was essential during the long drought, for there was no water within a half mile. The creek bed was dry and the Missouri River was too far away for the heat-stressed wildlife to get to, no matter how thirsty they may have been, not unless they could pick up and fly there. Even in its shrunken form, its water level far below the high-water mark sketched by the varying strata of grasses and aquatic plants, the pond was a magnet for the birds and animals that populate my eighteen acres. Their tracks were everywhere. Skunk and raccoon and squirrel, badger and woodchuck, waterfowl and songbird, all left their graffiti in the soft mud or marked the weedy bank with their urine. The messages they left one another piqued the interest of the neighbor's dogs, which snooped amongst the mingled odors like the busybodies they are.

A watery magnet is useful; it attracts things you might not otherwise see. A glossy, red-brown doe, drawn to the coolness of the pond in the midday heat, stood submersed to her knees; I watched in silence, scarcely breathing until she had drunk her fill. She eyed me warily across the narrow expanse of water, then with an ancient dignity retreated up the bank, never bothering to flash her white tail at me at all.

The pond changed color like moiré silk in the strong March winds. Normally a mirror image wearing the darkening blue of the sky, now it was mossy green shot with light and sky color. Lighter green algae thickened the water near the shore, adding a monochromatic color note; at this season of the year, the stuff seemed dense as floating peat, scummy and bubbling. In a month or two it would sink without a trace—until the water cleared enough to see it lurking there just beneath the surface. It always came back, rising from the depths like something from a gothic horror novel; even the grass carp someone stocked here long ago to eat these pond weeds can't make significant inroads against the burgeoning algae.

In the protected upper area of the little pond, the water was nearly still. Long, elegant reflections of the still-bare trees were drawn in angular, art nouveau scribbles. Frogs made a series of full-bodied splashes as I walked the pond's edge, betraying their position; a frightened "eep!" as they went for deep water was their only conversation. They turned and came to rest facing me, imagining themselves invisible.

Something cut the water deep below the surface, too deep to see anything but the emphatic arrow of its wake. It must have been one of the huge carp. These long directional signals offered the hope of spotting the old lunkers, but they stayed too deep. Only the little bluegills and crappie visited the surface as though out of youthful curiosity. These enthusiastic breeders have taken up all the room in the pond; successive inbred generations are smaller and smaller. To remedy the situation, the Missouri Department of Conservation suggested we fish them all out—a statistical impossibility given the limitations of time and willingness (what do you do with a thousand or so tiny, tiny bluegills?)—or drain the pond and start over. A friend proposed I accomplish the same end by poisoning everything, then restocking. That's not likely. I liked the mixed community of fish and frogs and turtles that I found; we leave the bluegills to their breeding and do the best we can.

The pond is none too useful for providing meat for the table. The little sunfish are tasty but hard to clean at well under three inches long. I've lost my fishing edge, at any rate; nearly four years have passed without my line ever getting wet. "It doesn't hurt them," my father always said as I watched a fish writhe and flop on the bank. "They're cold-blooded." It was the fight my dad enjoyed; you can't miss the fact that you've connected with something live, and wild, and determined. That thing has a mind to be *out* of here. But a kind of terminal softheartedness seems to have set in. I buy my fish in the market and let others make their temporary inroads on the bluegill hordes.

There seems always to be that point at which you've had enough; I became wary about strangers at the pond. One weekend I found a pickup-load of teenagers fishing from the dam, ensconced in lawn chairs, drinking and making out. I didn't know them; I didn't like the casual, proprietary mood they had established—a party on my land to which I was not invited. I stared hard at them as I drove by, then turned around in the next driveway to give them another look.

I should have stopped, gotten out, asked their names, and told them I didn't allow strangers to fish here. I should have taken down their license number. I should have done about anything but just drive by and scowl, because the next day as I again walked the woods behind the dam I found the clear evidence of their disregard. There were Styrofoam containers, bait cans, chewing tobacco cans, and enough empty beer cans to render the driver incapable of handling that fancy pickup truck. And much of this litter was thrown off behind the dam into the brambles and wild rose bushes—it wasn't enough to just throw it on the shore or in a ring around their picnic area; it had to be inaccessible among the thorns.

If I had my way, I'd make them clean up their mess, instead of pushing my way through the brambles to do it for them. I'd like to see them hip deep in mud and up to their eyeballs in stickers and ticks. I'd love to watch them poking through the stinging nettles, picking up the evidence of trespass. Community service was in order.

Our local feed store has Fish Day twice a year, spring and fall. You can order anything you like—grass carp for pond maintenance, channel cat, crappie, bass for the table, and elegant hybrid male bluegills that grow up to ten inches long without ever interbreeding with the locals. The thought of ten-inch bluegill jump-started my fishing fever; tempura-battered fillets called my name. So I ordered fish and planned to pamper them like the well-bred creatures they were.

Fish Day dawned with a curdy gray sky; the night before it poured rain, and it would have helped to have gills myself. Harris and I drove to the pond through a renewed drizzle and slogged down to the water's edge, bearing buckets and plastic foam coolers to fill with the water to transport our mixed bag of imports.

"How much do they need?" Harris asked. "We're not going all that far."

Getting from here to there with brimming water containers seemed like a feat in itself, and the fish would be small; we opted for half-full and fastened the lids down as well as we were able with bungee cords and rope. Even with our gum boots and slickers we were wet in less than five minutes.

There was a line at the hatchery's tanks; the rain had let up and the sky was reduced to an occasional drip. I queued up for my fish, listening to the banter of the farmers and pond owners. I had put in for fifty hybrid bluegills, ten channel cat, and three new grass carp—a paltry order, but when I remembered the strangers that fish my pond I wondered why I was spending the money at all.

It was a small enough order in comparison to these others. Near the front of the line, a man wearing bib overalls and a plaid shirt announced—somewhat sheepishly—that he had ordered 400. I watched them counting the little fish out, one by one; that lumpy gray sky looked ready to open up again at any time—and it did. By the time I got my little order of fish loaded precariously back in the car—the cooler full of bluegills in the back, the two buckets of channel cat and grass carp under Harris's feet in the front—it began to rain in earnest. We broke the top of the cheap cooler putting down the lid of the trunk, and I drove slowly, deliberately, hoping not to find the hold full of squirming, two-inch fish by the time we made the four miles back to our pond.

At last, we topped the last hill and parked; Harris carried the broken cooler and waded out into the water to free the little captives, wishing them well; I toted the bucket of catfish down the slick, weedy bank. By the time we walked back up the hill to the car for the carp, I could hear the flopping of fish; one had pushed the lid off the bucket and was throwing itself disconsolately about on the floor of the car.

There was no harm done. Our car is old, sans plush carpets or class. The carp, none the worse for the adventure, followed the others, disappearing without a trace.

Hatchery fish know what to do, once they hit new territory; growing and eating, mating and nesting and egg laying are up to them; the hybrids have nothing to do but eat and grow fat—not such a bad life. I trust to what I can't see there beneath the cloudy surface of the pond. The residents seem to manage just fine; why think less of these store-bought creatures?

I researched the common Missouri pond fish along with my new purchases, just to get an idea of what's going on beneath that opaque surface; I want to know what's what. And sure enough, just inches under the water there is a world of invisible activity.

Only the male channel catfish fashions the nest, choosing a natural cavity protected by piles of brush or logs. These sought-after creatures are as opportunistic as many mammals; they'll take over ready-made digs, nesting in the underwater dens of muskrats and beavers; and doing only a bit of redecorating to prepare the site for the young: semidarkness and seclusion are prime requirements. I read that this bewhiskered fish may attain fifty pounds and eyed my pond with some expectancy.

Catfish are mostly night active, searching for prey by sense of smell—or by feeling along with the fleshy, whiskerlike barbels that give them their name. I watch for them in the last light of evening, but the bottom feeders keep their own council.

Sunfish build homes for their young, spawning in the late spring or early summer in nests violently swept from the muck with tail fins of the male sunnies; a Spanish dancer could fan with no more emphasis. These deep-bodied fish vigorously protect their nests from predators, the male fish especially on guard to keep eggs from harm. In a few particularly paternal species of sunnies, Dad even sticks around to protect the fry.

The water near the shore churned in the unmistakable action that meant nesting. Fish were busy making more fish; it would be crazy to let every trash-strewing kid with a pole in to pull them out. Maybe I'll get out the rod and reel, after all, to see what hides beneath the water; I look ahead to progeny, generations of fish to come.

That might have been the end of it, except for the rain. Usually there's no way of knowing what has become of your charges once you've stocked a pond; they lead secret lives in alien environs, hidden by opaque reflections on the water. They might as well live on Mars and breathe a different atmosphere altogether, for all we see of them.

But the rain didn't quit. It was as though it made up for the drought all in one week. The pond was a giant rain gauge, marked in gallons and feet instead of inches. The creek down the hill, suddenly audible from the pond, was a muffled roar that made me just slightly uneasy. The tiny drainage ditch that passes through suburban backyards up the road — normally carrying scarcely more than the gutters on the houses — escaped its banks and inundated half the road; the runoff from the next hill flowed under the culvert just by our pond and filled it like a bathtub. The spillway was river-full, its clamor counterpoint to the creek's angry voice. I surveyed our dam with some alarm as the water continued to rise against it; I didn't want to lose the pond. It had failed twice in the past — and I'm not surprised. The dam is a ten-foot-wide corridor of earth meant — with luck — to hold against the pressure of tons of relentless, building water.

As I drove up, I was relieved to see the sparkle of light on water through the screen of trees; my imagination had been on fast-forward, and I had wondered about the abandoned muskrat's hole near the top of the dam — if it went all the way through and if it would act to relieve the pressure or as breach. There is a seep at the bottom of the dam that oozes water in all but the driest weather; I imagined that wall of earth some fifteen feet above the seep and wondered if there were a nearby Dutch boy willing to put his finger in this backwoods dike.

The runoff from the spillway coursed along the old tractor road and spread out across the floor of the grove on its way to the creek. The tiny path

Bluegill young
washed out of the
pond by high water.

that leads from the grove down to the water's edge was a miniature creek that ran as briskly as a small river.

The dam held. The spillway's waters slowed and cleared until it was more like a sparkling Ozark spring coursing through the woods than a muddy flood. And in one of the pools on the old tractor road, 500 feet from the pond, I found a hybrid bluegill swimming as unconcernedly as though this shallow puddle were its natural habitat.

Damn. Why did we free them so close to the spillway? If we had carried them to the opposite side of the pond, they might have found a safer home, away from the relentless suction of the spillway's drain. Tracing the stream uphill, bucket in hand to recapture as many of the little fish as I could, I puzzled to see that the one that swam in the shallow pool in the drive was the only one to have survived its adventure. The woods were full of dead fish. At each logjam or natural dam in the little stream, there were rafts of them, shining silver in the weak gray light. Hybrids, natives, bluegills, crappie, bass; there were hundreds of them, far more than the fifty little hybrids we stocked, all under two inches long. Had only the little fish suffered in the deluge? The catfish and carp were not among the casualties, and thinning the pond's population had been accomplished courtesy of Mother Nature. Raccoons found the bounty, and the corpses disappeared in less than three days.

I took it philosophically enough. I might never have seen them again anyway; who's to say I'd ever actually drop a line in that murky water?

But before I took my leave of the creek and headed back up the hill to the pond, I paid my respects to the big pool by the limestone slump block. The water was still murky with equal parts rich brown topsoil and gravel dust from the road to the north, but I could see something moving there. It was dark brown and moved slowly up and down like a sawyer, a log imbedded in a riverbed that bobs beneath the surface, moving with the current. On closer inspection, I could see a second line of brown and discern a graceful lateral movement; the first brown object was the tail of a huge fish, the second the line of fins along its back.

This thing was immense. The pool is only ten or twelve feet long; the fish seemed to take up a quarter of that length, a freshwater Moby Dick. Could it have run the same rushing gamut the little bluegill did, washing from the pond down the long spillway through the woods, banging into rocks and logs on its way to the creek? I ran to a phone to call Harris; was my father's old fish net still in the closet? It was; I drove in to pick up my husband and the net and we returned to the pool, up to our knees in gum boots.

The creature was still there, slowly plying the water with its tail. I could see the light body in the clearing water now and waded into the stream behind it, making as little disturbance as possible. The water was still swift, and the big fish faced into the current; I moved as slowly as a heron and slid the net carefully over that big snout.

The fish felt the tickle of the net and arced away, circumventing my boots to outmaneuver me downstream, but the water at the far end of the pool was quick and rocky—there wasn't enough draft for that stocky belly. I tried again and again, muddying the pool with each lunge, but at last the net slid over the big fish's head; I turned the handle to fold the webbing over the body and raised it up in a single motion.

It was a huge carp. Sure enough, there must have been a giant in our pond; it bore the marks of rough passage down the spillway and through the woods. The head and sides were raw and abraded. The fish stared at me with its round moonstone eye, resigned, trapped.

Harris helped me carry it up the woods path to the pond; it must have weighed twenty or twenty-five pounds, and its shifting bulk was awkward. The fish net was made for a much smaller creature; this carp was nearly a yard long, deep bellied, and strong.

The net couldn't hold it. I had forgotten how old its knotted strings must be; my father had been gone over fifteen years, and I don't know how long before that he last used the trout net. The string was rotten, and as we moved quickly uphill I felt a sickening rip, then another. Before we could stop it, the big fish had fallen through and flopped there on the duff. "A fish out of water" took on personal meaning; the fish looked the graphic illustration of helplessness.

"Damn! Now what do we do?"

We were too far along to abandon the effort now, and too far from *anything* to find a sounder receptacle, at least one large enough for this lunker; fish can live longer out of water than I can imagine, but this one was badly stressed.

We were only a couple of hundred feet from the pond; I picked the carp up in my arms like a baby and made the run, moving as quickly as possible with a slick, wet twenty-five-pound fish. That round eye still stared balefully up at me and the huge, inch-long scales felt odd against my bare arms, but at last I clambered over the dam and waded into the water with my burden. I expected more fight, more resistance, but the big creature was quiescent, almost trusting. I lowered the fish into the water and held it there a moment, allowing it time to recover from the shock. It didn't move, for what seemed an endless time. But at last it waved an emphatic farewell with its tail and cast off into deep water, leaving a familiar arrowed wake to mark its passage.

And a week or two later, as the pond cleared to a crystal window, the carp was suddenly visible, swaying through the shallows, dining on algae, trailed by three or four much smaller fish — its young? The small carp we had stocked? I couldn't suppress a grin to see it there, obviously alive, obviously healthy, obviously at home.

A thin film of water has formed over the ice on the pond. The alternate freezing and thawing has scripted a time-lapse series of changing surfaces, from inviolate ice to unbroken snow to a maze of tangled tracks. The ice that showed through each footprint was darker in color than its blanket of snow, and that small difference was enough to catch and hold a minuscule warmth, like a tiny, frigid solar collector. When the snow finally melted, this warmth turned out to have been enough to leave behind it incontrovertible evidence of its presence, though the frozen veneer felt as cold as ever to my touch; the surface was pocked with icy depressions drilled into the frozen pond. This new melt, affecting ice as well as snow cover, had produced an odd effect, as though the pond's water was itself marked with tracks; the icy ridges at the surface of the film of water were just tall enough to leave phantom prints, as if someone had indeed walked on water and left the evidence for a bemused tracker to find.

For the most part, the winter pond is all but deserted. The turtles pocket themselves in the mud to sleep till warmer weather revives them. The frogs are silent, as though the blood in their veins turned to ice. The birds that normally seek out this source of water and the rich veldt of insects that frequent the airways at the water's edge have disappeared, heading south for the winter or finding open water in the moving creek. Only the tracks that mark its frozen surface tell me that anything moves here at all, but they are enough. They remind me that life will return.

And return it does. The fish are the first — though they haven't gone anywhere. They've only waited in a half torpor at the bottom of the pond for a break in the ice. At the first sign of open water, their wakes mark the surface in a cryptic script that reads "fish." The turtles are not far behind. When the mud reaches wake-up call temperature, they shoulder their way to the surface and raft on the water, ducking surreptitiously when I come too close. On warm winter days they pile onto the flat surface of an old stump, sunning themselves. As the weather warms they will stake a permanent claim on this stump and the two others that appear as the water level drops.

Sliders aren't choosy about their homesites, as long as they have mud and aquatic vegetation in abundance—just so their basic needs are met, the water is fine. When the sliders are in residence on the big stump, it's lying room only; there's more turtle than stump. If I am careful to slip up behind the screen of cattails, I may catch them basking, piled one on another like a casual stack of tea plates, taking siestas that last from midmorning till late afternoon.

Last year, a huge snapper stopped dead center in the old tractor road and would not move for any amount of prodding—until we devised a bait-and-switch con game to tempt the irritable beast to lunge at one of us while the other nudged her off the road from behind. I offered the snapper the end of a stick in lieu of my hand, and each time she made for it she moved a bit farther off the road. With each lunge, our friend Greg prodded her in encouragement. When she grabbed my stick in earnest, I was able to pull her gently off the road and we hurried by with a respectful nod in her direction. (And it was a she. In egg-laying season these primarily aquatic creatures abandon lakes and ponds, traveling overland, looking for mates and soft, deep soil in which to lay their eggs.)

Someone had killed one of the pond's big snapping turtles before we bought the property. In my rambles I found the evidence; a few stubby, powerful turtle bones and the remains of the broad skull, the maw of that formidable mouth still impressive in death. Arrayed in a perfect pattern were what was left of the chitinous outer covering of the carapace, thin plates of translucent tortoiseshell, glossy as amber when I washed them in the pond to remove the thin, dried scum of algae. There were bits and pieces of the harder, bony carapace; nothing more. The murder weapon was a big rock, dropped from above on the hapless turtle; perhaps the beast blocked a fisherman's escape on the narrow shore between water and the thick stand of willows and brush. "It was self-defense, Your Honor, him or me."

I kept the skull and a bit of tortoiseshell; I polished the amber fragment with oil and put it up in my window, where it filters the light like stained glass. The rest of the pieces I put by for safekeeping, lodged in the crotch of a low tree where I could find them later—or so I thought. When I returned for them, they were gone.

The frogs that stare warily at me from the pond weeds are mostly bullfrogs, green frogs, and southern leopard frogs, all members of the family

Ranidae; the tiny spring peepers just over the ridge look for fishless ponds to safekeep their eggs from predators. They racket away at the tops of bantam lungs in full daylight, a cappella in the slough on the hill.

From spring to fall, each time I walk beside the shore, disgruntled bullfrogs launch themselves into the water with an Olympic thrust of muscled thighs and disappear with a series of heavy splashes. If I sit quietly, screened by the lush grasses above the water's edge, the bullfrogs forget about me and return to section off their territory; they claim it with emphatic vocalizations, blowing air through extended bagpipe throats. I can almost find the demarcation lines of these patchwork properties, down to the inch; Frog 1 owns the bank just below me, a space of some ten or fifteen yards; Frog 2 owns a commensurate acreage along the edge of the dam; Frog 3 takes up residence on the far shore, hidden in the fringe of cattails.

One afternoon all was quiet except for the occasional light splash of a feeding fish or the musical song of a redwing—or the loud *cherk* of a belted kingfisher that patrolled the pond's edge. That is, until one of the bullfrogs suddenly felt an inexplicable urge to announce ownership of his particular bit of shore.

"Ba-*rum*, ba-*rum*, baa-a-a-a."

The bull on the opposite shore joined in, breaking the truce: "jug-a-*rum*, jug-a-jug-a-*rum*."

This was too much for the dam-site bullfrog, and he put in his succinct opinion: "*rum*." All the while I sketched, these three announced, taking turns or making a trio of it, then falling silent all at once, as though—once territorial boundaries were reasserted—there was no further need to press the issue.

The birds that make my pond home—or camp here fleetingly—are attracted by the protected expanse of water, ringed on two sides by trees, on the third (the pond is roughly triangular) by the dam. A fringe of trees just behind this monolithic earthwork provides still more limbs for nesting or perching or watching for prey. The full contingent of dragonflies and damselflies must look tempting from that vantage point; these big, primitive insects prey on smaller ones, in return. Mayflies and midges are prime.

Bank swallows cried and swooped above the water; the plaintive call of a killdeer echoed overhead. A great blue heron stalked the shallows, slow and magisterial. His dignified gait was reinforced by his subdued plumage and by his humped, sepulchral shoulders. When he had eaten his fill he dozed, half-hidden among the uprights of the drowned cattails, his neck looped back to rest on his shoulders as though his head had become too heavy to bear upright.

One day I put one of these big birds up as I crested the dam, and it split the air with a harsh, primitive "*scronk! scronk!*" (great blues are among

26

the least sociable of the heron clan). Neck pulled into a recurved S, it stroked the sky with a cadence as deliberate as its gait. The wing beats looked too slow to sustain flight, but their span was huge, perhaps as wide as I am tall. Those aerodynamic wings with long, reaching primary feathers lifted the five-pound bird with ease; he sculled off, seemingly without effort, and disappeared beyond the next hill.

Waterfowl don't seem to find my pond so inviting; a pair of mallards visits on occasion; a few Canada geese have made it a stopover on their way to roomier accommodations; and once I saw a trio of wood ducks, polished and painted as figurines. Their white chin patches glowed like candles near the shadowed shore. I bought a pair of inexpensive decoys to moor there, to coax visiting waterfowl in; they were imported Italian plastic decoys, found in a flea market for $6 each. I wondered as I tossed them into the water at the prices these "collectibles" have attained (some hand-carved and painted models sell for $300) and did my best imitation of Bret Saberhagen, pitching the decoys as far as possible into the center to prevent pilfering; no easy task with a weighted decoy, a length of rope, and an anchor.

There is some more subtle decoy that attracts me to the pond; I need no coaxing. A powerful bond of curiosity and love, discovery and exploration keeps me coming back, wanting to know more, wishing I were home here, wishing I could stay.

July Meadow –
Bergamot, Black-
eyed Susans, & Red
Admirals.

...eadows

The meadow v ...   ...rees just beyond the pond was
an irresistible ...   ...lowing in wildflower waves in
the hot wind. T...   ...the fiery itch of chiggers and
nettles to push ...   ...d brush that choked the dam,
gaining entry to ...

It had not be...   ...dence pointed toward extended desertion. The...   ...ls suggested that no hay had
been baled here,   ...ar or more—probably much
more. I could har...   ...where a thick mat of tiny yellow cloverlike flow...   ...e with wiry stems, and I tried at
first to maintain a kind of marching step, lifting each foot high over the tangle of stems. Game or dogs had forged a narrow path, perhaps six inches wide, and I followed as best I could, wending after their long-gone wraiths.

The ground rose sharply from the pond; I could look back at it and at the road from a vantage point swept with a blistering wind that dried my sweaty face in an instant. From here the pond looked even more inviting, winking sky-colored beyond a screen of pale-limbed young cottonwoods. The woods that surrounded this tiny, two-tiered meadow were deep and black with shadows; they would have been oppressive if I were another kind of walker, but instead they beckoned like the mouth of a cool limestone cave. It looked the perfect place to build a home, overlooking the limpid pond where I had seen so much evidence of wildlife—if it weren't for the fact that the only way to get here was across the narrow dam. Just to the west the neighbor's fence crowded the pond; there was no room to maneuver past it; to the east were the spillway, a sharp drop-off, and more forest. The dam was the only egress to the meadow wide enough for more than foot traffic and that only with care.

Foot traffic is plenty good enough; shank's mare is my favorite mode of transportation, inviting exploration, demanding response. I see far more afoot than when I whiz by in my car. Once bought, the meadow was mine to explore, and I crisscrossed it summer and winter and spring like Livingston searching for the headwaters of the Nile.

This meadow is sparsely covered with dead weeds and wildflowers. The bald weathered limestone is visible at each step between the scant vegetation; the path itself is paved with tiny, flat cobbles that crunch like spilled popcorn underfoot. Where these horizontal layers of prehistoric seafloor have weathered long enough, chipping away into smaller and smaller particles and mixing with the meager organic matter that has managed to find a foothold here, the new ground shines gold, like the rocks. But the gold does not betoken richness, not here—the poor soil offers little in the way of nourishment, and vegetation is only the most hardy. In summer, weeds with rough-whiskered stems nearly as tall as I am find these challenging conditions to their liking.

It's Winterset limestone, here on the hill, a thin-flaking brownish rock that weathers out to mimic a chunky shale. But the texture is of a hard sandstone; I could hone a knife point on one of these stones and strop it to a razor edge. The color of this split-personality stone is gold, stained with iron oxide, which dyes the rock with shades of red and tan, and if it weathers long enough—as it has in my meadow—it becomes ochre. Hidden between the flakes of layered rock are finely preserved fossils, held like the pressed flowers between the pages of my grandmother's field guide: crinoids, brachiopods, horn coral, and the like.

The weedy meadow with its bald rock pate showing through is lovely nonetheless. Lovely and useless. Totally without redeeming social (or financial) value. No good for row crops, no good for hay. Useless—that's why I bought it.

There's no temptation to productivity here, no niggling guilt about plowing or planting or running stock. No need to worry about finding someone to bale hay in a timely fashion or whether the rains fall in proper order. Just a great place for a ramble among the rococo tracery of weeds and the thick stand of broom sedge that seems to suggest a usefulness that does not exist.

Andropogon virginicus likes my poor, dry soil; thrives on it. It's thick as Kentucky bluegrass in the meadow and down the old tractor path, a lush watermark of land good only for Queen Anne's lace and bee balm and the occasional cottontail—and broom sedge. My battered copy of *The Grasses of Missouri* says that broom sedge will grow in old fields, waste ground, and even sandbars, painting them in autumn with lion-colored manes.

The basal leaves curl tightly to the ground, soft and springy, inviting. We lay in comfort on that thick mattress and watched the night sky for shooting stars; the stones were cushioned with sedge. The clear evidence of poor soil didn't bother me; the richness of the sedge's color was fine compensation. I had no agenda for the meadow other than to study its varieties of plants and animals, to crawl around looking for clues, getting to know my territory— and the russet broom sedge is just another bit of mystery to unravel.

It is beautiful, that lusty sedge. In autumn and winter it is tawny and red-gold and whispers secrets to the wind in a small, dry voice. At each joint of its grasslike stalk, it produces fine stemlets and silklike milkweed, tiny bits of blowing light in the afternoon sun to carry its insignificant seeds to new territory.

Andropogon is a proud family whose members include some of our most historic prairie plants. Their names are a litany of a time before human occupation, before the way west came to be: big bluestem, or turkey-foot, taller than a horse; little bluestem; silverbeard; beardgrass.

Broom sedge must have been common in the Missouri of prehistory. At one time, upwards of a third of the state was tallgrass prairie. A map of presettlement Missouri shows the long, flame-shaped fingers of grassland reaching down each river drainage system, intermingling with the deciduous forests that grew along these rivers and streams. Here in the rustling tall-grass, the bluestems shared space with switchgrass *(Panicum virgatum)*; wild rye, or *Elymus canadensis*; Indian grass, or *Sorghastrum nutans;* and side oats grama *(Bouteloua curtipendula)*. In the lowlands, bluejoint *(Calamagrostis canadensis)* and the common reed *(Phragmites communis)* joined the general milieu; I found an uncommon canary grass among them, its panicle tightly knotted with small green seeds.

The first year we had the place, there were dry-ground orchids among the sedge. I had seen ladies' tresses only in books, never in the field; these stood tall on their ten-inch stems, tiny white flowers arrayed up the stalk in a delicate helix as though wishing to be found. A scent of vanilla led me to them, a sweet, remembered odor out here on the hill. I followed my nose to the lovely white blossoms that sometimes grow in stands of a hundred—but here were only two proud orchids waving in the grass. *Spiranthes cernua*, the plant's botanical name, suggests its habit of growth: *Spiranthes* is Greek for the spiraling or twisted stalk, and the Latin *cernua* describes the drooping white flowers. They can be found in a variety of habitats; in grassy swamps, in marshes, upland prairies, and limestone glades—and on my dry meadow that first year. After that they disappeared; I've never found them again.

The sedge hill forms a kind of break—or perhaps brake—for the takeover plants that crowd in from the edge of the woods, the brambles and sumac and hawthorn. From here to the old tractor road that divides the lower meadow from the upper, only sedge and a few hardy weeds book space

Yarrow
smells
like
sage.

—fleabane, sage-scented yarrow, and Queen Anne's lace—and these only sparsely dotted among the thick stand of sedge. British soldier lichen covers the ground between the plants; in late winter I lay here on the springy hummocks of broom sedge to admire their fine branching forms and ruddy heads held at attention all of a quarter of an inch above the ground. Pale, bleached bits of shield lichen looked like drifts of out-of-season snowflakes on the dry ground. They crackled softly when I rolled over on my back to admire the turquoise sky. The hillside absorbed a thin, wintry heat, mitigating the cold wind that swept the tops of the nearby trees; I luxuriated in the clean scent of sun-warmed sedge and drowsed on the mattress of thickly woven basal leaves. Wild geese flew far overhead, yelping their familiar, ancient messages.

This section of the meadow is a graphic re-creation of the postglacial age here in Missouri, the ground scraped back to bedrock and extremely poor in nutrients as it was when the last ledge of ice receded some 15,000 years ago. The ground-hugging lichen was probably among the first plants to repopulate, going about its work in patient, timeless fashion. Half alga, half fungus, lichen was uniquely fitted to its task, carrying out photosynthesis with its algal part while breaking down the solid rock to extract the sparse nutrients with the fungal part. With the weathering action of water and cold weather, the rocky sedge hill should become rich loam in a few millennia.

The limestone that glows in the warm light of sunrise was once covered by a skin of decent soil like the upper meadow, which hosts a different plant community, one more finicky about the availability of nutrients and moisture. The lower meadow was scalped when the pond was dug, the thick stand of grass and weeds and intertwined root systems peeled back by the bulldozer's blade. A man-made ridge, straight as a roadbed, runs along the edge of the woods, and a pile of rock and dirt was shoved clear across the meadow, sprouting little but moss on its north face. In winter it holds the snow longer than anyplace else, calling attention to itself like a white flag. This rough, rocky patch is much like what the Paleo-Indians found as they followed the retreating glacier or settled in its newly vacated outwash; perhaps they hunted the mastodons and red-haired mammoths that eked out a living on the sparse vegetation here or found a dire wolf on my hill. I held the teeth of mastodons in my hand, fleshing out the beast in my mind, recreating the clues to the history of this place like a sleuth, like an archaeologist; the midden piles are few, but they can be read.

Lilliputian game trails snake through the thigh-high weeds and brambles at meadow's edge, and I feel like Gulliver when I pick my way through their arched and spiny tops; going must be easy at ground level where the bodies of small animals have bent the weeds in an ankle-high tunnel. I knelt to peer down a tunnel and found it as branched and complex as an English gardener's maze. These tunnels provide safe passage for the field mice, voles, and rabbits that construct them—and it's a good thing. The meadow is under constant aerial surveillance by hovering hawks. The scream of a red-tailed hawk splintered the air overhead and I scanned the sky, eyes shaded, until I could find the broad-winged shape against the glare.

The blackberries that once only edged the lower meadow in a thin barbed-wire fringe have reclaimed half its breadth, the first step in the meadow's long march to becoming young forest; their canes are singular rather than clumped, as they grow in a more hospitable soil. Sumac and wild plum and rough-leaf dogwood sprouts have joined them in their ragtag procession to meet the woods on the other side. These young dogwoods—or *Cornus drummondii* if you prefer formality—are not the lovely flowering white dogwood that make for spectacular springs in the Ozarks; their flowers are less showy. Instead of the huge white bracts that fill the woods with low-flying cumulus clouds, these appear later in the summer as tiny white blossoms held in a fairy bride's bouquet. The waxy white fruits are borne on coral stems and twigs; it's as lovely in winter as in summer, and I was pleased with its presence.

As if it cared; nature can't wait to reclaim whatever ecosystem it had in mind for a particular plot of land. Making decisions based on climate, soil conditions, and available moisture, nature chooses what will grow in a specific area without regard to our designs. When a clearing returns to forest, it is because of succession. Brush and young saplings gain a foothold, shading the soil and providing new and hospitable conditions for plants that can handle less light. As those plants prosper and the saplings grow tall, ever more shade-tolerant plants move in and those that need the sun wither away. In a generation, what was grassland becomes forest.

In my part of the Midwest, the common oak and hickory woods moved in once the tallgrass prairie's hold was broken. It appears they have every intention of reclaiming their territory if I don't intervene. At the edge of the woods and encroaching everywhere on these old meadows are the young shoots of white and red oak and the fernlike leaves of hickory. Here and there, black locust sprouts are abundant; if the woods on the north hill are any indication, I have only to wait. I'll have eighteen acres of forest in a heartbeat.

Except perhaps where the broom sedge is thickest, where its tangled mattress of leaves allows little competition. Here, conditions may replicate the ancient tallgrass, which stayed as it was for centuries. Fire helped maintain the broad grasslands, searing off encroaching brush and trees, but it was the grass itself that perpetuated the prairie. Thick, entwined root systems up to a yard deep allowed no interloper a foothold. There simply wasn't room in that closed society for change until we broke the monopoly with our agriculture.

In the green-shaded woods I had just vacated to get here, my footsteps were silent as a deer's. Damp soil upholstered in acid-green moss muffled any sound. When I moved dreamlike through the dry meadow, limned in sun and shadow, each step crunched as through a crust of snow, a sonar that made stalking impossible. Everything that lives in the meadow heard my approach; they didn't need the grapevine.

Close to the woods' edge in the dappled half shade is a mat of wild strawberries, enough at least for a bowlful to dip in Maywine and sugar from this wild garden of earthly delights.

Disproportionately large leaves umbrella these tiny, bright red berries, half hiding them from view. These clever plants seem to have another protective ploy as well: the lower leaves hug the ground and turn as red as the fruit—and about the same time, as though to confuse a hungry berry lover with their chameleon camouflage.

Like the brambles, these are rose family members; their five-petaled flowers are white, resembling a smaller multiflora rose; the center is a tiny green knot that enlarges, softening and ripening into the finest of the wild fruits. But the wild strawberry is not really a fruit—or at least it's not the part we think of. The "berry" is instead the receptacle, embedded with dry, seedlike fruit. Tart-sweet, small as my fingernail, they are nonetheless some fine eating—if you can beat the turtles and birds to them.

The box turtles that forage here prefer open woods and grasslands; I find them hotfooting it across the meadow or lumbering across the road during the heights of spring breeding season. The carapace resembles a tiled bowl inverted over the body, but it's illusion; it's all one with the turtle itself. Unlike a snail, a turtle doesn't shed its shell or leave it for a larger one; the bones are fused directly to the outer carapace and plastron. Age lines are

female
box turtle
(brown eyes rather than red)

scribed on its back like the crow's-feet around my eyes; you can almost count the rings like a tree's yearly record—the turtle that made its way through the sedge to lay its eggs in the loose dirt of an anthill may have been sixty to eighty years old. This shell is incredibly strong, supporting 200 times its own weight. No wonder a predator has a tough time finding turtle meat inside that armor. It's a design perfected by the eons; these dinosaurs haven't changed in 250 million years.

Now in early June, it was unseasonably cool, unbelievably, exquisitely perfect—more like Maine than Missouri at this time of year, when usually the wet slap across the face of saunalike heat is coupled with humidity you could swim in. The rich plant smells contained in this crisp, clear air rose in visible undulations against my white paper as I drew, shimmering like heat waves over a blacktop road; without that unmistakable visual aid, I wouldn't have been aware of heat at all.

A pair of northern orioles barreled across the open meadow to hang ornamentlike at the forest's edge, singing their eccentric duet. It was a good year for orioles; I've no idea why. Here and in town and in the nearby state park, these bright birds took up residence en masse and acted as though such things were commonplace. The woven pouches of their nests hung from the branches like Guatemalan hammocks. Young birds begged for food, their feathers spiky and comical as though they had used too much mousse.

Painted ladies and red admirals worked the wild garlic—butterflies,

35

these, not members of a Communist navy and their concubines. A burnished copper skipper landed lightly on my page, wings folded upright for a moment before dropping them—along with his guard. He allowed me to watch him there for the better part of a minute before taking off again to drift across the field. A hackberry butterfly accompanied me on my rambles, landing on my arm and unfurling a long proboscis to taste my salt. I often find a battery of them clustered on animal droppings, mining the minerals or the salt they find there, and wonder why their presence on my flesh doesn't bother me, as it does when a fly lands on my face. Later, when the meadow is in full bloom, it will be woods edge to pasture break with their fellows: monarchs and tiger swallowtails, zebras and giants and tiny, tailed blue hairstreaks.

I sat in a well of quiet, once I ceased my rustling, crackling progress along the path, a quiet made more palpable by the whir of grasshopper wings on a three-foot trajectory; I heard the arcing flight as much as saw it. The sound of flies was a half-heard conversation, a rise-and-fall whine, elusive and tantalizing.

It was so still I could hear the helicopter buzz of a snake doctor's wings thirty feet away. I jumped when a car passed on the road; the sound broke protocol, and I felt like a monk in an order pledged to silence when someone inadvertently sneezes.

After days of howling wind, the gentlest of breezes still excited the two young cottonwoods, and they madly waved their polished leaves in response. Unlike the redbud's heart-shaped leaves, these are stiff, leathery, and wave at the ends of long, flattened stems; they react to the slightest air current with a sustained dry whisper: "The wind! The wind!"

The deer like this meadow, fringed on three sides with woods, providing safe access to the pond; the brambles yield a favorite browse. My neighbor says he often sees the whitetails at sunset, standing calm as cattle on the hill. I follow their tracks, shallow-drafted here on the rocky soil, and find the small, brown beads of excrement, only slightly larger than a rabbit's. These ruminants make good use of their brushy browse, wasting no nutrients.

Bluebirds like these living arrangements, too—an open area for flying practice, a nearby woods for cover, and plenty of food. We nailed a new birdhouse to a cottonwood by the pond to attract the bed-and-breakfast trade; the birds had inspected the house in the walnut grove, but we hoped the woods might prove sufficient barrier to entice two families instead of one to nest. Optimum space between bluebird territories is as much as a quarter mile, but we had already bisected that with last year's offering in the walnut grove, and it was too late to move it now. I held my breath and hoped for successful nesting in one house or the other—or both.

Perhaps the barrier of meadow and woods would be enough—today when I walked across the dam and entered the meadow, I was delighted to find a male bluebird protecting his new territory with a lilting, distinctive call. The sunlight glinted off those sky-colored wings and found the warm russet of his breast. The more drably attired female was at home, peering at me from the new house, but she wasn't in the mood for company, even so circumspect as myself; she swooped across the meadow to the fence and sat there, hunch-shouldered and disgruntled.

I didn't care. I was glad she had accepted my hospitality, however ungraciously.

The blackberry brambles that ring the meadow form a lethal border, a break between weed and wood that discourages casual entry. These things are armed and dangerous — though tempting enough in July when their spiked shoots are hung with ripening berries as big as my thumb. The birds and squirrels and deer and I keep watch; I taste the sweetness in my mind and roll it around on my tongue. But for two long years the rocky meadow sabotaged us again; it dried out quickly after the sparse midsummer rains, absorbing and radiating the heat long after the sun had set. The fat globes of the blackberries mummified in the superheated air.

The third summer we owned the place it was different. Six months of moisture, not only normal but far above, refilled the earth's subterranean stores; a month after the rains had stopped the berries continued to ripen until the canes hung heavy with them. Still, even as I collected the ripe berries I couldn't imagine what it must have been like to be an early hunter-gatherer, dependent on these fickle food sources. There would have been two berryless years followed by this more abundant one, but after picking in the sun as long as I could stand it I still had only a cupful of berries in my pail; the others were not yet ripe. If this year had been like the last two, my stomach would have pinched with hunger.

It's the same with other wild foods. The stand of wild garlic near the pond seems lush and rich, and so it is if all I want is an occasional condiment. If I were dependent on it to keep me fed it would shortly be gone. Wild onion is scarce at any time; I found a few plants near the tractor path but only enough for a single salad. Black walnuts were as scant. The pond has its small fringe of cattails; a week's steady eating and they would disappear. The strawberries that seemed to flourish in the drought the first year, providing me with bowl after bowl of sweet red fruit, were almost nonexistent in the third year's lush summer — who can say why? The life of a hunter-gatherer would have been difficult, largely taken up with collecting only enough for that day. The idea of putting by enough for winter astounds me. No wonder they were seminomadic; you would have to be to follow the game and the locally abundant wild foods — the idea of staying on one's own eighteen-acre plot would have been suicidal. No wonder, too, that during the Woodland Indian period people learned habitat management, burning off the underbrush in the woods to increase their luck at hunting; invented the bow and arrow; and utilized the bola, a pair of weights connected with a cord that was thrown to entangle the feet of small animals or birds. Perhaps they even learned a rudimentary agriculture, disturbing the soil to encourage the growth of edible plants like pigweed or lamb's-quarter, abundant in my garden. During the Woodland period these same people developed basket making and pottery skills for food storage and grinding tools like the metate and mano. I've found one of the latter near my creek, its side flattened by use. These hints suggest they were learning how to provide more food for themselves than nature was willing to provide.

This day in early July the berries closer to the ground ripened first, shaded by their own leaves—or perhaps they were just hidden from the hungry birds there. They were wild tasting, with only a hint of real sweetness, cool in their self-made shade, refreshing as ice water in the hot afternoon. The sun had bleached a whiteness into the sky, but so far it hadn't burned the blackberries.

It is hot in the meadow. When I vacated the shadowed wood for its openness, the temperature jumped like the cottontail rabbits I startle as I come up the path. In this grasslands microclimate where not much tempers the heat, there is nothing beyond the spindly stems of wildflowers to provide shade. It may be ten degrees warmer in the space of only a few feet as I leave the woods for this sun-beaten spot; at ground level it is hotter still.

The scent of this unremitting heat on meadow plants is oddly pleasant, like potpourri. The haze of violet that hangs over this lower meadow is not just midwestern humidity; it's thousands upon thousands of bergamot flowers—bee balm, horsemint, call it what you will, the spice scent has gladdened me from childhood; Chanel should bottle it to dot behind my ears and at the backs of my knees. Even in winter the dead stems release the heady scent when crushed against my palm, and I breathe full summer on the frosty air.

This day, the air was noisy with the hum of fat bumblebees unfurling their long proboscises into the nectar-filled trumpets of wildflowers; their honey must taste of spice, but who ever tastes bumblebee honey? They hide their honey pots in holes in the ground, and only the brave or the foolhardy will dig for them. Unlike honeybees, these bees can sting in multiples.

A friend once had a nest of bumblebees in an old burlap bag that was wrapped around her pump to keep it from freezing in the well house. Since the old pump had to be replaced, the bees had to be moved. I volunteered.

This is not quite as rash as it appears. I'd learned to handle honeybees with no ill effects and had allowed hornets to explore my hands and cheeks without mishap. These last have a reputation at least as unsavory as the bumblebee's—how different could these furry insects be?

Plenty. These bees cared little for the fact that I wanted only to move them, not harm them; they didn't care a whit that I'd talked friend Roger out of the wasp spray; they couldn't have been less impressed with my exploits with honeybees and hornets. They were *mad*. And they showed their displeasure with an unforgettable show-and-tell that stuck with me for what seemed like weeks. Longer; twenty years later, I haven't forgotten my lesson.

One particularly defensive bee flew up my pant leg and let me have it, right in the knee. The joint swelled to twice its normal size, as red and glossy as an oversized apple. Bending it was out of the question; I walked with a limp for a week. A single bee had found itself trapped between flesh and denim and knew which to attack. There must have been five stings in that knee alone.

Now I hold hornets in my hand and sit nose to nose with honeybees, but the big, furry bumblebees have my utmost respect. They can *keep* their honey, bergamot-flavored or no.

I shoved my way through the winter-killed brambles to the woods and found my jeans spiked with thorns as if I had encountered a porcupine. The canes looked somehow less forbidding, less impenetrable stripped of their thick leaves — as though it were the leaves that inflicted the damage. Bramble thorns must be tipped with poison, like a South American Indian's arrow; when I prick my fingers on these dead, dry points, infection is almost sure to follow.

Next summer there may be other flowers to tempt the bumblebees in the meadow, planted by sheer clumsiness, not design. One winter day I lugged a ten-pound bag of sunflower seed down the hill to the walnut grove; the icy path was my undoing. I dropped the paper bag of seeds and it exploded as though packed with blasting caps. After trying without success to cram them back into the ruptured bag, I sowed the remainder on the wind.

Who says the only birds to be fed should be those that cluster in the protected grove? Why localize the prey for hungry falcons and my neighbor's opportunistic Siamese? I threw seeds as far as I could and watched for the next few days to see if they were found.

At first they went undiscovered; the snowy ground looked as though it were covered with dormant box elder bugs. Then one day every seed was taken, the snow swept clean as with a good stiff wind. I wish I could have seen the feast: Come and get it! Sparrows or juncos, quail or cardinals — I wonder which were the lucky recipients of my disaster?

At any rate, summer may bring a few sunflowers among the bergamot, if the birds overlooked a seed or two, and self-sowing birdseed is always to be praised.

The weeds and wildflowers that give the meadow such a pleasant mien in summer are not through once icy cold blasts them. They bloom instead with the intricate tracery of seed heads and pods, a fine-drawn beauty that might have been executed with a crow quill pen and ink but for the variety of hues. If you imagine winter plants to be dull and monochromatic, you have not walked a January meadow. There are the tawny henna of broom sedge, as though I had mixed burnt sienna and yellow ochre on my palette to paint them; the frosty gray-blue of the bergamot; and the subtle gold of the wiry flower baskets of Queen Anne's lace. Where curly dock has made good its intent to colonize, rich, brown seed heads glow with color like the eyes of a fox. Encroaching sumac holds tall, maroon standards to the sky, covered with lemony berries I suck as I walk to the woods.

There's another kind of color here, as well—the kind that deepens as you learn more about your chosen place, the kind of local color only long association can reveal. The bare winter weeds tell me much about what shares this land with me. I find tiny birds' nests lashed to the branches of sumac and woven among the weeds. Goldenrod stems bear round or elliptical galls that suggest occupancy. The oval-shaped ones capture my interest; they are more rare, caused by the larva of the *Gnorimoschema gallæsolidaginis* moth, an exception in the insect world. Few moths cause galls, but this one has injured the goldenrod plant when it laid eggs on the stem or lower leaves. When the eggs hatch in the spring, the larva burrows into the new goldenrod shoots and tunnels into the stem; the plant responds to injury by swelling around them, inadvertently providing the insect's young with both food and housing.

More often I find the goldenrod ball gall here, a marble-shaped swelling caused by a tiny, spot-winged fly *(Eurosta solidaginis)*. Again, the egg of the insect hatches, burrows into the stem, and the gall forms around it for a well-insulated home. Or that was the plan, at any rate. Here and there a gall has been vandalized; a larger, chipped-looking entry reveals that a downy woodpecker knew where to look for sustenance. One quiet winter walk I could hear an odd chipping and followed the sound until I could see the tiny bird hard at it, clutching the weed stem for balance and hammering away at the gall. It found its quarry and flew to the next gall as though on a moveable feast.

How galls form is a puzzle except to say that somehow—by the secretion of chemical irritants or the physical irritation of forced entry itself—the gall maker induces the plant (whether a goldenrod or an oak tree) to respond with a variety of deformities. The insect doesn't look at them as such; these are happy abnormalities for the opportunistic insect: home sweet home.

In the upper meadow, overlooking the pond, the complexion changes radically. Here the soil is deep and—by lower-meadow standards—rich as butter. Grasses grow breast high. The lower stratum is crowded with a low yellow clover family member, tangled together so tightly Harris's weed machine gave up the effort after making only negligible inroads. It was the same low plant that tripped me up the first day I made entry into the meadow; I was not surprised at its deceptive strength. The spinning nylon blades choked and stopped, tied tight. I didn't care; these tiny sweet-smelling flowers are like calico. Who would want them cut? They were visited by hundreds of honeybees as I sat up to my shins in them, their sturdy little stems — so deceptively slight, so wiry — unaffected by the weight of the feeding insects.

Everywhere I looked, the prehistoric shapes of dragonflies — darners, skimmers, and clearwings — poised on weed stems or flitted from place to place, more kinds of these primitive insects than I could name. I have seen their ancestors as fossils, turned to stone in ancient rocks.

The brambles in this upper meadow were much further along. Below, a galaxy of white flowers still starred the green. Here, each armored cat-o'-nine-tails cane was hung with developing berries, hard and green and waiting. If the rains continued there would be wild, sweet fruit in plenty — enough for us, enough for the birds and field mice and deer, enough for a browsing box turtle. As the season progresses, the tall, lusty wildflowers of summer crowd in: Queen Anne's lace, black- and brown-eyed Susan, and

Deptford
Pink (*Dianthus armeria*)

grows like
carnation — naturalized
European. Hot pink
flowers, usually with
white spots, although
these seem to have
darker spots instead.

dog fennel, as we used to call the tiny, daisylike flowers of fleabane. Among these taller flowers, hot fuchsia Deptford pinks bloom from May to October. These are tiny members of the *Dianthus* family; it's Greek for "flower of God." God must love it; it is such a pure, bright color you can't miss it for all its crowded conditions in the meadow. It expects to be appreciated, and it is. My mother loved these best of all, and I carry her fondness. The leaves of Deptford pinks are hairy, grasslike, but the flowers are pure simplicity, a pleasure to draw.

The east meadow at the far end of our property is as different in character as it is possible to be. Unlike the pond meadow, with its exposure to the road and neighbor's gaze, this upper meadow—Rachel's Meadow, named for my next-to-youngest godchild—is hidden all summer by a fringe of trees on all sides. In winter it is barely visible and that from the distance of a quarter mile; it would take binoculars to see what happens there. The pond meadow is easy to reach; Rachel's Meadow is attainable only by effort, no matter which direction you choose to approach it from. From the upper road, you must wade through a rough band of climax meadow well on the way to becoming forest; a barrier of young trees, most of them black locust and hawthorn and as staunchly defended with thorns as Sleeping Beauty's castle, and although these haven't grown for a hundred years, they are nearly as impenetrable. I like it that way; it discourages trespass and the thoughtless

Meadow Grasses

traffic of all-terrain vehicles (ATVs). The old tractor path, looping in toward the meadow from the north road, is nearly as overgrown. Only a slight difference in the circumference of the trees here suggests a onetime access.

It is through the woods uphill from the creek that the going is easiest, the strange open woods with their transparent gauze of slender saplings that reach and reach without ever branching, punctuated by an old giant here and there. It's a lovely place to sit and dream, to walk, to camp—and a fine approach to the upper meadow.

This meadow catches the sunset in its tree-rimmed basin and basks in it. In summer, the air has the honeyed sweetness of multiflora rose. I can see the far, blue hills from here; it is the highest point on our property, 950 feet above sea level. I come here when I need to see beyond my ordinary affairs, when I need a bit of perspective; distance seems to help.

The soil is different, too. By the pond, the soil is thin and rocky; here it is deep and rich, black as Cajun coffee. Earthworms and other underfoot denizens love this hillside; a spadeful of moist summer earth squirms with life. The difference in soil quality makes for a different plant community; it became "Rachel's Meadow" when Rachel and I sketched the lovely multiplicity of weed heads, seeds, and insect galls here on winter afternoons.

I find a variety of fungi in my meadows, but my favorites are the puffballs. Big as a softball in the grass, these catch my eye with their simplicity of shape and color. That's not all I love them for; they are among the most delectable of edible mushrooms. When I find them along the meadow trail, I pray they are fresh; once they've begun to dry out it's too late for that particular treat, but when I slice them through to find a fine, featureless whiteness, blank as paper, I know my dinner is made. Sautéed in a bit of oil or the guilty pleasure of bacon grease, there is nothing finer to put on a plate, and I eschew steak without a whimper.

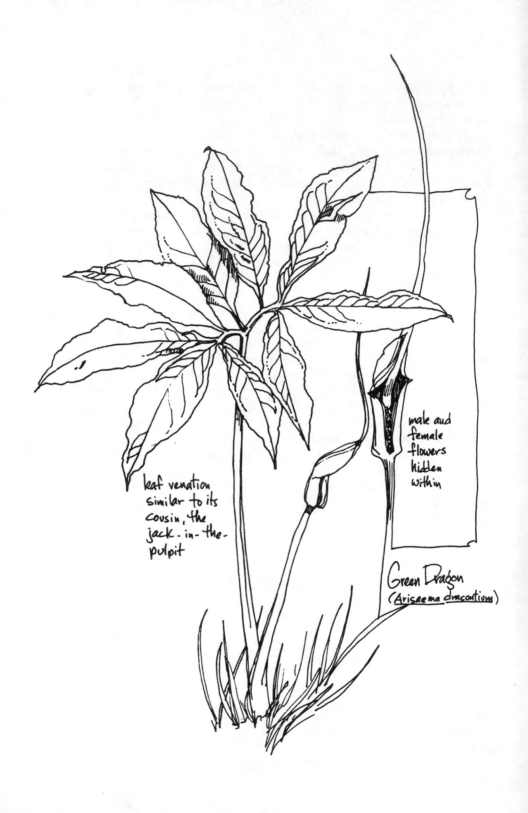

leaf venation
similar to its
cousin, the
jack-in-the-
pulpit

male and
female
flowers
hidden
within

Green Dragon
(Arisaema dracontium)

4. The Woods

Beyond this point there be dragons. The ancient maps of the world bore this legend at the demarcation between the known and the unknown; it's as good a description as any. That elusive place is more internal than external, more psychological than physical. I like to read into the words not so much a warning of concrete danger—who since Saint George has seen a dragon?—as a notice of a certain sense of possibility, a realm of great promise among the tangled branches of the trees. Beyond this point, you don't know what you'll find: adventure, mystery, untold riches. Dragons.

There are dragons in the woods beyond the pond. This is not mere fancy; these are green dragons, wildflowers of the arum family, which includes jack-in-the-pulpit, wild calla, and arrow arum. They are untold riches, unexpected as diamonds on the ground, and I watched their development from sprout to oddly shaped leaf to even odder flower with a growing interest. These green dragons—like gryphons, like unicorns—are comparatively rare (much more so than their cousin, the jack). They're subtle, hidden from ordinary view by their choice of color; in the spring woods, flowers of camouflage green go unnoticed among drifts of bright yellow, lavender, red, and pink. These other plants—the mustards, the sweet williams, the roses—spend a fortune on advertising; the solitary green hood of the dragon hides beneath the understory, waiting private and self-contained for discovery.

I don't know why I recognized the tightly folded shoot as a relative of an old friend. Jack-in-the-pulpits have been vaguely magical to me as long as I can remember, but I don't remember ever seeing one at ground-breaking stage. This blunt new sprout, its leaves wrapped around it like an umbrella, emerged rather like a mayapple, but it bore a family resemblance to the jack's clan in the habit of growth, in the pattern of the veins on the leaves as they opened. Like the jack arum, the veins began as parallel lines taking off from the midrib. Then, as though changing their minds, they turned back before reaching the margin, joining with the next vein in a kind of interior scallop. When someone suggested it might be green dragon, the bells went off in my head, and I looked in my field guides for confirmation.

They weren't much help. So far, all I had to go on were the leaves, which most wildflower books view as secondary. The photos were ambiguous at best. I'd have to wait for the main event to be sure of what I was seeing—but that was not that far in the offing, according to Edgar Denison's *Missouri Wildflowers*; here they bloom from April to June.

Now I found the dragon itself, a slender green shaft with a slightly larger swelling at the head, ending in a long, pointed unicorn's horn—the "dragon's tongue," Audubon calls it. There was an opening along one side of the hood that showed the rest of that horn (the spadix) cloaked in the leaflike outer spathe. Tiny yellow male and female flowers concealed themselves within, clustered along the spadix—as secretive as the dragon itself. Perhaps that's why I like them; this shy secretiveness—this mystery—appeals to something childlike in me. I know something that those who drive the road in their cars or bucket through the countryside on ATVs will never see; I'm in on the secret. I know that there are dragons in the woods, and the dragon slayers are not allowed trespass on my land.

There is something in the forest that stirs a primal response. The trees mask as much as they reveal; it's vaguely unsettling. Americans like to know what they're up against. It's in our culture; we're open, we're straightforward—and we're spoiled. We like things the easy way. In the woods there is always more to see, more to discover there beyond the screen of leaves, the tangled limbs, the graceful, angular lines of the trunks—something that must be worked for. It's never given away without effort.

The meadow tells all its secrets—or appears to—but the trees keep me guessing, peering into their depths, trying to penetrate their mystery. In winter they seem almost to give it up. The bare limbs are like mist against the bony hill, and I can see far back into the woods. But it's concealment enough; I am left, still, longing for more, trying to break the code, trying to read their cryptic messages.

Trees obscure the path that leads back into a filtered green stillness; it turns between two forest giants and is gone. One false move and I am delightfully lost, wandering in search of a new path or forging my own; blue-eyed grass watches me pass without comment, nodding its head as if in approval.

Between the road and the walnut grove are ranks of trees, hundreds of them in various life stages. I am amazed at their variety, astounded by their

46

loveliness. Our farm had only a narrow strip of woods between a wild, rough pasture and a river-bottom field. Here, whiplike saplings indicate this woods is fairly young or that cattle once ranged here, keeping the underbrush down. Old giants, twisted and arthritic with years, veterans of many storms, are full of war stories written in lost limbs and woodpecker holes, owl nests, and the fine sawdust of carpenter ants. There are stumps and blow-downs in various stages of return to the forest floor.

There's a mixed community of trees here. The oaks spread iron branches, unmoved by the vagaries of life. After the worst of the storms last spring, I found no downed oak limbs; only rot or lightning seem to affect these angular giants. Here and there a black locust tree reaches lacy leaflets in a broken canopy overhead. One, along the deer path, is so thickly spiked with thorns along every inch of its trunk that I shudder to think of losing my balance and reaching out for support anywhere in the neighborhood; I still bear stigmata where the fallen thorns stabbed through the soles of my sneakers. This year and last, I didn't catch the scented sweetness of locust flowers

on the wind and wondered why these trees had not borne the long racemes of legumelike blossoms, but they must have done—the treetops are hung with long, green ornaments.

Ghostly white sycamores mark the creek's passage down its long draw to the Missouri River. From the east hill I can trace its path by them, like a mist in the hollow. One giant tree has been dead for a long time, but still it stands against the wind, only occasionally surrendering a branch. I leave it where it stands; woodpeckers have excavated here, and cavity-loving birds and squirrels benefit from their labors. (One day as I sat beside the creek to cool off, I heard a querulous keening overhead. Looking up, I found a female red-bellied woodpecker peering from a hole in the tree, whining that my presence down below made her nervous as she sat on her eggs. I took my leave in deference to motherhood.)

Osage orange trees show evidence of their usefulness as fence posts, iron hard and rot resistant, written in the ledger of cut stumps, rock hard and unchanged after all these years. One, as big across as a luncheon table, must have been an old-growth giant. Like the locust, *Maclura pomifera* has thorny twigs. My parents used to call this hedge apple; *pomifera* refers to the light green fruit, convoluted as brain and big as softballs. In the fall, the squirrels find these "apples" to their liking, dining on the table of the hedge tree's stumps. Scraps of scattered hedge fruit suggest a late-night party.

This is the *bois d'arc* (or bodark) of a frontier naturalist's journal, named by the French and used by everyone who found them; "bow wood" tells one chapter of the story. The native Americans made sturdy, resilient weapons from this tree. When I saw through a branch for my fire, the blade smokes and the surface of the wood is as smooth as though sanded and varnished.

The understory at the forest's edge blooms with the foamy white of Missouri hawthorn; I can't begin to tell you which species. My eastern forest field guide lists thirty of these trees and nearly as many offshoot nicknames. "Missouri" is not among them, though this small tree bears our state flower. According to Jerry Monterastelli, urban forester with the Missouri Department of Conservation at Burr Oak Woods, there are more than fifty varieties of this spring-blooming tree in our state alone, providing cover, beauty, and edible berries for the birds.

The piercing rose of eastern redbud, or "Judas tree," accompanies this early-spring blossoming, painting the woods with showy color. Bare twigs of *Cercis canadensis* are covered with hot pink blossoms, followed by tender, tiny leaves — in a good year, that is. One year a freeze caught the leaves just as they were emerging and turned them as dry and brown as though hit by lightning. I hated to see them lost, but a few weeks later transparent green had sprouted again and the understory colored; the heart-shaped leaves bobbed and swam in the currents of air that moved slowly down the hill. The leguminous flowers are not so resilient; this year a hard freeze blasted them to tiny, dried-up balls and they fell off, unrealized. There were two or three viable flowers where usually there are thousands, and I missed their blush in the woods.

A miniature grove of young pawpaw saplings, tall and skinny, look nearly unable to support their large, moccasin-shaped foliage. These leaves are simple — without a toothed margin — they have a clean, bracing aroma when I crush them in my fingers. My field guide differs with that description. "Bruised foliage has a disagreeable odor," says the *Audubon Society Field Guide to North American Trees;* perhaps. It smells green and fresh to me. In the spring, the little moisture-loving trees bear large, bisexual flowers.

They're exotically beautiful, the color of polished mahogany. Three yellow-green sepals protect the bud, and the flower itself is convoluted, lined. *Asimina triloba* looks like a carved mahogany jewel box, inadvertently left open. To sketch them I bent a sapling down with one hand and inched my way along the slender trunk with the other, until I could break off a single, flowering twig.

My grandmother called the fruit "custard apple" for its mild, sweet flavor; you may know it as soursop, sugar apple, false banana—it resembles that tropical fruit, measuring three to five inches long, if the fruits make at all. Weather and latitude are major factors.

They are not nearly so common as they were when de Soto first described them to European society in 1541; once there were so many that pawpaw jam and preserves were an everyday part of our forebears' larders. Now you're lucky if you find a single bearing tree; we've cleared too much of their habitat.

Beside the creek, two trees entwine rough, twisted trunks to lean across one another, as though each held the other back from falling into the water; perhaps they do. In flood their roots are relentlessly undermined, and still they stand there as if fully intending to stay. Each has lost a limb or two, to decay, to damage, but endurance has a rough beauty of its own. They persevere.

And if I didn't get the message the first time, I have only to wander downstream another twenty feet or so. There, a huge limestone slump block has let go its hold and fallen into the creek. I don't know when this occurred. I have no way to guess the hour. But I know it was long enough ago that a sapling sprouted in the crevices between the sandwiched layers of limestone, sprouted, and grew full sized from the trace of soil and the scanty moisture pocketed there. Now there is only a broken stump, big around as a good-sized shade tree. I wish I could do as much with as little.

In the woods near the edge of our property is a huge post oak, its trunk so big around it would take three people to reach. I sat by it in the winter woods, hugging close to that corrugated trunk between two huge roots, and fell asleep in the leaf-filtered sunshine. When I woke I was more refreshed than I had a right to be, as though I had absorbed the oak's strength while I slept. At its base, the layered ruffles of hen-of-the-woods fungus grow each fall, like a fat brown chicken with her feathers fluffed—delicious, so they say. *Grifola frondosa* may grow in clusters up to twenty inches wide and weigh an astounding 100 pounds. If I gathered all of these specimens, they'd fill a bushel basket—but they looked as though they'd been fresh some time last week; now the feathers were dry and curling. Perhaps next year.

There are thousands of mushrooms and other fungi in the woods, from early spring to late autumn; apricot-scented chanterelles raise ruffled caps beginning in July. In winter, a variety of hard, dry shelf fungus takes up the slack. Some are edible, some are not, but all have a kind of mysterious attraction. They're enigmatic, relying on no photosynthesis for their growth, waiting for the right combination of moisture and felicity to strike out on their own, leaving their delicate, interwoven mycelium underground and coming up for a look around. Mushrooms produce millions of microscopic spores (that's what you see floating off in a green cloud when you step on a dry puffball); those with the goods to germinate develop into white, thready hyphae, or mycelia. It's not so simple as all that, though. Now two compatible mycelia must meet, join, and form mycelium containing cells with not one but two nuclei. This double-nuclei cell is the vegetative body; after a few more permutations, maturing and expanding, it makes mushrooms—if the signs are right, or the moon, or the cards. I picked a selection of serendipitous fungi on a hot August day and painted them with my watercolors until the light was gone and my subjects began to dry out. In morel season I can think of little else but those fine, smoky-flavored mushrooms.

The walnut trees in the grove are tall and slender, with minimal branching until near the top of the canopy fifty or sixty feet from the ground. They move in the invisible current of the air; I touch a gently swaying giant and feel wind under my hand, caught in the fibers of the wood. The least breeze sets them quivering seismically in response; a fresh wind sets them swaying to their roots, describing funnel-shaped arcs against the clouds.

They were planted too close together some forty or fifty years ago, these walnut trees—or crowded by an accident of nature. There is little room for side branches, and the picture of *Juglans nigra* in my field guide shows nothing that resembles them. Someone has marked them, long ago—perhaps the walnut thieves our neighbors told us about. There is a rough blaze at the bottom of most of them, grown over with scar tissue, a swollen rim of

Apricot-scented
Chanteralle—
Somewhat
the worse for
a night or two
past sprouting.

smoother bark like a doughnut encircling the wound. Here and there a stump is cut nearly flush with the ground, clear evidence of the successful raid—the thieves didn't plan to waste an inch of that valuable lumber.

I wouldn't have imagined these trees worth stealing; in the shadowed grove they've never gained much girth as they reached hungrily for the light. There wouldn't have been that many board feet in any one of them — from all of them put together. Each year when I see the lumber trucks rolling through town, shortly after the inevitable ad appears in our local newspaper —"We Buy Walnut Trees"—I am amazed at the size of these monsters, four and five and seven times larger in diameter than our slender string beans. But these trees didn't belong to the perpetrators in any case. They'd have been pure profit even if they were only inches around.

The walnuts are the last to leaf out in spring and the first to drop their sparse canopy in the fall, as though they know their beauty lies in the dancing, wind-borne grace of their long trunks. Their crop of nuts, held stingily out of reach overhead, is paltry. Each tree has a very minimum of limbs at the end of that long, long trunk; few limbs means fewer small, greenish flowers, a minimum of nuts. There's not enough to bother with; last year I picked up less than a peck and gave them back to the squirrels.

The squirrels are everywhere in autumn, leaping acrobatically through the trees, harvesting the landslide of acorns against the long winter. I followed a furry piper up the hill towards sunset, the squirrel apparently enjoying the game as much as I—it never got more than twenty feet ahead, nor did it seem to try to outdistance me by more. Just as I imagined I knew where it was or where it would appear next, the squirrel surprised me, popping out from behind a completely different tree as if to give a Bronx cheer. Who wouldn't get into the spirit of the chase? I took to tracking like a fox, moving only when the squirrel moved, walking as silently as possible, finding a tree large enough to mask my intentions and moving up rapidly behind its bulk to peer out at the little rodent. When finally I became too bold for the squirrel's peace of mind, it leaped into a shingle oak tree and was gone—but not before handing me off to another light-footed trickster.

This second squirrel led me astray, made me forget my errand—and the time—as it skipped a few feet over the golden forest floor, stopping for a frenzied dig, then scampering off a few more feet before repeating the whole performance. I never saw it actually bury the nut it clutched in those curved front teeth. It just carried it from place to place, looking for the perfect cache safe from interlopers like me.

These western woods are rich in wildflowers. Ferns grow here in abundance—triangular rattlesnake fern, bracken, northern lady fern. The understory is well developed, varied. Buckbrush fills the spaces between the trees from April to November, forming an imagined barrier; in the winter, when these pink-berried bushes shed their leaves, the woods open up to my explorations.

The owls have staked out a favorite tree on this hill to raise their young; I hear them in the late evening and on rare afternoons, begging in strange, scratchy voices to be fed.

One summer day I could stand the summons no longer; I had wandered up the creek to find respite from the pounding heat, wading upstream toward the owls' tree, and again I heard that whispery creak. "Shhhhht! Ssssshht!" Had it seen me? Was this warning or greeting? And most important, was it an owl at all? I had never found the author of these strange noises I assumed to be *Strix varia*, the barred owl; this time I was determined. I stalked the sound to the edge of the woods, never looking at my feet at all but keeping my eyes nailed tight to the source of the sound. My quarry would escape without my ever knowing where unless I watched it go.

The noises continued as I circumnavigated the thick brush, and I wished I possessed the owl's uncanny sonar skills. Still, I gained the woods path and moved as slowly there as I did in the creek, wading through the weeds like they were water. Each time I neared the sound it seemed to fade a bit, and at last, by slowing and assuming a more effective stalking mode, I managed to see why. The owl looped silently off through the trees just ahead of me, the sound of flight muffled by soft, fringed wings.

Each time it flew, I took the opportunity to move up while its back was

Barred
Owl –
Strix
varia

turned until at last it stopped and turned to watch, bobbing its head to get a bead on me. I did the same. It was a young barred owl, marked with the cuneiform dots and dashes that give it its name. The huge dark eyes pinned me to the ground, and I stopped where I was to stare back.

It wasn't enough. I wanted to be closer, to be as close as I could to wildness. So I tried on the owl's own conversation, trying to match my human "sshhhhhht!" to the big bird's. It seemed amused—or puzzled; it turned its head nearly in a circle to get a better view of this strange, two-legged impersonator. Perhaps curiosity got the best of the owl. At any rate, it allowed me to come closer, closer, until I was just under the limb it perched on.

It's hard to end a conversation with an owl. I began to realize I had to get back, but the bird kept me mesmerized. It seemed unthinkable to simply turn my back and walk off after intruding on its privacy. I stood there a while longer, shifting from foot to foot, uncertain how to break off the relationship. Lacking a better solution, I thanked the owl for its patience and retreated down the path, repeating our common word as best I could. I looked back once to find it still staring after me as if in disbelief.

I wasn't that bad at it.

When I hike to the owls' nest tree in winter, when the ground is bare and easy to read, I find the remains of their meals: the skulls and bones of small prey animals and owl pellets, wads of hair, and tiny bones regurgitated as indigestible.

Owls are not the only skull makers. Accident, old age, illness; who knows how these bones come to be? I found a smooth-domed skull close beside an oak tree and wondered what it was; the eye sockets were almost nonexistent, the skull plates tightly knit, with a bony ridge that bisected the forehead. The skull itself was impossibly thin; I could see daylight through it with ease. Where the bony details were clearly visible, the structure was open, lacy.

This ivory skull bore tiny, repeated hash marks that showed where some small rodent had found a source of free calcium. The opportunistic little mammal had destroyed evidence; it's hard to place a partial skull. There was nothing left of jaw or teeth—or, as I suspected, a bill. This looked more bird than mammal, and I took it in to show Pete Rucker, one of our veterinarians, for his opinion. I thought it would be an easy ID, since Pete is licensed to care for wildlife, but the skull was far beyond care and in bad shape. This much we agreed on: it was a bird. Probably, given the size and shape, a raptor or young turkey vulture. I took my prize home, grateful for any bit of information I could get; I like those big black birds with their sailplane grace. Without the vultures we'd be up to our eyeballs in carrion.

The birds that flit from tree to tree—the goldfinches and towhees, the grosbeaks, indigo buntings, brown thrashers, and Carolina wrens—form a population constantly in flux. One year I saw summer tanagers in the walnut grove; this season we have squatters: brown-headed cowbirds. Ladderback woodpeckers swoop from tree to tree with their peculiar looping flight and land again four trees over.

It's a jungle out there—or so it seems. Vines are everywhere. On one tree alone I counted such a dizzying variety of these clinging, woody plants that I was amazed the tree could support their weight. There was a swarthy poison ivy vine, clamped close to the trunk and holding tight with the aerial rootlets that resemble a bad toupee; I never laugh out loud at this vine, though—it's capable of revenge. *Rhus toxicodendron* is tricky, a master of disguise. If I avoid only this thick, hairy vine, I can still run up against the slim, shrubby version or the low, sprawling plant.

I used not to be allergic to its venom; then later, only a tiny rash would appear. Now I can itch from fingertip to elbow and wake scratching in the night.

Wild grapevines twined and arced against this same tree, defining grace. Their bark was rough and loose and peeled away easily; the birds found it an admirable nesting material, tying basketlike homes tight to their supports with strings pulled from the vine. In the summer the air is thick with the scent of the inconspicuous whitish flowers, an overpowering sweet odor, cloying in the extreme—but the tart grapes are ample reward for tolerance, both for me and for hungry wildlife.

A plethora of wild vines in the woods.

Virginia creeper clings to the tree, contrasting its relatively smooth vines with the rougher grapes and poison ivy. The vine has developed a unique growing method: its tendrils reach out, grasping at a support; when they find one, they develop tiny adhesive pads that glue the vine to its host, whether it be tree bark or the side of a house. When you pull away the vine the tiny eighth-inch pads remain, stippling the host surface with dots.

Providing a fine-line counterrhythm, catbrier lay delicate hold on the larger vines. My fondness for things feline encourages me to use the vernacular "catbrier," but when I look this *Smilax* up in my field guides I must remember to look for greenbrier instead. The tender growing tips are crisp and fresh as buttercrunch lettuce from my garden. This plant is an important food source for wildlife in spring—when it is attractive to me as well—and later in the year, when I no longer can touch its woody, thorn-spiked shoots. Deer don't seem to care how thorny it gets; they'll nip it to the ground. I found marks of the feast nearby and recognized the culprit by the rough ends of the vines—deer have no incisors and must tear their food loose, macerating it with large molars. (I imagined deer molars to be like ours, mostly flat and meant for grinding; instead, they are closely fitted like the teeth of my saw blade and engineered to fit, top and bottom, much like the teeth of a zipper. The surface of each tooth is uneven; on the upper jaw, the molar's front edge rises sharply in a V-shaped wedge; it's just the opposite on the bottom, where the inner surface rises higher. The teeth of the two jaws overlap one another, perfectly fitted to their ripping, cutting task. I let the tiny fawn that my friend Pete rescued nurse on my fingers one day, expecting a gentle suction, and yanked my hand away hurriedly—it hurt! I can imagine what a fully grown deer could do to a finger.)

Large-leafed moonseed, a common vine with poisonous black berries, tied the tangled picture together. It was as though there was not enough room on the crowded forest floor; the vines opted for altitude, but it's light they're after, not room. And that's to be found overhead, where the leaf canopy thins to allow fingers of light to shine through.

Sketching this confusing tangle took time; I brought my folding camp stool and sat quietly in the woods, batting away mosquitoes. A difficult subject like this one forces me to slow down, to push back my normal tendency to perpetual motion—to stay at it as long as it takes. Ordinarily I passed this strangled, trussed tree with a quick glance, appreciating the rhythmic lines of the variety of plant forms that clung here, but never doing more than snapping a quick picture on my way to the walnut grove.

This day, there was time. I heard the music of the forest: the kettledrum beats of a woodpecker just overhead. He had found a huge dead tree to bang on; the sound reverberated, I am sure, for half a mile. A hermit thrush fluted deep in the transparent green shadows. A migrant warbler of some kind or another added its vocalizations to the general symphony. Something big flew from tree to tree, making a harsh, primitive *kwawk*, an atonal counterpoint that reminded me of Bartok. I tracked it briefly to try to determine its identity: heron or turkey buzzard? But it had the advantage; I can't fly. Each time I got almost close enough to see my quarry clearly through the thick leaf canopy, it heard my approach and took off, leaving me frustrated and hot, watching its direction, and renewing the hunt until I gave it up and returned to my drawing, trying to keep the sense of all those interwoven vines.

Today as I searched the woods on the hill to learn the identity of the big red-orange-colored leaf canopies I could see from the road (black maples, not oaks; score one for Harris), I reveled in this quite different habitat. There is a wet-weather seep on this hill, a huge stain of dampness that covers an area as big as my lawn at home. Moisture-loving jewelweed sprouts here in drifts but to no avail, surely; there can't be enough sunlight to allow full growth, flowering, and seeding.

But how, then, do they appear here in the murk? Jewelweed spreads by giving its seed a spectacular send-off, propelled by a seedpod spring when inadvertently brushed; hence the perverse name "touch-me-not." Someone wasn't thinking when they dubbed that plant; in order to spread seed and prosper, this plant is more likely to say "please touch."

A thick stand of tiny ferns blankets the hill just down from the seep; even in drought they cast soft angora lace over the ground. In the spring, miniature fiddleheads tempt me to try just one for their crisp, fresh flavor, all the better for a winter of store-bought greens and tubers; they are so small I don't have the heart to gather enough for a salad.

This hillside shows signs of long-ago use scribed along its lateral dimension. Another tractor road, overgrown with redbud saplings and poison ivy, is barely visible, bisecting our property and joining it to its ancestral plot. Before the road, before the cul-de-sac, before the mobile homes, this was all one huge holding, acres upon acres of hills and fields in the hands of one family; my land is the disinherited scion of a backcountry estate. Uphill, near the south fence, a rough rock wall is thrown up beside the road—whether to clear the way or to provide a rough barrier I have no way of knowing. Lichen has claimed this old wall; the rocks glow with a paint-box array of yellows, oranges, greens, and blacks. When it rains the colors are as intense as a child's drawing.

Rocks have tumbled back into the roadway, and when I opened the path this spring with Harris's weed whacker, I sent its white nylon teeth shooting off into the woods each time I failed to see a stone hidden among the ivy. I picked up the largest of these and replaced them on the wall, wondering who might have done so before me, and when.

Above the rock wall is the oddest wood of all, most recently open from the look of things. There are a few giant oaks here, a shagbark hickory or two, a hedge—but mostly there are thousands of thready saplings reaching for the light. None is more than three inches or so in diameter; none is much taller than fifteen feet. They are close together, an explosion of onetime growth, perhaps seeded all at once when cattle no longer grazed here, when the fence fell and the owner of the ancestral plot broke up his holdings.

It's a magical wood; dragons—arum flowers—sprout as they do on the west hill, but here there is little competition. Understory is nearly nonexistent, shaded out by the thick adolescent leaves of the close-spaced saplings. It is a clean place, open; it has no secrets like the other woods. If a deer moves here, I see it. If a squirrel scurries overhead, I can't miss it.

Harris and I say we will camp here in these guileless woods; who would worry about snakes or coyotes or ticks in such an open place? I could see a tick coming for a city block and a deer for a mile.

The deer are elusive as smoke, like a dream on waking. Their cloven prints mark the woods where nothing was the day before. They had been here, occupying the same land I occupied, breathing the same air I breathed, watching as I watched for them. Unlike the casual herds in the nearby state park, which stand and stare with unjudging equanimity until I am quite near, then bound away with a belated snort of alarm and a flash of white tails, the deer that co-opt my place prefer not to be seen. They've got the skills to elude detection.

I follow them; they follow me; the paths I enlarged for our use, from the pond and meadow through the woods, from the creek up the old tractor path beside the stone wall, are as convenient for the deer, and I bend to touch their prints along these green arched thoroughfares.

The deer are here. I sense them; I smell them. I see their deep-etched tracks in the fresh mud and find where they slipped coming down the hill where the wet-weather seep makes the footing difficult. I read their messages and long for their presence—but like the dragon in the woods, they are elusive, secretive as spies. They wear their camouflage well.

Tiny Waterfall
after a good
rain

5. The Creek

Scoured limestone lines the bottom of the creek near the open slickrocks, level as poured concrete. Some 300 million years ago these rocks were beachfront property, the receding edge of an inland sea. Scraped and abraded by the last glacier, stones bear striations scribed by moving ice. Like the nearby Missouri River, they are the orphaned children of another age. They've adapted well.

Now they are wraith pale and studded with the fossilized remains of small invertebrates, trace fossils, and primitive plant forms; I can scarcely pass them without walking bent like a crone, nose to the earth to see what I can see. The slickrocks themselves are mystery; my footsteps ring with a slight hollowness when I walk across the blanched, rounded surface. The sound is more pronounced when I tap their skull-like smoothness with a loose stone, and I wish I knew what airless chamber was secreted there. Limestone is soft and malleable as rocks go. It can be worn by water into a billion veins and pockets, gargoyle shapes, chutes and hollows and caves; beneath the slickrock, an incipient cavern may be waiting to mature.

Tiny aquatic creatures lived and died beneath these prehistoric waters, slowly turning to stone as the silt hardened. Folded into this finer matrix are the bodies of crinoids and brachiopods, ammonoids and corals. One odd rock, a *Chætetes* coral colony, turned up near the creek. The tiny, hairlike tubes that fur the nucleus rock had held living corallites, each of which sealed off its living quarters behind it as it grew, lengthening until it waved in the sea like grass. The animal with the longest reach got the most food, and competition was as keen then as ever. Now they are recrystallized and as delicate as gypsum; each time I handle this fine, ornate specimen, I am dusted with bits of crystal prehistory.

Here and there, a trilobite stares back at me with stony eyes. The sea that drowned my corner of Missouri was home to billions of these creatures; the limestone bones of this landscape attest to our watery genesis. I am astounded by the persistence of these ancestors of the horseshoe crab; I can grasp the fact that hard-shelled brachiopods and mussels survive intact, in some cases still maintaining bits of the original shell material. What strains credulity is the fact that trilobites were arthropods; their "shells" were chitinous, like the casing of a beetle—like our own fingernails, but far thinner. How could such a thing have remained intact throughout the processes and pressures that lead to fossilization?

I like the idea of the patient endurance of these sturdy little tourists from another age; I keep nose to ground looking to meet those hard, buglike eyes—evidence of survival in spite of apparent weakness.

We may have something in common, it seems, the trilobites and I. Paleontologists Loren Babcock and Richard Robinson at the University of Kansas have theorized, on studying thousands of trilobite fossils, that the little creatures may have been right-handed. There are an inordinate number of fossils with a bite taken from their right sides (the work of their arch-foe the *Anomalocaris*, a prehistoric sea predator), indicating, perhaps, a trilobitic tend to the right. These distant relatives of life in general may have shared the characteristic that compels me to lift my hammer or write my notes with my right hand.

The land snails that stud the rich dark earth here show a marked tendency to the right, as well; their graceful helix appears on that side of the shell. The left may reveal a bit of spiral deep in the interior; it may show none at all. The fleshy foot of this common land gastropod is oriented to the left, apparently to balance the heavier, protuberant spiral. What this means I can't imagine; how it relates to brain function is beyond me, though handedness seems to have a bearing on brain hemisphere dominance in humans. But in all the shells I've picked up in the woods, not one has been left-sided. Oddly enough, the ones in the creek itself are bilaterally symmetrical, without a sign of handedness, like their ancestors the ammonoids. Perhaps evolution noted their relative weightlessness in water, obviating the need for counterbalance.

We need the limey skeletons of bedrock that girdle the earth, appearing in virtually every landmass. Eons ago, when they formed beneath primordial seas, the small, calcareous bodies that made up this fine matrix gradually locked up much of the carbon dioxide in the atmosphere, making our environment hospitable to life as we know it. If some unimagined disaster were suddenly to dissolve all the Earth's limestone, CO_2 levels would rise and the greenhouse effect would be no longer threat but reality. This thought amazes me; I owe my life to the rocks beneath my feet.

In my wanderings I find a rockful of perfectly preserved brachiopods,

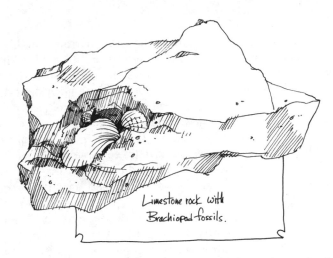

Limestone rock with
Brachiopod fossils.

their graceful clamshell shapes still as finely and elegantly marked as the shells we toted home from Maine, turned to stone by the slow passage of time. One shell, still whole and double-sided—open just a crack like a sleepy eye—is filled with a quartz translucence as if the body of the shellfish had crystallized. Perhaps it did, though more likely silica filled the empty shell and by a process of shifting of atoms became this glittering loveliness.

There are two kinds of brachiopods visible in this particular rock; one, called *Antiquatonia,* is marked with simple linear striations. The other is busy with flourishes, tiny protrusions that mark the position of erstwhile spines—variations on a theme. Sometimes one of these fossil shells weathers free of its stone matrix, as perfectly formed and whole as the mussels in my pond. I start with pleasure as though I'd discovered great treasure; I've never gotten used to finding stone seashells loose upon the ground.

The beadlike stems of crinoids, common to this part of the country, are the segments of a prehistoric creature with the name of a flower: sea lily. When I am lucky I find bits of the flowerlike head as well.

A rose-colored stone flecked with feldspar, rounded by its long passage beneath the belly of the glacier, had traveled far from its place of origin hundreds of miles to the frozen north. It is Sioux quartzite, one of several types of rock to have passed southward under glacial ice. A lighter stone bears linear scrape marks; it was imprisoned between the glacier and the bedrock below, a gigantic mortar and pestle that made small rocks of large ones and wrote the story of their travels on their sides in long, straight traces.

The nearby slickrocks are Bethany Falls limestone, named by geologists for an outcropping first studied near a waterfall in northwest Missouri. Each layer-cake bed of rocks is named—some for their place of discovery, some for a nearby feature of the landscape, some for their discoverer; it's a taxonomy of stones.

Downstream from the slickrocks the creek narrows, jumbles with a million rocks tossed together or piled one on another in a kind of manic stonework. Water is the casual stonemason, each time it rips through the narrow draw that contains the creek. Coupled with gravity, moving water has power I can scarcely imagine—without a rather graphic visual aid, that is. The catch pool below the tiny waterfall changed shape entirely after the latest high water, and a boulder washed downstream, lodging at the far end of the pool. It was immense; it would have taken three strong men to lift it, and now it appeared like an island, dividing the creek in two and making of the single stream a two-headed snake before it joined again downstream.

Before upstream farms and towns tapped the aquifer and stole the creek's water away, it may have held a more generous flow like other nearby streams. The limestone bluffs that stand back from the creek are separated from one another by hundreds of feet, suggesting that the eroding width of water was once considerable—or that the streambed has changed course wildly over the millennia, wearing away the space between the rocks.

These woodland creeks were a magnet for the various native Americans who left their mark on Missouri's prehistory, and I am always alert for messages encoded in the stone or salted through the gravel bars. I sat by the creek in early September browsing through the millennia like the Sunday paper, looking for whatever there was to find—fossils, glacial erratics, artifacts. On this day of butter-colored sunshine and early turning leaves, I looked to find what may have been uncovered by the flood—arrowheads, perhaps, or scrapers. Our place is peppered with flint and chert, weathered out of the Winterset limestone on the hill. Trekking down through the centuries from the land bridge at the top of the continent, the first arrivals to this area found these rocks useful, perfectly suited to cutting and scraping. I tested a tiny chip of grayish flint against my palm and cut myself on its edge.

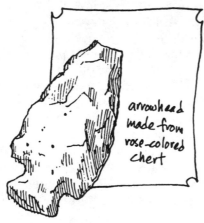

arrowhead made from rose-colored chert

These random bits and flakes of siliceous chert were probably the first cutting tools; our Stone Age forebears recognized the utility of such an edge. Later, they chipped away at the natural edges, stone on stone, to make tools of great beauty and sophistication.

Flint, chert; some geologists explain the difference in rock names in this way: chert is the rock itself in its untouched state; flint is chert that has been worked. At Nebo Hill, a few miles to the west, a flint mine provided the locus for a population that spanned thousands of years. Tools—scrapers, knives, drills, spear points, banner stones—are found along the rivers of this part of the state, wherever a land rise near convenient water suggests a good campsite.

Twelve thousand years B.C., Paleo-Indians utilized this cream-colored chert; archaic-period peoples followed. Woodland Indians, most populous at Nebo, scattered tools like pop cans. They traded with other peoples from as far away as New York—that characteristic flint found its way here to lie undiscovered beneath the sod for 2,000 years; it turns up bit by bit after each spring rain.

I never pass the creek without looking for the evidence of use, a connection to the past to help me find my place in time. And just as I was about to get my nose up off the ground and get back to business, I saw it: a napped edge, chipped to a sharpness that could only signal intent. That edge was no accident. It was meant for scraping.

The piece fit my hand as though I had designed it myself. A natural depression in the flattened, oval stone received my thumb perfectly; the wide, blunt lip fit into the hollow of my palm to provide leverage, a comfortable pushing surface with no sharpness about it at all—the tool maker, like me, was right-handed. I fingered the piece with satisfaction and felt the long string of prehistory tug at my afternoon.

The creek bisects our eighteen acres across along its north-south axis; it's the needle in a compass, pointing north from the walnut grove. This linear feature in the landscape is a geological marker, both time line and lifeline of our small quarter section of Missouri. It acts as a sundial's gnomon, channeling light deep into the woods to tell the passing of hours as it marks the passing of millennia.

But no matter where the creek itself points, life certainly arrows toward this nearly year-round source of water. The creek is an immense squirming nursery. Mosquitoes bred prolifically when the water level dropped and moving water stilled to stagnant pools. The shrimplike young boogied beneath the surface of the water, and I slapped a syncopated percussion at the hungry females, greedy vampires that needed my protein to formulate more eggs.

A moving cloud of midges danced above the surface of the water, sprung from some microscopic life-passage invisible to me. Mayflies hatched from larval dorotheas, and I thought of my father's delicate feather trout flies that mimicked the preferred food source of his elusive, epicurean prey. Dragonfly larvae scooted through the shallows, scuttling away from the threat of my shadow on the water. Here and there a water bug swam below the surface or hauled out for a moment on a fallen leaf; predatory water striders sculled the edges, looking for meat, laying their eggs in secret. Their thready legs dimpled the water's surface and cast round, sparkling shadows on the limestone floor of the pool. They're irritable creatures, as territorial as cats; one strider sneaked up behind another and jumped it, clearing the surface of the water by nearly a half inch; there was a short, nasty scuffle before the loser broke free and retreated.

An emerald damselfly escorted me up the creek, stopping at points of interest like a guide and flexing jet black wings as though to dry them. Crayfish and fat tadpoles scattered as I waded upstream; one callow tad mistook my dirty canvas shoes for the scoured limestone it normally shelters under and made a dash for my foot. I caught it easily, lifting it to my face for inspection; the tad was soft as butter on a summer day, and I returned it to the creek before I injured it with my touch.

At each small riffle, the rocks were whiskered with short stems of dark gray-green algae like a three-day growth of beard—or so I imagined at first glance. Bending closer to see, I found these were animal instead, attached to the rock at one end, just where the water broke over a tiny turbulence. Their eighth-inch-long, tube-shaped bodies responded to the creek's current, but there was something else afoot. Each tiny creature seemed to have it in for its fellows, and after a peaceful interlude, head downstream with the current, one would suddenly reach over and tweak its neighbor. Perhaps it was a mating ritual instead, but nothing seemed to come of it. Each stayed firmly anchored to its rock, each—perhaps wisely—an eighth of an inch from the next. Later, when I described this ritual to Department of Conservation fisheries biologist Phil Jeffries, he was as stumped as I—were they leeches or larvae? But when I returned to gather some samples for identification, the water level had dropped and there were no tiny green hairlike creatures to be found; the mystery remains.

There's a great deal of birthing and dying, of eating and being eaten going on here; the food chain is forged of pretty solid links, and on a summer day when the rain has been constant it seems productive beyond measure.

Spring peepers, the tiny three-quarter-inch *Hyla crucifer*, find their way to the creek's slow-moving pools once mating season has passed. Earlier they congregated by the thousands in the neighbor's fishless pond near the road. With the slow turning of the seasons, they retreated deeper and deeper into

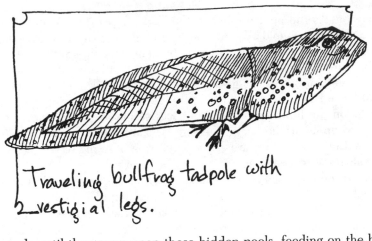

Traveling bullfrog tadpole with 2 vestigial legs.

the woods until they came upon these hidden pools, feeding on the bounty and settling back to digest in peace. All summer and early fall we startle one another as I pass; they always seem to see me first. But if I am patient—and silent—I find them perched beneath the edge of a leaf, imagining themselves unseen.

After the flood the creek was alive with the big gray-green commas of bullfrog tadpoles washed over the spillway of the pond. Their bodies were sumo-wrestler fat, but their tails were translucent as a silk scarf. They didn't look capable of the power they must in fact have; this gossamer appendage propelled the tads across the pool almost too quickly to follow.

A larger green frog, *Rana clamitans* Latreille, inhabits the big pool by the fallen limestone monolith, diving for cover beneath its leading edge. The frog is streamlined as a fish as it pushes away from the bank with muscular, Greg Louganis legs. We are at the edge of this frog's range in Missouri, living as we do at the southernmost border of a plain once beveled by glaciers, and it's an uncommon pleasure to spot one.

Today, I sifted through the stones of the gravel bar, half in preparation for an upcoming class in geology of the Kansas City area, my thoughts occupied by the bits and pieces of prehistory I could hold in my hand. Suddenly, a green frog appeared literally at my feet, emerging from between two leaves like a bookmark in the pages of a diary. I had been still for several minutes, and it must not have seen me—or perhaps this soon before the long winter's hibernation it simply didn't give a damn.

The frog sat spread-eagled, chubby as a Buddha, not eight inches from my sneaker tips, blinking as if just awakened by a wrong number. I was directly in front of its snout; perhaps the eyes so prominently set on each side of the frog's head simply couldn't see what was right in front of its nose.

A large oak leaf was glued tight to the animal's side by the water's surface tension. As the pool rippled in the slight breeze, the leaf repeatedly touched that bronze-gold eye and the frog blinked to dislodge it, again and again. The leaf bobbed like a dinghy. I blew in the creature's face to try to send the leaf off across the pool, but too gently. I gathered my resolve along with my breath and gave it a good "whoosh!" and the leaf cleared the frog's eye and floated away, revealing the entire body with its subtle stippling and faint bars on the hind legs. The snout was yellowish green, and a double ridge stood up along the back. The big ear spots looked like the stretched head of a drum, which they are—the percussion of sound waves rather than drumbeats is the reagent.

I could see the frog's breath come and go in the wet nostrils and in the faint bobbing in the water. It was still oblivious to me although I had inched closer, glacier slow—so near that my sneaker was wet and my left hand was in the water. This must be how the great blue heron at our pond catches so many frogs, for this one hadn't even blinked at my approach.

I moved closer, careful to keep my shadow from falling across the ani-mal's face, stifling the impulse to pounce. "No, patience, be patient—see if you can touch it." I lowered my right hand into the water and left it there until it was cold as a frog's belly. I inched toward the frog, and still it stared at me—or just beside me, as though concentrating on deep thoughts of its own.

A limb crashed behind me, knocked to the ground by the wind, but I refused to allow myself to jump; too near, now, to the quarry. Gently, careful-ly, I touched the frog's back; it seemed not to notice. I stroked it, petting it as I would a kitten, and it remained supremely indifferent. I slipped a finger under the soft belly, then another and another, until the frog rested quies-cent in my hand, and lifted it level with my eyes.

I moved as slowly and deliberately as a Japanese Kabuki dancer, the frog still on my palm, unmoving. I could see each fine detail, every bit of frog spot or eye gleam, even to the gold-leaf limning of the dark pupil, and I dipped and turned my hand for a panoramic view.

That did it. The green frog was aware of me now, seemed to notice me for the first time; there was a dawning in its eyes, the amphibian equivalent of "oh, shit!"—and that was most definitely that. The frog leapt free, broad-jumped four feet across the pool, and disappeared under the edge of the tiny waterfall, lost in that small turbulence. I could breathe again and let out the air with a delighted whoop; I hadn't had that kind of fun since I caught tad-poles by the railroad tracks when I was seven.

On any given day, birds chatter in the trees that overarch the rocky creek bed. They use the open tunnel of the creek as a thoroughfare—as do the mammals and insects that populate our land; as do I. This line of least resistance is like a path, wet sometimes so that I must hotfoot it from rock to rock, dry as Nevada when the rains cease. I duck to avoid the spiderwebs strung across this busy insect highway; the spiders know where their next meal is coming from—up the creek, or down it. I wear their silk banners streaming from nose and cheeks and smudgy glasses; if I am careless, I wear the weaver as well.

Most mornings the signs are unmistakable; we share this land with others who bear an older deed by far. The soft mud by the creek, the night before a blank slate waiting to be written upon, bears the marks of green herons, opossum, and raccoon, small handlike depressions that explain the noises we hear in the night. I find the remains of the raccoon's meal, a crawfish as neatly and thoroughly shelled as a Maine lobster; even the tiny, chitinous legs are sucked clean.

White tailed deer pass beside the small waterfall; the story is written in muddy braille. Here a doe led her fawn to drink; the tiny hearts are strung like beads beside the water. My fingers read the message, and if the relative size didn't spell out the story, the shallower draft of the tiny hoofprints would tell me—this is a baby, light as thistledown in relation to the greater weight of its mother.

In the night, a large buck ran pell-mell beside the creek, pursued by dogs. Spread wide for traction, dug deep with the force of his stride, the big

Heron tracks near the little waterfall— I frightened it away, but it didn't go far—just to the oak tree.

splayed tracks of the deer are overlaid with the prints of maybe half a dozen dogs. I could almost hear hoof thunder and the excited canine yammering.

My neighbor confirmed the scenario: "I saw a bunch of those big dogs chasing a buck through your place last night," Donny told me. "I knew you wouldn't like it; I shot off a round or two to scare them off him." It must have worked, too. Donny said the buck went one way and the dogs another —nothing like a twelve-gauge shotgun to require one's immediate attention elsewhere.

Guns are a basic fact of life in the country. It's a rare weekend when I don't hear the repeated crash of target practice. This time I was grateful. "Speak softly and carry a big stick"—one that makes plenty of noise. Donny does, and the deer escaped unscathed.

He knows I don't but thinks that I should.

"Carry some of them big Black Cat firecrackers, anyway," he tells me. "They make a big enough boom they'd scare off anything or any*body*."

But so far I haven't armed myself with Black Cats, either; the image is too ludicrous. "Back off or I light the fuse, mister," as I fumble for a match. No, I guess not.

These limestone-paved tributaries contain death as well as life. When we first explored these miniature highways through thickly forested hills, I found the skulls and bones of animals that had died beside the creek—or perhaps in it, in a flash flood. A woodchuck's skeleton was perfectly laid out, bone on bone. I found the blunt, thick neck end of the skull still aligned with the first vertebra, and the next, and the next. It must have lain there untouched by any of the larger scavengers—a rare occurrence in nature, where nothing much is wasted.

Nor was this, in fact. Deathwatch beetles and botflies had arrived within hours and begun the grisly work of returning dust to dust. Even the protein-rich hair was useful to some creature or another. There was nothing left but these perfectly arranged bones.

Down the creek it was a different story. The bones of a Virginia opossum were scattered over twenty feet of creek bed and bank. I could find only bits and pieces near the skull with its long, bony snout. Coyotes or turkey vultures may have been the beneficiary of an unfinished meal.

These findings clue me in on what shares this smallholding, supplementing the testimony of tracks and scat and markings. Normally shy, these creatures hide from me by day or run like a gray-brown streak sketched against the thick underbrush.

I am no threat to bleached bones; they lie there patiently, allowing me to run a finger with impunity over teeth as sharp as flint bird points. I flesh out bare skulls in my imagination and check with my book of mammals to see what it is I've found. The startled woodchuck that pounded away by the hackberry tree isn't so trusting of my goodwill—nor patient with my endless curiosity.

My collection of bones and stones grows each time I wander down the creek; they capture my imagination, focus me in my ramblings. Their bones —and the limestone bones of the rock that shines as whitely in the moonlight—support me as surely as my own skeleton, tie me to the land with a common bond of calcium carbonate.

If the creek acts as a compass needle pointing the way north and away from the walnut grove, it is also a pointer towards. A temptation, an invitation to trespass—with low water, a rock-paved road seemingly meant for egress. The birds and animals and I are not alone in seeing the possibilities of thoroughfare.

So it seemed to our local contingent of ATV riders, at any rate. In the wrong hands, these all-terrain vehicles are the bane of private landowners and conservationists. Noise pollution is constant. Forest paths are torn up and left to erode; creeks are damaged; fish, frogs, and tadpoles are run down as though, by being invisible to a goggle-wearing rider, they are insignificant as well.

It's the mindless damage that gets to me. Donny told me that the barbed-wire fence at the back of his father's property has been cut three times simply because the sports wanted free rein. This isn't the American West; there are no public lands beyond the occasional park, and off-road use of machines is banned by law. Recent Missouri law states that these unlicensed machines as they come from the dealer cannot be used on public roads and highways—or on private property not owned by the ATV operator. It could hardly be plainer. Enforcement is another matter; catching the perpetrators as they bucket through the hills on these little buggies is impossible for a police officer in a car.

Too many places are scarred with ATV trails where they have no business being: along public highways; in parks and greenbelts; through old-growth woods; down fragile streambeds. Too many animals have been chased to exhaustion, too many ground-nesting birds and their young have been killed, too many spawning habitats in waterways have been destroyed in the name of recreation—at least when irresponsible people are at the wheel.

When I saw these hated tracks in my *own* streambed it was a massive shot of adrenaline. I was on fire, incandescent with anger—energized as though shot through with lightning.

I was in motion in a heartbeat, tracking where they had entered my land —my sanctuary—following to see how far they went. Did they find the slickrocks, the waterfall? Did they rip through the walnut grove, chasing deer or rabbits? I covered as much of the land as I could, scarcely noticing when I became winded or when my muscles began to burn. I was hot-wired, oblivious—furious.

If it were legal to spike trails, spiked they would be. If I could string fence wire at neck level across the creek, I'd do it—and may yet, but with a more reasoned and fluorescent warning sign hung at midcreek for visibility.

We had discussed new signs for months, of course, to supplement our old "no hunting" signs; ever since we bought the land at the tail end of summer we wondered what we should do. The insistent *ownership* of "no trespassing" signs doesn't work for me; I know too well how transient that can be.

But we had planned on new signs, something that would outline our expectations, something polite, if you will, a decent, simple sign that expects decent, simple compliance.

I must have been nuts.

I didn't care *what* the suckers said, just so they were up. Within twenty-four hours I had bought three, eight-foot treated-wood posts, cut signs, and painted my hasty message in permanent red: Private Property. NO ATVs. NO Hunting. No Fishing. (I'd have added "get out of my face, don't bother me" if I'd thought there was room on the sign; I was way beyond polite.)

I chopped and dug and scrabbled my way through gravelly dirt still locked in steely drought, carried an eighty-pound bag of concrete 600 feet from the road to firm up the farthest sign, and nailed my messages in place. I dragged brush and branches across the point of egress and dropped a thorn-studded locust tree across the trail with a hatchet.

I was beat but not beaten—just bone tired, all the anger-fueled energy sucked out by a cyclone of work. Tired, muscle sore, and covered with the worst case of poison ivy I had ever had in my life. Such are the dangers of war.

It's strange, when I think about it; I'd be hard put to find the logic in my feelings about trespass in the abstract—though not if the trespassers ride ATVs. I explore here myself; the barrier of a half-fallen barbed-wire fence in deep woods isn't much of a deterrent. If I can go under or over, I do, to see what lies down the creek. The waterfall Brigadoon is beyond the borders of my land, as is the big meadow on the highest hill around here, the one that Wendy calls "Starfield," with a nod to Edwin Way Teale. The rock shelter that marks another wet-weather waterfall is likewise somewhat past my perimeter, and I visit it when I can, wondering if archaic or Woodland peoples camped there.

The idea of ownership is oddly arbitrary. I grasp its meaning, of course; I pay my taxes and drive the road to remind myself that my land turns a corner at the east road and that this—all this—is mine. What I have trouble with is a deeper concept, one that has to do with time and occupancy. I own it now; I didn't three years ago. I call this eighteen acres my property; who will say that in forty years? It's not mine in the same way as early graying hair or introversion. The land has too much past, stretching back along the creek's time line to a place that's outlined in the fossilized shell of a brachiopod. Compared to the tactile millennia contained in one of these erstwhile sea creatures, my time here is a nanosecond; who cares who owns the land just then?

We have a lot to learn from our native American forebears; we may have to if we plan to survive. According to the great-grandmother I never knew, I am a part of all this. And rather than insist on my paper ownership, deeded and recorded, I recognize that it owns me—that I've come home.

Our late twentieth-century ideas of private property, the feeling that we can do as we will with land we've bought and paid for (whether our actions are good for that land or not) shows in the silent testimony of erosion. Missouri is the second worst state in the nation for that hard evidence of the lack of long-term care; ATVs and other off-road vehicles exacerbate the problem. If trees are in our way — if we want a new field, a better view, another shopping center, or firewood for our stove—we cut them; never mind that each tree contributes to the health of the biosphere. Our sense of proprietorship and our apparently increasing alienation from (or ignorance of) the natural cycles that keep us alive join forces to further cut us off from true relationship—and from recognizing that relationship. We are not separate, however comforting our forebears might find the thought.

In the Midwest of 150 years ago, the land was wild, covered with tallgrass, bristling with trees. We found it oppressive, untamed, and set about to do something about it. What we did has had far-reaching consequences, not only for the land itself but for our own sense of belonging.

I don't own the land beyond my property line. I pay no taxes there, post no signs, mend no fences. But its wildness reminds me of that older Missouri, and I make my forays deeper and deeper into the woods down the creek, trespassing on property not my own. Not, however, on an all-terrain vehicle.

PART II:
BUILDING
ON A DREAM

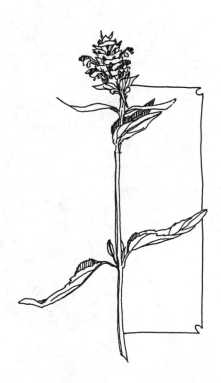

A pair of entwined
oaks — they've
withstood a lot.

6. Dreamseeds

I hadn't intended to build when we bought the land. It was simply to be a getaway, a place to be alone and think, somewhere to walk without anxiety or enforced sociability.

In this isolated wood, there would be the chance to discover the small changes that move across the face of the Earth and the immense transmutations that draw their designs on the seasons, the effects of storms and droughts and the coming of winter. I planned to track them like a meteorologist and to note their impact on the birds and animals and insects here. I wanted to get to know the creatures that held first deed and to share their lives.

I like to learn; in that, my family taught me well. My mother enjoyed her mind; my father reveled in his, building his mental muscles like a weight trainer. My mother's father continued to study a variety of subjects until his death at ninety-five; we're not big on boredom. My gray matter is my best physical attribute; it beats blue eyes every time. Just having a place to unearth the wheels within the wheels of the varied habitats and to make my own discoveries was enough; I didn't need a building to make it complete.

Our eighteen acres would stay as we had found it, or very nearly so. Maybe we'd put a bench by the creek; we visited the waterfall almost daily, carrying lunch and folding lawn chairs down the hill from the car and then carrying them out again. Often I came alone, sitting by the creek or watching the surface of the pond ruffle in the wind, noting the slow raftings of turtles, tracking the progression of plant communities. I sketched, making entries in my field journal as I got to know my way around the land, taking inventory. It was the first time I had felt so at peace—so safe—in years. Why would I need more than this?

But the walnut grove sprouted a phantom cabin in its midst. It was as if it wanted to be there; it felt right—or so I imagined. There was a certain spot, a place between the trees that seemed to encompass everything I loved about the place. The path that Harris had cut around the grove began and ended there. I could see the place where we first saw the deer at the edge of the grove; just beside it was a tree wreathed in bittersweet. Before it was the creek and the big limestone slump block and the waterfall. And leading directly to it was the old tractor road I had walked that first day. There had to be a cabin; there already was, in my mind.

I'd think this phantom place a mirage that shimmered in my imagination, but it wasn't just me; others had seen the thing there, too. Our neighbors walked back to meet us when we first bought the land; as usual, we were in the grove, admiring the nearby creek and its tiny waterfall.

"Are you going to build here?" Donny asked. "We always thought it would be perfect for a house—a cabin, anyway."

The young couple who had owned the place before us had loved the grove, too, and wanted to build there before complications intervened and they moved to another state. His father is our neighbor across the road; when I talk to him I see the reflections of their dreams for the place in my own.

And when I brought Rachel here with me to sketch, we walked the perimeter of the grove and inspected the waterfall before crossing the little stream. We took the old tractor road up the east hill that overlooks the walnut trees across the creek. I'd said nothing to her about building or where such a thing might be.

We paused at the place where the overhanging trees frame the wooded landscape. "Look," she said, pointing across the water. "It looks like there ought to be a cabin right over there."

She was right.

The walnut grove was a kind of meeting ground for the wild and the just-touched-by-humans. These tall, straight trees didn't grow here by themselves, or so I surmised. At nearly the same height and circumference, it was as though they were planted by someone with visions of profit—a plan we, by leaving them be, circumvented. Walnut is a dense wood, satiny, the color of a sable mare in shadow. Since colonial times people have utilized this hardwood; in southern Missouri, where it is plentiful, it finds its way into handsome salad bowls, hand-carved gun stocks, and sculpture.

In summer the trees pelt us with the immature fruits as though to drive us out, raining down hard little knots that will be black walnuts. We sit well in the open to avoid the worst of the shelling and watch the wind direction carefully. These nuts have deadly aim, and as they mature they may be two inches across. They're encased in acid green husks that turn slowly to a deep brown if allowed to ripen fully; if you touch them your hands will take on the same dark hue as the wood.

There is no understory here, beyond a young redbud or two and a few baby oaks. If the mixed community of wildflowers and weeds were cut, it would resemble an English greensward, a bowling green beneath the trees. The floor of the grove is carpeted with wildflowers like a medieval tapestry; I half expect to discover a unicorn sleeping among the brown-eyed Susans and heal-all.

The grove abuts the creek and reaches nearly to our back fence line; from here I can see the limestone rocks that bracket the old, fallen fence that marks the end of our property. Here I watch for the fat woodchuck that likes the slight clearing and pick the bright orange bittersweet that hangs just within reach. This woody vine begins in anonymity, nondescript among the other vines that climb nearly every tree in the grove. Its leaves are simple, yellow-green; the flowers are nondescript. Our native *Celastrus scandens* is losing ground in our northeastern states to Asiatic bittersweet (*C. orbiculatus*), a pushy relative as emphatic as kudzu. That it survives at all is amazing; every fall when the scarlet fruits of the female vine—fleshy seeds, in fact—open with their stoplight colors on the roadsides, we see cars lined up to pick it for floral displays. And if the country nostalgia buffs don't get it the birds do; bittersweet makes fine winter food. This vine of mine is too isolated—and too high in the tree—to be in danger from any but the birds; I applaud its perspicacity.

The grove had just enough of the human about it to suggest a series of

Heal-all
(*Prunella vulgaris*)
purple flowers,
glossy leaves.

questions. Who came here and to what end? Who owned these acres? What were the plans for this place, what were its uses? How long has occupancy— some degree of occupancy, at least—laid its inevitable mark here? There was the weathering evidence of the Boy Scouts, the square nail Wendy and I found near the creek, the scraper napped by native Americans, and the blazes cut in the bases of the walnut trees, barely heard whispers that made the place seem hospitable, inviting; wild, but not wilderness. This place had the stamp of my kind already on it, a brand, a radio collar with a signal I could recognize and respond to.

There may be marks of the human here, but it is owned by the wild; the place bears indelible watermarks. Summer tanagers and indigo buntings own the trees; the burring of a Carolina wren and the flocks of bright, chipping cardinals claim deed to the colder months.

The seed of an idea grew, as deep-rooted and lusty as the burr oaks that sprouted on the hillside; it had the persistence of weeds. And why not—its log-cabin image is imbedded deep in our American consciousness with the ancestral wanderlust of the pioneers. Earlier, in the 1600s, our forebears built tiny settlers' cottages of timber beams and hand-split clapboards, a New World copy in miniature of the peasants' houses they had left. Earlier still, Leif Eriksson and the Scotsman, the Earl of Sinclair, who walked our shores in the fourteenth century, may have built temporary shelters in the East.

Thoreau's retreat kept the idea alive; in March of 1845 he left the refined company of his fellows to build his own tiny cabin at Walden Pond. It cost him all of twenty-eight dollars and twelve cents (and a half); this grand sum was all it took to perpetuate an ancestral leaning toward simplicity that has captured our imaginations throughout our New World history. It's never too far from our consciousness, no matter how many condos and town houses we may build.

Landscape; land; country; wilderness; most of us respond to those words as to a note of music or the wild fluting of a hermit thrush and, most of us, positively—if only in the abstract. Americans like the idea of space, of room to stretch. We can't help it—there was so much when we were new to the land. Compared to the crowds in the cities and villages of Europe, America appeared wide open. Space—distance—must have seemed endless, without boundaries, as if there were room enough for us all; as if there would always be.

There was a time when it was said that a squirrel could run to the top of the forest canopy in Maine and not touch his feet to the ground again until he came to the Great Plains. That open vista, that whispering, insect-song prairie, was an ocean of grass. The tallgrass prairie was covered in some 40,000 or more species of native plants, some as tall as a man on horseback,

Walden — Henry's cabin — not much smaller than mine.

blown in wildflower waves in the wind. It stretched from the state of Missouri to the foothills of the Rocky Mountains. Beyond were ranks and ridges of jumbled peaks and the West. This was our wilderness, these millions upon millions of acres of marvelous emptiness—an emptiness filled with such infinite varieties of loveliness that we can only imagine them. You might not see another human for days; your territory—by deed or simple fact of no one to rub shoulders with—stretched as far as the eye could see; now it runs smack up against your neighbor's back fence, if it gets that far. Somewhere in the backs of our minds, we remember how it was. We want to go home.

This common thread, this desire to own a piece of the landscape—and a cabin, don't forget the cabin—is imbedded in our psyche, I suppose; it has found its way into our written history. Thoreau's cabin at Walden, John Muir's *Slabsides*, Henry Beston's *Outermost House*, Anne LaBastille's cabin at Black Bear Lake—I've read about them all, devouring every book that even remotely fits the genre. They're popular with a lot of us; the vein of interest runs deep as Missouri's icy underground rivers. Who hasn't toyed with the idea of stepping outside of normal life, stripping wants down closer to one's needs and reveling in the rough simplicity, rediscovering fire and wind and the smell of a rain-wet morning, listening to the conversation of chorus frogs? Perhaps now more than ever it seems an antidote for the complicated tangle of life as we find it, fast closing on the last decade of the century.

Cabin, shack, shed, retreat, shanty, cottage, summer place—whatever you call it, it has an odd power for something so small. It's homeopathic, a tiny pill to tuck under your tongue when you need a hit of peace, but a pill with a nitroglycerin punch. The desire for such a place—and the reality— takes almost as many forms as there are those who dream it. In my case it was a naturalist's interpretation, an eccentric spin on the basic concept. I envisioned a place that was almost all windows; the view is everything, and I didn't want to miss a thing. My cabin would act as an observation blind; I imagined myself watching the world outside the windows that opened onto the creek and grove and tractor path or sitting on the deck to explore the spaces between the trees. I could see the wildlife there accepting my presence, ignoring me and going on with life.

I needed a place to work under cover, with the sound of rain on the roof overhead. I needed silence, and distance, and that intangible perception of separateness that sets my senses free and fills me with a joy and a bone-deep peace that I feel only occasionally in the noisy neighborhood I call home.

And I needed to fashion my own nest here in the woods—build it myself, not simply pay to have it done. It wouldn't be enough to hire someone else to do the job, visiting each evening to see what progress had been made; I wasn't interested in a client-contractor relationship, adversarial, aggravated by isolation and misunderstanding. I didn't want that distance— both psychic and physical—between me and the place I had dreamed of all my life. This should be mine in every sense, from planning and designing to hammering the nails. I remembered Thoreau's advice: "If you have built castles in the air, your work need not be lost; that is where they should be. Now put the foundations under them." I wanted to lay my own cornerstone.

The idea took hold like an infection and ran rampant through my system, setting my veins on fire, throwing up visual images on my brain like the hallucinations of fever. I had no antibodies for this particular illness; it was a weakness I carry from birth, entangled in my DNA. For as long as I could remember, my family had searched out these tiny cabins in the wilderness. When I was young, there were four choices. You could travel in style— which we seldom did—and stay in a hotel. You could find a little mom-and-pop motel, bright with a racket of neon by the highway, pull in, and plop down on the bed or take a shower in the narrow metal stall. You could camp out, which we did, and often. Or you could rent a cabin.

This last was my favorite. Camping is wonderful; I still enjoy the atavistic closeness between myself and the earth. But a cabin was like stepping outside of ordinary life just far enough to be exciting, like trying on a *different* life, a different home; like playing house. I could pretend I owned the place, as I never could a motel or hotel; the sounds of other people just beyond the walls reminded me of that. Those shared spaces were like a dormitory, a hospital—a place to be slept in only under duress. The private little cabins seemed intimate, inviting—and well within a realm of possibility. I felt at home.

No matter what the view—the smoky blue hills and deep, rugged hollows of Tennessee, the pine-scented peaks of Colorado, the big lakes of Minnesota and Michigan—the cabin itself always seemed to fit me like a favorite pair of jeans. The little log cabins, the tiny clapboard dollhouses themselves—they had a charm that became a part of me, a happy malaria that must show up encysted in the blood.

At Bramwell's, at Bennett Spring in the Missouri Ozarks, chuck-will's-widows, the Ozark cousin to our whippoorwills, called on the hills behind these cabins, filling up every inch of the night with their songs. We sat on the tiny screened porch at night to listen, hearing the wild, comforting sounds mingled with the more homely ones as my mother bustled around the cabin; I leaned on Dad's arm, inhaling the mingled odors of tobacco and whiskey and wood smoke, and I never felt so safe—nor so at home, not even in my own bed. The place was magic; nothing could touch us here. Little wonder cabins have hold of me.

If indeed I was going to build something—and it was beginning to feel as though I would—I tried to want a cabin somewhere more accessible and less misanthropic than the walnut grove; it was as far from contact with other people as possible. I tried to think of resale value—my mother-in-law's old advice. I tried to envision the place close to the road, where electricity would be easy to get, where we could drive in in the winter, where water might be had for less than crown-jewel range. I tried—and failed.

Our neighbor Greg is a carpenter; I showed him the land in the autumn, walked him all over it to the various building site possibilities: in the pond meadow, close to the road on the east hill: in Rachel's Meadow where electricity had already been installed. All we had to do was tap in.

I couldn't pull it off. Even Greg agreed. "It needs to be in the walnut grove, Cathy. You'd have protection from the wind. You'd have privacy for your work. It won't be that hard to get building supplies down here; those guys can deliver lumber almost anywhere. You don't *need* to be practical; you're not going to live here. This is a dream we're building."

And so I embarked on planning for a cabin in the woods.

Plans do have a way of going awry—or so it seemed at the time. The idea of a separate place from our house in town (two houses, essentially) seemed remote, almost indecently impractical. So, instead, we explored the possibilities open to us, thinking to build something we could live in; we could always

81

sell our sweet old Victorian, though not for as much as we might like since the neighborhood had skidded downhill into rental properties and the occasional drug house.

Almost everyone has a log cabin stuck somewhere in their craw; say "cabin" and your listeners will supply the word "log" in their minds, I guarantee it. We—and the country—have grown up with the idea. It seemed, in our case, not only most practical but most possible, like putting up a set of childhood's Lincoln Logs, only heavier. How difficult could it be? We knew little of conventional construction techniques—I couldn't imagine what it took to build a frame of two-by-fours with all the attendant angles and corners and cover it inside and out with structural and finish skins, the siding and drywall that made a completed dwelling. The planning of conventional windows and doors and thresholds and sills, floors and ceilings and lighting systems was beyond me.

Why I imagined logs to be so much simpler, I can't fathom—except for the fact that with logs the finish, both inside and out, is in place as soon as the logs are up, with no need for more than a bit of lacquer. Other than that, the complications should have been obvious. I've certainly cut and split enough logs for my wood stove. I know about the odd twists in grain that tell something about the tree's previous incarnation and give it an almost willful resistance to my designs. I understand green wood and the necessity of long, slow seasoning. I know how difficult wood can be to work, how heavy it is— I've lifted tons of the stuff. No matter; this seemed like the obvious solution at the time.

Nearly every day's mail brought a new packet of slickly produced plans and full-color renderings of log homes, from Canada to California. I used the long-distance lines so often to discuss my ideas with log-cabin companies that my phone bill resembled the first stages of construction.

One outfit had a lovely little cabin right in the parking lot of a huge mail-order sporting goods store and a two-story log cabin inside the store. They had also built a slightly larger log home just a few miles from us in Roosterville, they told me, and we drove by to have a look. It was enchanting, sophisticated and rustic at the same time, built of aged, standing timber from the West—mostly fir and pine. It was almost big enough to live in, but it cost $25,000 just for the kit: the logs and windows and doors. We'd still have to provide a foundation, a roof, room partitions, flooring, wiring, heating, and labor—it was out of the question.

We ordered every book we could find on building with log—from our library, from our favorite bookstore, from the ads. We pored over magazines and discussed the various types of corners, the advantages of square-hewn logs against round ones, the Swedish cope method of joinery against tongue-and-groove logs; considered the various methods of caulking; discussed the merits of short-wall construction, flirted briefly with stack-wall methods, and formed a growing body of opinion as to what we wanted; what would last; what pleases aesthetically; what was suited to our climate.

My design evolved with each new bit of knowledge—always, it seemed, in favor of some slight change that made a monumental difference in cost. The problem with being an artist and sometime designer is that changes take only moments on paper and cost nothing; once I had conceived them, they were set, fait accompli, in my mind. I *wanted* French doors; I *needed* a screened porch to provide a place to watch unmolested by mosquitoes as big as military helicopters. I liked the idea of a dormer to provide headroom for a loft or second story, though I hadn't lived with one for twenty years and remembered how hard it was to climb those stairs at the end of a long day.

As I sketched my ideas and discussed them with carpenters and log-cabin companies, the possibility began to seem as distant as the first evening star. Each addition that lifted this little shanty into the realm of livability boosted the price seemingly to the tenth power; each modification complicated the process. I gave up as much as I could stand to: no screen porch, no round-top windows, no dormer, no French doors, no deck. What I had originally thought might cost $10,000 still ballooned to $35,000 and $50,000 and beyond, for a house just over half the size of our present one, even with our doing part of the building. These brave plans seemed suddenly foolhardy as I discovered complications I hadn't known existed, terms that might as well be Chinese calligraphy for all the sense I could make of them.

Each book espoused a different theory; each log company touted its own methods. Green logs were fine if you use heartwood—or you needed standing dead timber from the mountains. Oak was great; oak was awful. Round logs invited water infiltration as surface tension wicks moisture up between the joints—or they didn't. You *could* nail vertical frames to the logs and set windows and doors immediately—or that was dead wrong and you had to wait months (years, if your wood was green).

There was no thought of building with logs from our place as the first white settlers had done. It takes an incredible number of logs to put up the smallest place, and those logs must be straight and true. The only trees that halfway qualified here were those in the walnut grove, the lovely, graceful trees that made the cabin site so inviting; there wasn't a chance I'd cut them. Besides, I didn't have the time or expertise to create snug-fitting dovetail corners or flat, hewn logs from raw timber.

And thinking of building from scratch, with my limited knowledge of construction techniques, rendered that plan stillborn before it took its first breath. The books weren't that much help. No, I wanted a kit, with instructions and technical support and pieces already cut to fit; I wanted to build my dream with a jigsaw puzzle.

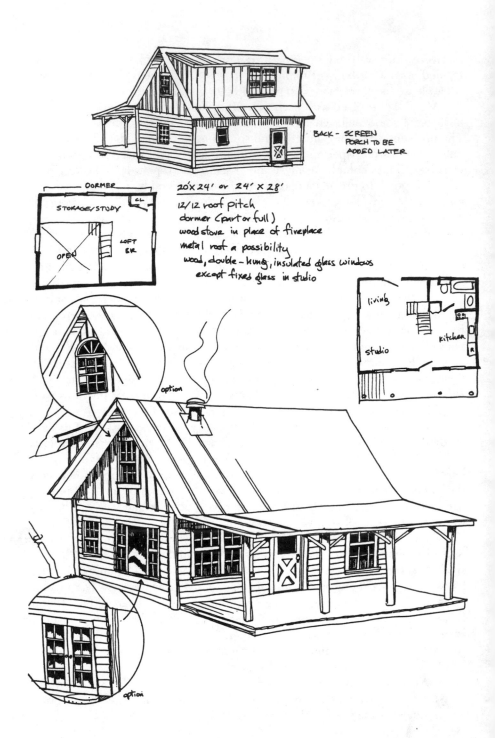

BACK - SCREEN
PORCH TO BE
ADDED LATER

DORMER

STORAGE/STUDY   CL

OPEN   LOFT
BR

20'x 24' or 24' x 28'
12/12 roof pitch
dormer (part or full)
woodstove in place of fireplace
metal roof a possibility
wood, double - hung, insulated glass windows
except fixed glass in studio

living

studio   kitchen

option

option

It was as ridiculous as it sounds. And when I faced the simple physics involved in lifting any but the lowest logs as gravity pitted itself against us, or in the force needed to drive a spike through a log with a six-pound sledge, I began to despair of my plans.

The obsession was getting to me, interfering with my work—interfering with my sleep. I began to wonder if the cogs were slipping in my brain; my judgment was certainly impaired, and I felt unable to make a sensible decision —or any decision at all.

Greg stopped by to look at my rough sketch.

"Why does it need to be log, Cathy? I could build something like that for you for $16,000—complete with carpet and cabinets."

But I was stuck in tunnel-vision plans hewn from logs and only giving them up completely could shake them. And so I let them go, with the last bright leaves of autumn. Snow drifted down to cover the dream, obscuring the outlines of the logs.

Garden Shed

7. *Close One Door…*

The dream of a cabin in the woods refused to die. The hard facts of limited finances and of our physical capabilities when it came to building with logs dealt it a staggering blow, but nothing changed. Over the winter I tried to be practical (again) and failed (again). That we couldn't afford it seemed not to matter at all, and though the log cabin we thought would be the perfect answer turned out instead to be impossible, the urge would not go away; it was incurable. It was only dormant, storing strength for the new year.

If I wasn't going to be able to exorcise this thing, then there had to be a way. There was something I wasn't seeing, something just past the rim of consciousness, elusive as mist.

The cabins of my memories wouldn't let me rest. They're harder to find, these days, the little cottages at seaside or tucked away in the mountains. When I conducted a workshop recently in the Ozarks, I thought it would be easy to find a rustic cabin to stay in; it was not. We searched for the better part of an hour, only to find that most of the little tourist courts were closed, shuttered tight against a pervasive vandalism, or gone altogether. When we finally settled into a little sixteen-by-twenty-foot cabin, it was as though I had dropped thirty years. I handed over my rent, took my key, and felt like a kid again. I explored every corner, stepping it off in delight: just big enough to hold anything you'd need. This was my kind of place.

Returning with fresh eyes from the Ozarks, I saw new possibilities everywhere; maybe a log home wasn't in order—or a home at all. These few remaining cabins, discovered on a long afternoon drive—none of them much over the size of the one we stayed in—reopened my eyes to a different possibility, and I remembered E. F. Schumacher's famous line, "Small is beautiful." So it is. Beautiful, and perhaps possible.

There was something about the new wooden garden shed we had had built, and I stepped out to look at it, time and again. I contemplated its sloping roof and simplified construction as though it were a code I was just about to crack.

It was. The shed *was* a cabin, if a tiny one. It was simple and do-able, with its modest size, small window, and big double door. What more would I really need? If I had such a place in the walnut grove, at least I could sit under cover to work; we could store our tools side by side with a writer's basic needs: a desk, a chair, a cot, and a tiny heater of some sort. With a couple of extra windows and a kerosene lamp, it would work. How much could it cost?

(The question doesn't apply. How much the garden shed cost had nothing whatever to do with the final cost of the cabin in the end—but at the time, it seemed perfectly reasonable that we could build it for only a few hundred dollars more than the cost of the shed. When I thought of my retreat, I imagined it as simple as this bare-stud and plywood-sided edifice. It turned out to be nothing of the kind.)

This new germ of a plan seemed practical enough—as though "practical" was a word that applied to building such a thing in the first place. A naturalist's cabin is not exactly necessity, except perhaps to me. But the pragmatic angle helped justify it in my eyes. If we ever *did* build something more permanent, the shed would be there for storage. To pull this off, all we needed was a bit of guidance, a little information—and a lot less money than the log homes we had looked at. The more I thought about it, the more the idea took hold.

The plan was clinched by a chance call to Dinah Henderson, a friend who co-owns a great little bookstore where I dispose of my disposable income.

"We gave up on the log cabin, Dinah—got any books on shed building? We thought we might scale down drastically."

"Well, no, but I've got a book called *Tiny, Tiny Houses* you might like to see."

"*Send it.*"

You might know my answer would be a literary one. Everything I ever wanted seems to have come from some book or another. This one was full of little places—cabins, retreats, earthquake relief shacks, studios, sharecroppers' houses, slave quarters, beachcombers' shanties, old ones, new ones, dumps, and charmers. Thoreau's Walden was here and Thomas Jefferson's honeymoon cottage—and a tiny architect's studio that turned the tumblers in my mental lock as if it were made to fit.

It was shed shaped, like my half-formed plans, but it had a rustic elegance: rough cedar siding, stained-glass window, and, across the front, a huge bay of glass made from recycled storm windows where my garden shed's barnlike door was. I couldn't stop looking at the photos; in the evenings, after work, I sat with the book in my lap, turning the pages from photo to framing plan to floor plan to the elevations of all four sides. This could be it—with our modifications. *This*, we could pull off; a dream scaled down to fit our circumstances.

We called Greg again, five months after the first time.

"Forget the log cabin. We're on to something else. Come by and see what we've come up with; maybe you can give us a bid."

By the time he arrived, we had taken off from the book's plans, personalized it to fit our needs—a big observation deck around two sides, room for a kitchen corner (is there a writer who can function without coffee or tea?), and space for a cot so we could spend the night and monitor the nocturnal wildlife. The studio in the book was nearly twelve feet by twelve feet; we had already realized that wouldn't be big enough and enlarged to fourteen by sixteen. The roof pitch looked too short for Harris, too—my husband's six-foot three-inch frame has made for several adjustments in living arrangements over the years, ever since he split open his head on the ceiling-mounted light fixture in our old farmhouse. Remembering, we upped the height of the ridge beam to twelve feet.

My rough drawings looked almost simple enough to pull off by myself, even with my limited building experience, but I didn't trust my math. The roof angles were complicated by the bay window abutment at the front and the shed-style roof designed with one short plane and one long one. Toenailing had never been my forte, and fitting windows looked like a job for a pro—at least if I wanted them to open and close and keep out the weather.

We had made photocopies of the little building in the book and of my modifications, for Greg and for the other builders we planned to ask for bids. It was only a jumping-off point, but it was the best cliff edge we'd been on so far.

It wasn't easy, we found, to come up with someone willing to let me work. It amounted to their taking on a novice assistant and spending extra time for on-the-job training. Some wouldn't even talk to us about it, wouldn't come to give a bid. Most carpenters or builders wanted to arrive on the site with their own crew, get the job done as quickly as possible, and get out; that's how they make their money. Charlie, our only other serious bidder who had worked on our house in town, figured that's how we'd work it, with us doing only the finish work—painting, varnishing, and so forth.

That's not what I had in mind at all. I wanted my hands on every board. Sweat equity for the satisfaction of it; I needed to experience the physics of construction on my own, to see and feel and know what it takes to build a dream.

Greg's bid was a good one—too good to be true: he estimated $1,400 for materials and said that he could do the work for about $600 in labor. I doubled the bid in my mind, just to be square on the side of reality, and that doubling put it in the realm of the difficult but still possible.

Then there were those deciding factors. Greg is a friend; we were comfortable with him—and he was willing to let me work. Not just the finish work, but the be-there-from-the-beginning, teach-me-what-to-do stuff. I could have the experience of putting the foundations under my modest castle, learn something of the art of building, and save money as well. After all, the going rate here in the Midwest—for home construction, anyway—was about $55 a square foot, or about $12,320 for a cabin this size. That figure takes into account that a house has plumbing and a kitchen with cabinets and stove, which the cabin would not, but still—I expected some worthwhile savings.

Greg had a different set of priorities from most builders we had talked to. Instead of home construction, he was doing small jobs now, decks and gazebos and such. The fact that he'd be getting free (if inexperienced) labor couldn't hurt either, since he had gotten out of the business of contracting houses—my labor would relieve him of the need to pay an assistant during this project. Add in the fact that we planned to use recycled materials where possible and his bid (with my doubled modification) seemed ballpark. We gave him the go-ahead and added our names to his waiting list.

These smaller jobs kept him plenty busy; he does good work, and the word had gotten around. It would be another month before we could start on the job; now that it would be a reality, I could scarcely stand the waiting. I felt like a five-year-old in the last weeks before Christmas, watching the days inch by with all the speed of evolution.

The only way to stand it was to keep busy—the search for building materials helped. We made it a treasure hunt, and the windows seemed an obvious place to start. I chose used ones to save money as well as for character, and besides—this was a cabin in the woods, not the Missouri Taj Mahal. But what I saved in dollars I spent in time and effort—it took me nearly a month to recondition my random finds, sanding, scraping, bracing a wobbly corner, replacing glass where necessary, learning to lay a smooth bead of glazing compound around the dozens of little panes, painting the frames a soft sky blue to complement the warm cedar siding we had chosen—and their setting.

At first, some of the old windows looked almost beyond repair, like the old square window with colorful stained glass rectangles down each side, leaning with a stack of its rotting clones against a bureau in an antiques mall. But for $10 I was willing to try restoration. If I failed, I could always use it in an outbuilding, later.

I designed the cabin's fenestration, finally, around the windows I found —it was a symbiotic situation, watching for windows to fit my spaces, designing the spaces to utilize the odd-sized windows. Shed vernacular architecture makes for an interesting variety—there is the possibility of tall windows in front and low, wide ones across the squat back wall. On the gable ends, anything was fair game. I was loath to give up a millimeter of view, and in the woods there is something to see in all directions; the cabin took both shape and orientation according to these expanses of glass. Each new find modified the plan; half a narrow double-hung window, separated from its twin, seemed to demand a place beside the antique front door. Its four-paned visage doubled the view to the north.

As my finds collected on the back porch, it looked as though I might build a greenhouse instead of a cabin. But the big bay across the front, where I planned to spend my time watching whatever wandered through the walnut grove or trailed up the wooded east hill, was harder to fill. I even advertised in our local shopper and lined up two possibilities over the phone —but both were uncomfortably far to drive with such large panels of glass tied to the top of the car.

But when I went to pick up the double-hung windows at an antiques shop near home, I browsed one last time through a hoard of possibilities and outright junk that Bob Carter kept in a constant state of flux in his barn. This time I was alone and unhurried. Harris had stayed home, Bob was out, and his wife, P.J., was minding the business at their antiques shop a few hundred yards away. I could look in peace, sifting through the barn like an archaeologist. And there, buried far at the back, were stacks and stacks of tall, beautiful, old, eight-paned French windows, complete with hardware. I wouldn't even need to buy locks and catches. (I had already discovered the endless expense of this small stuff.)

The windows were slightly out of square and furred with exposure to the weather, the unprotected wood grain raised to a fine cellulose nap, but they had character. Eight small panes per window were not nearly so daunting to transport on my cartop carrier as single large panes would have been. The price was right, with the investment of time to refurbish them.

And time I had. Greg was still tied up on an elegant ten-sided gazebo complete with hot tub, refrigerator, and a knockout view of blue Missouri hills. I watched its perfect progress in an agony of impatience, as my carpenter/mentor cut every carefully fitted floorboard and shingle, each bit of rococo trim. I watched—then went home to attack my pile of antique windows with a vigor born of frustration.

I knew from the number of windows I wanted that I could spend $1,600 or more if I went for factory models; French windows and round tops don't come for pocket change. If I wanted a new window comparable to the antique stained-glass job, I could take a second mortgage on the house. I checked out the price of a small round-top at my local lumberyard, a $300 tariff that made me flinch as though struck. When I discovered instead that the antique semicircle of glass and wood that I had carried with me for twenty years perfectly fit above the width of my $10 find, it was obvious that the studio wall would have its focal point for pennies. A beautiful old Victorian door, sans glass and hardware, was a pittance compared to the cheapest new models. Like the windows, it cost little more than my time.

Each time Greg stopped by to check in with us, I escorted him to the back porch to show off my finds: he hid his skepticism well. A far cry from modern factory-mounted windows, with dimensions as accurate as an engineer could make them, these were a ragtag bunch with a kind of organic quality to them: decay arrested by my chance adoption.

It wasn't until later that I discovered that he had never worked with windows or doors in this state before but only with preframed ones, ready to mount, and square as a Rubic's cube.

"First time me, first time you," he said; "We can do it."

In the end, the timing just seemed to fall together; as I finished the last window and put the final coat of paint on the ornate door, it was time. Greg was ready. We ordered the first load of lumber, wrote the first checks — already for over a thousand dollars — and planned to meet to unload the wood on Monday morning.

After nearly two years of drought, on Sunday afternoon it rained. I didn't know whether to rejoice or curse. I rejoiced, grudgingly.

But still, after a day the tractor path had dried enough to give it a try — with care and a backup plan. We called the local service station — the one with two big tow trucks — to see if they would come pull Greg's half-ton hauler out if we got it stuck; they agreed, and we prayed we wouldn't need them.

Greg brought Daniel, his usual assistant, to help us unload, and the kid reconnoitered the rough driveway. "I think you can make it," he said, and the truck began to move — slowly at first, then picking up speed. We watched Greg barrel down off the north road and between the trees, almost forgetting to breathe in our excitement. It was close; the track was still muddy, the grass wet, and the big wheels began to slide perilously near the edge of the gully that is our pond's spillway. I imagined Greg and his truck and a thousand dollars' worth of treated lumber dumped unceremoniously down the hill. But he gunned it, straightened, and blasted on down the drive. We followed, hopping down the track behind the truck and whooping "He *made* it. He *did* it. All *ri-i-ight!!*"

Once there, we looked in amazement at the big truck in the suddenly small grove of trees.

"Wow. If a truck takes up this much room, how big is the cabin going to look?" I asked no one in particular.

We found rocks to pile on the ground and brush to lay across them, impromptu palettes to keep this expensive lumber out of direct contact with the ground; the treated stuff absorbs water easily and will warp if it's not cared for properly. Check writing still fresh in my mind, I wanted to hang it from the *trees* to keep it from the dampness.

When we finished unloading and stacking everything, the piles looked far too small.

"This isn't all of it, is it?" I asked.

"Oh, no. This is your deck, floor joists, rim joists, and foundation pilings. We don't want the rest of it out here without protection until we need it."

Oh, boy. That big check was only for the subfloor and deck; suddenly I didn't see the rest of the materials fitting into the $1,400 materials bid. This was no garden shed. I was beginning to get the picture.

But at last we were started. We marked off the corners with sticks and string, laying out the dimensions of my dream, finalizing orientation in the walnut grove. The cabin would just fit; the size we had chosen would allow us to shoehorn it between the trees without cutting a single one. If we had built the livable-sized log cabin instead, at least two would have had to go. I wanted very much to have a low impact here; perhaps the size wouldn't be too overpowering after all.

We had brought our posthole digger for the foundation holes, an old auger-style tool that I have found to work most efficiently with my short legs; physics again. Greg scowled at it in half-kidding disdain.

"*Nasty*," he said, holding his forefingers up in a mock cross to ward it off. He prefers clamshell diggers, which don't work for me—upper body strength is not a woman's usual area of muscular efficiency; I work best with my legs and back. But I saw now why he liked them. He slammed the double spoon-like shovels down into that soft, black earth, squeezed them together, and pulled up six inches of soil at a time.

The dirt is rich and soft here and smells of walnuts. We stopped to stick our noses in the hole, inhaling with delight; the roots we sliced through were aromatic with sap.

We expected to hit rock near the surface; the massive outcropping across the creek couldn't be too far underground, and the limestone is exposed only seventy yards away at the slickrocks. But we just kept digging deeper into that bottomless black soil and never hit more than a random rock. The concrete would have to hold the cabin steady; I crossed mental fingers.

By the end of the first day of real building, we had corner foundation posts in place and rim joists attached to them. Suddenly, the cabin seemed to have undreamed-of elastic properties, a certain Silly Putty reality that changed shape and size at will; now, instead of overpowering the walnut grove as I feared it might, it looked as tiny as the garden shed in my backyard. It was dwarfed by its setting.

Day two, we progressed by leaps. The silence of the forest, woven with the voices of resident birds, was shattered, surprised by our sudden noise. The gasoline-powered generator we rented to run the power tools hummed loudly in the clearing; rock and roll blasted from Greg's truck radio, and our shouts and laughter and curses added to the cacophony.

I hauled the long two-by-sixes around, holding them in place for Greg to fasten. Floor joists joined rims together like giant yellow-pine spiderwebs held in place with long screws instead of an arachnid's protein glue.

The rims of the big deck that runs along two sides of the cabin's floor followed; the spiderweb grew. Harris and I nailed the joist hangers in place here—a get-your-feet-wet job we couldn't botch too badly. The top of the U-shaped metal hanger should be just flush or a hair below the top of the rim joist; ours wriggled up and down slightly, but Greg assured us they'd do fine; they did. When he fastened the deck boards in place, our tiny inaccuracies disappeared beneath an edge as straight as a ruler.

After a while, I began to feel a growing impatience, an itch that began in my mind and set my fingers twitching. I came here to work, to *learn*, not to do jobs a child could accomplish.

"I can do that," I said, watching Greg fasten down the deck boards with long screws. He fit the end of the screw onto the Phillips-head bit in his heavy electric drill, slammed it into the wood, and drove it home, all in one fluid motion.

"I can do that."

Not like he does, perhaps. There are a lot of years' experience contained in that quick motion. My attempts were clumsy; I fell off the screw head and drove the bit into the board. I stripped the threads of the screw or snapped off the Phillips head with misguided vigor. Greg tried not to laugh; Harris, and Greg's father, who had come to kibitz, had no such compunctions—I wasn't paying them.

I didn't care. I had developed my own system, a somewhat half-cocked technique that worked, nonetheless: I started the screws with my hammer, driving the point into the wood as an old friend and carpenter taught me, then drove them home with the big drill. After a while I sped up my technique, assembly-line style, starting a section's worth of screws, leaving them bristling from the board, then drilling them in one after the other.

It worked fine. Greg fastened the closer screw all along the boards to make sure they were in their proper places, working the warp out as he went and butting them snugly against each other—they would shrink to make the drainage cracks between. I came along behind to do the second screw in each row, fastening the boards permanently to the joists. The partially clad deck looked great; I walked along the smooth, bull-nosed lumber, imagining my bare feet here in summer, luxuriating in the wooden coolness.

This newly flat surface across the broad front of the deck gave us a place to work, a place to put the tools up off the ground, a fine surface to stack

The bay marked on the floor — I can see the cabin's shape beneath my feet.

lumber on to keep it from the dampness. We had left an open space where the bay would jut out onto the deck, and I took care not to miss my footing and step between the open joists.

The next day, we continued laying the deck boards and slapped on the treated plywood subfloor, carefully measuring and cutting the angle of the bay. I could see my cabin in mind's eye, outlined in this flat silhouette, and danced across the floor as though it were a done deal. When I hunkered at the back corner of the cabin, I could see what the view would be from those big bays, out across the grove and toward the limestone rocks.

Harris joined us for the lunch break, and we sat on the new deck like country squires, sprawled in our old nylon deck chairs. Ham sandwiches and chips never tasted so good, and I was reminded of the correlation between work—the expenditure of energy as calories—and real hunger. There was no gormandizing here, no delicate satisfying of imagined appetite: give me *food*, and plenty of it.

The fat woodchuck that occupied a den under one of the young trees at the edge of the grove was our cleanup crew; I made my offerings of bread crusts at his doorstep as though paying a tariff, a land-use fee to the rightful owner. He accepted my payment in kind.

As long as he didn't see me, that is. Finally, I was sitting quietly on the deck when he appeared in the grove. The old groundhog advanced, then caught my scent; stopped dead; and whipped his head around in my direction. Then with an almost audible "yikes!" he streaked away into the woods, rattling the underbrush. The ground thundered with his footsteps and I didn't know whether to laugh or apologize. I never got the chance. That was the last I saw of the old chuck. He abandoned his den near the cabin; my offerings turned stale, molded, and ants found them.

The large sheets of four-by-eight-foot plywood helped determine the final dimensions of the cabin; they required very little trimming as we laid them in place, alternating the seams like bricks in a wall, their ends just meeting at a floor joist. We fastened the plywood in place around the perimeter and snapped a red chalk line where the joists were, so we could follow along them with more screws. These yellow zinc-coated construction screws will not rust, an important consideration given Missouri's infamous summer humidity; the treated plywood was chosen to withstand dampness—and insect damage—as well. They tell me this treated wood should last decades; I hope so. The cabin rests on pillars of the stuff stuck into the ground.

When we finished for the day, I was tired but deeply satisfied; muscle tired, only. My brain was on a kind of euphoric fast forward.

Day by day, the bits and pieces of my vision came together. The second load of lumber—two-by-four studs, two-by-tens, and rough cedar siding—made it more real yet. The cold-water shock of the lumberyard's bill assured me I was awake.

When I arrived, the flat expanse of the subfloor and observation deck seemed suspended over the valley floor like a raft. I couldn't believe it was there, at last. I couldn't believe that today we would raise walls.

One wall. It was all Greg and I, working alone, would accomplish in one day. He was surprised, I could tell, that I was still here, nail belt slung on my hips, hammer in hand. I hadn't cried uncle—not yet, anyway.

He kept Daniel, his assistant, in reserve, waiting for me to fade. Now, first week of unloading and stacking lumber, sinking foundation pilings, constructing rim joists, floor joists, and deck behind us, I was still here. "Bloody," as my father used to say, "but unbowed."

Bloody it was, too. While fastening down subfloor, the heavy drill slipped off the screw with all my weight behind it. There was no time to avoid drilling my finger. The Phillips head bit through flesh like a hot knife through butter.

Not about to give up so soon, I wrapped the thing in a rag and went back to driving screws; funny—when you're putting the foundations under air castles, pain is incidental. My subfloor is measled with drops of sacrificial blood.

Later, I helped to dig a secondary foundation hole, one of several meant to provide additional support for the deck's weight and the long run of the joists between the corner posts. Rather than dig these holes beforehand and hope to sink the posts in a straight line with only a flexible string to guide us, we sunk the corner posts first. The rim joists are fastened to them, in a perfect square. We began the secondary holes every eight feet or so, banging the posthole digger into the ground as close to the two-by-twelves as we could get. It would be an easy matter to sink the six-by-six pilings, snug them to the joists with three-inch galvanized screws, and then secure the bottoms with concrete and fill.

Easy, but not foolproof. It was fine as long as the holes were shallow and the Y-shaped handles of the clamshell digger protruded far above the joists. As the holes deepened, knuckles drove closer and closer to the edge of the rim boards. Impact was as inevitable as income tax.

Pain is strange stuff. At first you don't really feel it, then it makes your eyes water and your knees buckle into a half crouch. Your body bends around the affected member as if to protect it—somewhat behind the beat. "Ow" doesn't begin to cover it. Now I had *two* bandages, one on each hand, and I wondered briefly at the wisdom of risking the hands I use to make my living, type my manuscripts, and do my illustrations. Greg was sure I would quit, then—too sure.

I'm not accident-prone, but I'm hardly an experienced builder, either. I expected a disaster or two; I was glad to have them out of the way early on. It helped to be anesthetized by six months of planning and dreaming.

A few days later, my hands had mostly healed. I kept a box of bandages in my nail belt and a tube of antibiotic ointment. The unexpectedly hot April weather that made for sweaty palms and blistered fingers had turned cool, a fine, crisp day for work.

This cabin would be built the simplest way possible, using methods that two people could pull off with only the small generator to run the electric drill and worm-gear saw. Short of a hand saw and screwdriver, we were planning basic building strategy: Cabin Building 101.

It was a bit more basic than Greg had originally hoped. The generator was too small to run his air compressor, so the fast and modern nail driver was out. It spat the nails sullenly against the wood as if they tasted bad; there was no question of driving them home. It was a mixed felicity; it meant I'd be paying for much more of Greg's time than either of us planned, driving the cost of the cabin far above his estimates or mine. It also meant that I would have the satisfaction of having my hands on virtually every board and nail in the cabin—or a good half of them, anyway.

The two-by-fours and structural skins I had so dreaded when I thought of doing it alone, imagining logs to be simpler, now looked less mysterious with Greg's experience to back us up. It was simply a matter of knowing how, then doing it—Greg knew how and I could follow instructions.

It was a long day of measuring and cutting, nailing and more nailing. We

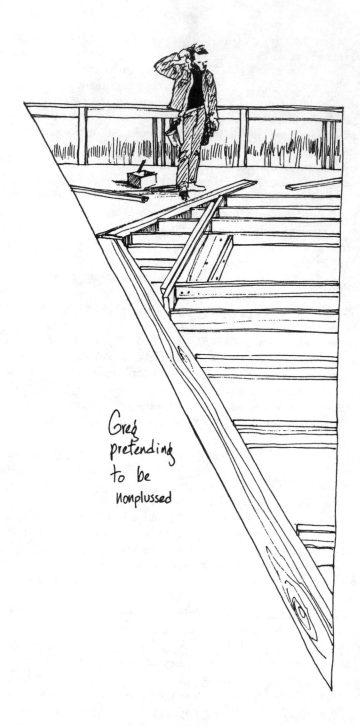

Greg
pretending
to be
nonplussed

worked flat on the subfloor, constructing the skeleton that would be my studio wall—the one with the antique round-top window that turns its back on the road as if it has better things to see.

This building of a stud wall flat on a deck, then raising it into place, is "western style" construction; if putting it up bit by bit in the air is eastern, I don't know it—Greg just says "the old guys still do it that way." It seemed easy this way; no need for ladders, no uncertain footing far above my normal height.

It was fun to watch Greg work. He's a patient young man who enjoys teaching. Now that he knew I was in it for the long haul, he showed me tricks he learned from his mentor, Jay W.—"Old Poophead." I heard a lot about Jay W. in the weeks to come—colorful sayings, stories, the bits and pieces that make up a man.

I learned the height of wall studs—$92^5/8$ inches. Greg says Jay wrote it on the underside of his billed cap so he would never forget. I don't wear a cap, and the numbers dissolved from my short-term memory in minutes. I learned the distance between the studs (16 inches O.C., or on center) and how—at last—to toenail. This dreaded task turned out to be fairly easy, standing on the two-by-fours to hold them in place and whaling away at their ends with a heavy framing hammer, driving the sixteen-penny nails in at an angle to hold the studs to the top and bottom plates. Two or three nails on either side do the trick. The first nails knock the stud off its mark; the last push it back in place. Does it matter if a nail or two is less than perfect? I smacked another in beside it and went on; they are hidden inside the wall beyond the reach of judgment.

Greg's dad, Harry, stopped by again to watch and advise. When I couldn't make one of the four-inch galvanized fasteners go in, holding my big framing hammer with one hand and bending one too many nails to suit me, I resorted to a two-handed grip—to the amusement of all concerned. But it got the job done, teasing or no.

I learned to make headers to go above the windows. These are a double-layered sandwich of two-by-tens bracketed by two-by-fours and nailed together with clinched sixteen-penny nails. They bear the load of the roof and distribute it to either side of that fragile glass. The headers rest on short uprights that frame the window, with king studs to provide extra strength at either side, and everything is tightly nailed together. (I also learned that there are single headers and double headers, depending on how much weight they are expected to carry, and that they have nothing at all to do with baseball.)

Then we added the cripples, short lengths of two-by-four that support the wall below the window, nailed in place as ministuds. Cripples; that's a good term for these little amputees.

The further I got into this project, the more I threw around building terms like a jargon junkie, driving Harris — and anyone else I could buttonhole with my newfound knowledge — to distraction. It was as bad as my fascination with words in general, a new lexicon of nail driving: Constructionology.

The gable rafters determine the angle of the roof; these are strong pieces of two-by-six lumber nailed to the upper ends of the framing. I liked the cut of their jib; suddenly the place began to look like my drawing, lying there flat on the subfloor. Greg left a space between their ends at the top to receive the ridge beam. The jigsaw puzzle had an immutable logic.

The naked stud wall lay finished and waiting on the subfloor, and I assumed we'd raise it like that, lightweight. But I was wrong. Raising a stud wall without at least a diagonal two-by-four-inch brace or two can be disastrous; a rectangle is not a stable form, quickly becoming a rhomboid if you look away for a minute — or a pile of sticks flat on the ground if you leave it overnight without bracing. (A triangle, it seems, *is* stable, the angled points supporting one another — thus a diagonal brace if we had intended to raise the thing bare bones.) The siding — whether a one-half-inch plywood skin, the newer sheet Thermax, or the red cedar car siding I had chosen — acts admirably to hold everything in square.

"We'll put the siding on where she is," Greg said. "It'll be easier."

As we struggled to "cheat" the tongue-and-groove siding into place, I saw why. It was warped. Most wood is, if it's been exposed to water or weather at all.

I started a tongue in the groove on one end and the board sprang free on the other as if willing mutiny. I tried again and the middle bowed up. It was slapstick carpentry, Keystone Kop construction. I was glad Harry had left; Greg had been watching with amusement, but he took pity on me and showed me how it's done: start one end, driving the tongue into the groove a bit at a time with a scrap of siding and a hammer, if necessary. When it's in place, you nail to the studs underneath — only the bottom of the cedar board, though, not the top. That comes later. We needed the free edge to make the next board easier to maneuver.

We forced a little more of the top board into place, slow and easy, and nailed it, then a bit more. Finally — "It's there," Greg sang out. "It's not going anywhere."

Some boards were so badly warped they had to be discarded. Still gofer as well as nailer, I trotted back and forth to the pile of boards.

"Bring me a *good* one," said my carpenter. What the hell was that? They all looked good to me — at first. But soon I was sighting down the length of the board, eyeing it for a warp too far developed to cheat into place or a bow that couldn't be flattened, checking for one too many loose knots. I know what a good one is; my pile of rejects grew to rival Greg's. Thank God the lumberyard took returns. I'd paid plenty for this woodpile, and until I learned we could take back the junk, I felt growing desperation and eyed the balance in the checkbook as it went down for the third time. This was still pretty fine wood for kindling.

Some of my "good ones" still had to be pushed and shoved, cajoled and bribed to make them fit. One recalcitrant board curved upward in the middle like an Osage hunting bow.

"We can fix it. No problem."

And so we did. Greg sat on the two-by-four studs above the bow and braced—hard, pushing against the arc with both feet until the tongue slipped into the groove—but only temporarily.

"Now!" he said. "Nail it!"

I hammered in a couple of good ones and was rewarded with yet another "It's *there.*"

It should be easy to nail the boards to the studs in a straight line. I could see the two-by-fours beneath each narrow piece of four-inch siding. I am a bricklayer's daughter, I reminded myself. Dad seldom needed plumb bob or level; he eyeballed it. But the skill died with him; my line of nails wandered up the wall, curving like the meanders in a stream; next to them, Greg's row looked as if he had snapped a chalk line to follow, as we did on the big panels of the subfloor.

I caught him looking dubiously at my nailings—"Kinda wormy, aren't they?"

Oh, well; it was the back side of the cabin. At least I didn't miss a stud altogether.

I worried more about the dents I made with each hammer blow when I drove home the nails, dimpling that expensive siding with my lightweight finish hammer—my "lady hammer" as I called the elegant little thing—and I didn't like it. But that, it seemed, was okay. Greg said the wood absorbs moisture from the air and pops back out flat.

So board by board, nail by nail, we finished the wall. Near day's end I was tired but full of a kind of sappy satisfaction. *Now,* I believed it. There would be a cabin.

"Great," I said. "I feel great. Tomorrow I'll get Harris out here to help us raise it."

"Oooh, no. I'm not leaving here until this thing is up. You don't think I'm going to get this far without seeing it standing, do you?"

Well, yes, I had. I was ready to quit for the day; I was sore and tired and not at the top of my form.

But I'm not a quitter. If Greg said we'd get it up, by God we'd get it up. I'd caught the fever, anyway. Against my better judgment, I wanted to see it too.

"Okay, then—where's your wall jack?"

"Don't have it. We can lift it," Greg told me.

Suddenly I was beyond tired. I didn't know how much a fully sided four-teen-foot wall, twelve feet tall, weighed—and I didn't want to find out.

"You're kidding."

I remembered my bad back. I remembered Greg's bad back, injured in a fall from a building. I imagined dropping the wall on our feet.

"You're kidding."

"Nope," he said cheerfully, "we can do it."

It was obvious that if I didn't help, the kid would do it alone. It was crazy, but I helped.

It's a principle of physics, simple enough on paper. We'd do it the same way they raised the monoliths at Stonehenge. Use a lever to get it started. (Good. I know levers. I understand that. Nail pullers, right? Crowbars?) Then just keep lifting.

We raised the wall the first few inches using a length of two-by-six; it was unbelievably heavy. Lift with your legs, I told myself, lift with your legs. The long muscles are designed for it; those delicate vertebrae protecting the spinal cord are not. Lift with your legs—but a *building*? I began to panic.

"Look, I'll go get Harris—it's only four miles. I'll call Wendy. I'll get a neighbor."

"Nope. We can do it."

And do it we did, inch by agonizing inch. My imagination kicked in—or maybe I was hallucinating. I tried to remember the principle behind the pulley and imagined my arms, with the muscles and tendons and bones, as a lifting machine: elbow as block and tackle, maybe. I wondered if the steroid scare is really as serious as they say and wished I had a few to pop like aspirin. I pictured Greg flattened beneath the wall when I couldn't hold it any more. I imagined what I'd tell his wife, his father; where was Harry *now*?

We lifted it again, each time propping it with a scrap of board, then a longer one and a longer one. It was my job to pick the scraps from a pile nearby and put them in place under the edge of the wall; some were only bits of siding, but Greg said they would hold. They looked like toothpicks, and I wondered if one would finally snap, shooting off like a projectile, dropping the wall with a crash. I wondered if it's true that there's a rush of powerful adrenalin when you need it; would I be able to lift the wall off this kid when it crushed him—and then pull him out? My mind was going warp speed in the echoing silence. There was no other sound than our grunts and an occasional "oh, *shit*."

"It'll get easier," Greg swore. "After a certain point it almost goes up by itself."

I'll bet.

But it did. At last, when our props reached four feet or so in length and we were bracing the bottoms with blocks nailed hastily to the subfloor, we could get under the wall and push with backs and shoulders and legs. I was all lever. The wall started to go at about seventy or eighty degrees, suddenly becoming lighter, moving faster and faster. Gravity was at last in our favor; the wall was almost buoyant. Would we push it right off the other side and into the walnut grove? What was going to stop it?

I must have missed the line of nails Greg drove into the bottom plate, holding the two-by-four firmly in place. The wall rose like Lazarus and teetered there, upright.

I was amazed. We did it, and neither of us had so much as a splinter.

"Check and see if it's plumb," Greg told me.

"Okay, I'll get my level."

"No, no, just look; you can tell. 'The eye don't lie. The sun and the moon may vary, but the eye don't lie.' Jay W. taught me that."

I heard that many times in the coming weeks, with varying degrees of accuracy. Maybe *his* eye don't lie....

At last we headed out, south wall braced precariously with two-by-fours and bits of discarded siding, nailed at crazy angles from wall to subfloor. I had a wall, hanging in the wind. I wondered if it would stand till morning.

The next day, for the north side, Greg brought his wall jack.

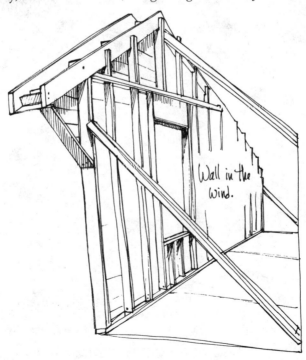

Wall in the wind.

Siding Instructions — "the eye don't lie," or so Greg says.

8. Building — and Beyond

The wall jack made the job of raising the second wall ridiculously easy. This wall, the one with the wide soffit end, had to weigh more than yesterday's project; the overhang that would provide protection from the weather added another foot and a half to the eaves. Greg's father came to help—but it was hardly necessary. The wall was flat on the floor one minute, fully sided and weighing as much as a bull moose; the next it rose into the air, lifted by the jack that looked rather like a giant rod and reel. There was a small pump-action handle attached to a ratchet; it looked capable of lifting a log, not a house wall. Greg fastened the hook at the cable's end to the roof peak— hooking our fish—nailed the other end of the jack to the floor, and simply reeled the wall up, pumping that red handle effortlessly. I hurried to prop the wall in place with a two-by-four nailed to the subfloor. The job was over in seconds, and I didn't know whether to laugh or cheer or brain him—we could have done this yesterday.

These two walls—the tallest ones, the eave walls—were heavy as debt but far more stable than a web of two-by-four studs. Once we had them up and well braced with wood scraps, the job seemed to have been almost easy —amazing how quickly mind and muscles forget pain. The front and back walls—the sixteen-foot-long walls—were even easier. We raised them both in one day. The back wall was low—just over five feet—and the bay on the front would remain open until we plugged the gaps with windows; because Greg had decided to side these shorter, more accessible walls once they were in place, they lifted up almost with one hand. We spiked them to the subfloor and to the corners of the gable sides in what seemed like minutes.

105

The front wall was only slightly more difficult to frame out than the back; the angles of the bay slowed the work but only a little. For Greg, who knows what he's doing, those angles and the overhang where the bay would meet the inside wall went together as if he had written instructions. In fact, he did not. There were no blueprints for this self-designed shack in the woods, and the triangles and rhomboids looked impossibly complicated to me.

I constructed the three tiny walls that made up the bay, nailing together Greg's cut pieces as if putting together a preschooler's puzzle. Here, the headers above the windows were single—the weight of the roof would be carried by the sixteen-foot two-by-ten tie beam that runs the length of the building. I had forgotten to spike the sections together from both sides, and Greg was getting bolder about telling me when I had made a mistake, at least when it was structural rather than cosmetic.

"I don't like *that*, Cathy—and you don't either."

But we rectified my mistake with a few quick nails; he soon had the bits of wall in place and was hammering the short two-by-four minirafters that connect them to the load-bearing two-by-eight-inch beam above the bay. There was no room to swing a hammer here; I shinned up the ladder to give it a try and found that when I pulled back for a decent shot, I hit the back of these snug angles with the claws of my hammer.

"How do you *do* this," I wailed; I hate not being able to do what looks like a fairly simple job. And it was—for Greg. He banged the short sections of studs into place as if he had four feet of swing space for his big framing hammer. Experience makes the difference; it's what separates impossible from easy. From the subfloor below, the joining looked perfect—or, as I found myself saying often on this project, "close enough for jazz." The bay was in place, and now the front and back walls waited to be sided where they stood; Greg had the back wall clad in the time it took for me to run to the hardware store.

He was careful with wood, trying not to order more than we needed for a given stage in the construction. I liked that—my checkbook liked it—but sometimes it meant that we ran out of a necessary board size and had to wait or make do with a patchwork of odd-sized bits and pieces. We used up some of the growing pile of scraps on the narrow areas between the windows, and I nailed a stack of them on the small, straight section beside the bay.

We improvised pretty creatively with scrap within the walls, where it couldn't be seen, but here, I wanted the siding to look good. To me, this was the front of the cabin, in spite of what you would see first as you came down the drive, no matter where the door was. But it was easier to will perfection than attain it. I was nearly to the top of the wall when I stepped back to survey my work and discovered that I had congratulated myself too soon. One end of the tongue-in-groove car siding appeared to have a decidedly uphill slant.

"I'll bet it looks fine. The eye don't lie," Greg reassured me when I leaned around the edge of the cabin to tell him my fears. "The sun and the moon may vary, but the eye don't lie."

Mine did, at least in the nailing stages. "Yep, I guess it looks straight to me," I said—but it wasn't; I lied through my teeth. Now, as I stepped back to survey the wall, my eye was disgustingly accurate; the level confirmed it. On the small, straight wall on the front of the cabin, the siding resembled a subtle game of pick-up-sticks. The lines of nails I fastened them with wriggled their way up under the eaves, no better than the ones on the back side of the cabin. Dad would have had words for this kind of workmanship; Greg just looked at me askance and kept nailing.

I had expected these short pieces of siding, at least, to fit easily together, the groove fitting tightly over the tongue and automatically creating parallel lines. Instead, it seemed it was still necessary to "cheat" them in place, even where the pieces were too short to be affected by warping. I had been too close to my work, not stepping back for perspective—and in too much of a hurry. And unless I wanted to wait for more wood to be delivered, holding up the schedule again, I was stuck with my own workmanship. No one will doubt that I had a hand in it; this was definitely amateur carpentry. Close enough for jazz.

The load of lumber arrived at last for the roof; two-by-six rafters, yellow pine tongue-in-groove siding, and rolls of tar paper to seal it temporarily from the weather. But just as the lumber truck pulled away, we realized there was no ridge beam among the piles—the one board you can't build a roof without, the one all the rafters are nailed to. A two-by-twelve-inch pine beam sixteen feet long is hard to miss; it wasn't there.

My carpenter dashed off through the woods after the lumber truck, yelling all the way. "Where's my ridge beam? Where's the damn ridge beam?" But it would be days before the delivery truck could come back our way with only one board. A piece of wood of that size was much too long to balance on my cartop carrier; Greg would pick it up in his truck the following morning. I was beginning to feel the frustrations inherent in the building game; today I had hoped to see rafters, the skeletal roof that would make me feel the cabin was progressing according to some loose sort of schedule.

But when the big board came, bouncing eight feet or so beyond the end of the pickup truck and waving a red flag, I couldn't imagine how we'd lift the thing into place twelve feet above our heads. Greg had constructed a pocket to hold the beam and a small, temporary shelf to prop it on, on its way up—and I realized this odd bit of jerry-built carpentry wouldn't have been necessary if he had an assistant who didn't mind heights. I assumed that he would use the wall jack to raise the heavy beam into place, but with Harris here to help we hoisted one end into its pocket with no trouble, with us below and Greg up above. My husband's six-foot-three height acted as just the bit of scaffolding we needed.

Greg had been scrambling up and down the tall gable ends, agile as a squirrel; now he walked the one-and-three-quarter-inch tie beam to the other end of the cabin like an Olympic athlete on the balance beam, casually smoking a cigarette. I couldn't watch. Harris and I lifted the other end of the ridge beam within his reach and propped it precariously on the little shelf. From there it was a short trip to the pocket in the other gable. In seconds it was spiked into place.

I drew the owner-builder line at the edge of the roof; as I said, I hate heights—unless I'm climbing a mountain. Don't ask me why that's different —maybe because if I fall off a peak I probably won't have to worry about much of anything after that. If I fall off a ladder, it could hurt.

I couldn't resist going for a bit more field experience as a builder, though. Greg had marked all the rafters with the proper angles to define the slant of the roof where they met the ridge beam. On the other end, they were marked so the edges of the vertical cuts would be neatly covered with the fascia board to seal the cabin from the weather. While he was occupied hopping up and down the ladder, I picked up his big worm-gear-driven saw and tested the marked line with the blade. It appears good tools help a poor

The little shelf acted as an assistant with no fear of heights — a temporary stop for the ridge beam.

carpenter; I cut the angle like a pro. With my own twenty-year-old radial saw I was likely to wander off the mark. The blade is hard to see, and keeping it perfectly aligned is more challenge than I am equal to.

I didn't let my success go to my head; this was no place for cockiness. I let Greg cut the little notches that determine how much roof overhang we'd have and how securely the rafters would sit on the sill plates. That I couldn't quite picture — the "bird's mouth" notches have to be just so. The seat cut must rest securely on the sill plate at the top of the wall; the heel cut fits snug up against the outside. I gave up the saw to its owner; I didn't want a wobbly roof.

Harris and I shoved the cut rafters through the rough-framed window openings, laying them out in place to hand up to Greg on the roof beam. He hammered them in place, first on one side, then the other, alternating rafters for strength. Physics applied to the craft of building was beginning to sink in, and I could see how this all would hold together, supported on each side like a bowerbird's nest. And once rafters were in place, it began to look like a cabin.

Yellow pine car siding topped the rafters, closing the rectangular view of sky I had become accustomed to, but the effect was wonderful. Growth lines scribe the pale golden boards, knots clearly mark where limbs once sprouted, and I realized that this exposed wood would keep me in touch with the process of building. Once the cabin was finished and the rough walls were covered with drywall, process would recede to memory; mystery would reassert itself. On the ceiling, the honest boards tell the story, straightforward as ABC.

Before we left for the night Greg tacked up more tar paper, whacking it in place with a staple gun to protect the new ceiling; until the metal panels came, this doubled as roof. The next day it rained, and I sat snug inside, the leaking sky unable to penetrate my nest.

It was weeks later before we were able to complete the roof; thank goodness for tar paper. I chose a metal roof for safety here far off the road. Fire protection would be difficult at best, though we signed up with the volunteer fire department and drew them a rough map to the cabin. We were still discussing the relative merits of a wood stove, still planning to install the one we had bought; the metal roof would be immune to sparks. The soft gray color would blend into the tree trunks, and when the wood of the cabin weathered it would be all of a piece, a soft gray with sky blue windows.

We had lived with a metal roof before; our old farmhouse was outfitted with typical corrugated tin, mellowed to a rusty sienna; as far as we could tell, it had been there for decades. In all the years we lived there, it never leaked as the shingled house in town did, and the drumming of rain on the roof was a heartbeat that lulled us to sleep.

It was a good decision, though we have yet to install the stove.

The metal of the roof expands and contracts as the clouds race across the clearing, keeping up a constant conversation with itself until the sun slips behind the west hill. I had imagined a cloistered silence here; I've learned to appreciate the distinctive clamor instead. The sighing of the wind in the bare winter trees and the creak of the metal roof are like the sounds in the rigging of a clipper ship with all sails set. I like a roof that talks to itself, that whispers tales of inland seas in my ear. But only the landscape beyond the windows is in motion, the tops of the walnut trees tossing like waves caught in the powerful tide of the wind; the structure itself is firm.

There are times when I can hear the cabin ticking and popping and whispering as I come to it down the west hill, and I smile as though I overheard the games of children. It's a welcoming sound.

We used three-inch-thick blue foam panels for insulation, laid on top of the pine car siding. The ugly stack of stuff had been sitting by the deck for weeks, and I was delighted to finally get it under cover, hidden away forever. And again, I reverted to client rather than carpenter; more roof work—more height. Daniel had come to help, and the two of them had the foam cut and in place in minutes.

It was great to have something go that quickly; it took forever for our roof to come in—we thought it had been ordered for at least a week (it must be cut especially for each project) and, in fact, it had not.

But at last, we were ready. Our only real snag was that with the thicker insulation rather than the two-inch specified by the roofing company, the nails provided wouldn't go all the way through to the wood. My job was to sit mindlessly removing the rubber washers from the nail heads and placing them on the much longer nails we bought for the job.

I left to get more supplies, and Greg and Daniel decided to surprise me by getting the roof on while I was gone. They almost made it, too, and when I came walking down the hill I was amazed to see what was beginning to look like a done deal.

It was a mixed felicity. In their haste they hadn't noticed that the nails were just that much too long and protruded through the car siding and into the cabin. The blunt ends of the nails pushed big splinters of yellow pine before them, so that in most places you don't see the points of the nails but flaps of wood instead. I ignore them; the nails are too high to hit with my head and no problem—once I discovered that the rain wouldn't wick down the nails and onto the floor.

While Daniel was here, he insulated the floor—reluctantly. It's a tight fit under the cabin and one job I was willing to pay someone else to avoid doing myself. The thin, pale sprouts of poison ivy were forgotten, until a day or two after poor Daniel's ordeal, wedged between the ground and the floor joists. I felt sorry for the kid. It was ninety-five degrees, and he was sweating and red faced. I cut the long bats of insulation and handed them to him under the edge of the cabin, listening for his voice.

"Cathy! I need more insulation," or "Yo! I'm out of staples." I kept myself busy with fetch and carry; at least I didn't have to lie on my back and crawl up into the area that's only six inches above the ground; there had to have been a better way to do this, a better time.

I read a new edition of Henry Beston's classic, *The Outermost House*, pleased by the similarities in our little retreats, granted that one big difference: location. His was on the seacoast at Cape Cod; mine could be called "the Innermost House" with some accuracy, close to the heart of America. It's sandwiched neatly between the population center of the U.S. at tiny DeSoto, Missouri, and the geographical center of the conterminous states at Lebanon, Kansas.

Aside from our common need for such a retreat in the first place, it's in our love of an unobstructed view that Beston and I are most similar. Beston had ten windows in two rooms; I planned for nine in one room — twelve, if you count the sets of French windows as two each. But their view is everything; I, too, have something "rather like an inside out-of-doors." We have no shutters here, far from the Atlantic's storms; the only time I mind the sun is when I'd like a bit more sleep after the nocturnal raccoons have enter-

View from the studio window — in progress.

The antique windows just match for width.

tained at 3:00 A.M.—those east-facing windows usher in every atom of morning light. Privacy is courtesy a tree-sheltered distance.

We left holes for windows everywhere; these odd-sized, odd-shaped apertures were a graphic demonstration of why we needed a professional's help. Studs I understood, cripples and headers were straightforward enough. Even that bugaboo toe-nailing turned out to be a skill like any other, mastered with only a little practice. But the windows were different, a difficult mix of sizes and styles and conditions requiring a working knowledge of these special apertures and a fine-tuned skill with power tools. Thanks to my purchase of used windows rather than factory-framed ones, it was necessary to rough-frame them with an eye to compensating for the fact that they weren't all perfectly square, not any more.

The variety of windows required a matching set of mounting systems. The fixed round-top was the only easy shot; I could have figured it out myself, without a blueprint. Still, I wouldn't have given any of them up; I was pleased with my finds and the spaces we had left for them.

The low windows across the back of the cabin were the only youngsters in the place. Compared to my collection of antiques, they were pristine—no missing putty, no layers of alligator paint—and no wavy glass. If you've ever lived with antique windows you'll know what I'm talking about; early windows were made of molten glass that was pulled like taffy, and the inevitable bubbles, imperfections, and variations in thickness caused distortion.

Now, early methods of glassmaking have been replaced in the U.S. by float glass, and just as it sounds, it's manufactured by floating a thin layer of molten glass over a bed of molten metal. It cools in place and produces an extremely brilliant, smooth product.

The quicksilver image seen through an old window is charming in its way; you know they are old. But it has its drawbacks. When I want to see the details of a specific bird, I weave my head around like a barn owl to get a clear look at my subject—otherwise the brown creeper outside my studio window appears to have a Quasimodo hump.

Greg groaned audibly when he saw the double-hung windows piled in single panels against the wall, neatly painted and ready to be rebuilt. I had packed them in down the hill with my nail belt and thermos that morning.

"These really gonna be double-hung, Cathy?"

"Yup," I said.

"Uh—okay. First time me, first time you," he said again.

"I've got faith in you—no problem." And oddly enough, given his propensity for repeating that last phrase, it was true.

My faith wasn't misplaced; the windows fit better than the original ones in my century-old Victorian in town. But double-hung windows now come from the factory already mounted in frames, with their wooden or aluminum channels already in place, counterweights hidden in the frame to control the degree of opening. There was a great deal more work involved in installing them than any of the others. The frames with their aprons and jambs, stools and grooves and stops were much more complicated than a hinged awning window with a single stop around all four sides—even with its down-sloped sill to drain water; double-hung windows must have that angle as well.

It occurred to me that my savings on these antiques were dribbling away with every hour it took to build their frames and mount them. I was beginning to feel the weekly pinch of writing the check for labor; we had agreed to $16 an hour, and I felt the hours fly by in contrast with the agonizingly slow progress as we built these frames from scratch.

"Did I save anything buying these old windows?" I couldn't help but think of the month of chilling work out on my back porch, sanding and puttying and painting.

"*Oh*, yeah," he assured me. "This would be close to $2,000 worth of windows. I don't cost *that* much."

He was right, too—if I didn't count my own time in reconditioning them, it was still a hefty savings; my finds had set me back just under $100. And time is mine to spend, interest free; even my bookkeeper agrees with that. It depends on how much sleep I'm willing to give up.

The ornate paneled door has seen a lot of life, opening and closing on someone else's history; its wood texture is accentuated by the weather even after sanding, and the panels were loose in their frames. When Greg mounted it in his perfectly square frame, the door balked like a Missouri mule and had to be removed from its hinges three or four times to plane it into submission. But once it was finally hung, it was beautiful. Greg fit the antique doorknobs and striker plates in place, and they looked as though they had been designed especially for this particular door on this particular cabin.

"We're just keeping honest people honest," he said as he installed the last window lock and the shiny new bolt on the door. "If they want in, they'll get in."

But I noticed that he moved his tools inside, under lock and key, at the first possible opportunity and seemed relieved to have them there. So was I. There was a lot of money sitting out in the walnut grove with only cheap plastic tarp for protection; the rented generator bothered me from the first. There was nearly a thousand dollars in that piece alone, and it belonged to neither of us.

"Are you insured against theft?" I asked Greg one day as we sat on the deck to eat our lunch. "I don't know if ours would cover it this far from home."

"Oh, yeah," he replied. "It eats me up, but you gotta have it. Never lost anything off a job site, though—isn't it amazing? It all just sits out, and it's all still there in the morning. People are pretty honest."

They must be. So far everything had stayed put in the walnut grove, and

I laugh to remember that Harris didn't even want to leave our five-dollar lawn chairs down here. There's been a whole lot more than five dollars sitting around on the deck.

I was beginning to miss the seemingly limitless time we had had, sitting in those old chairs by the creek or walking through the woods. Work seemed suddenly to be all I did; what must it be like to build a house? Building—and trying to keep up with my paying jobs in the hours between—had consumed everything else; spring passed without my noticing, and if I saw the woods at all it was as a barrier between the road and the building site, rough territory to be crossed with a backpack full of tools, a nail belt on my hips, a cooler full of lunch and sodas, and a head full of dreams.

I noticed the growing strain of working from dawn till bedtime, of too many decisions, of unaccustomed physical demands, of dwindling finances. My temper felt alarmingly close to the surface; my equilibrium was upset, as if I had an inner-ear infection.

Being constantly thrown with people was part of the problem; I was used to long hours alone. Now it seemed as though I'd moved in with half the county. Not just Greg and his dad—our ubiquitous overseer—but wives and kids and aunts and uncles; Daniel, Greg's sometime assistant, and his wife; delivery men, men from the electric and phone company, lumberyard people, friends, and a stream of curious strangers; I hadn't entertained so much in my entire life. One day there were over twenty people just passing through. There's something about building a cabin in the woods that touches everyone's dreams. I couldn't blame them for wanting to see. One fellow I'd never met wandered back through the woods to find out what we were doing: "I'm just being nosy here."

I couldn't blame them—but there were times when I didn't feel up to playing hostess for another second; I was never good at it. All I wanted to do was to work, to keep moving, to make progress—to get *finished.*

Finally, one day—a Sunday—Greg said he would be late, if he was able to come at all. Progress or not, it was fine with me; he works seven-day weeks, and if he worked, I worked. We'd been at it without a break for almost a month. But this day, anyway, I would have to myself, hours and hours alone in the windowless shell of the cabin that felt, already, like home.

I strained toward this time alone like a dog on a leash when a rabbit appears, holding myself together with sheer will and a patchwork suturing of promises, talking to myself: "You can do it. It's just a little longer. Take it easy." The sutures held, but barely. I wanted my life back.

But I'd made my escape. I was here. I had the place to myself; I could breathe again. I topped the hill with a long sigh...and there was Harry's car.

"Oh, noooooo! No! *No!* I can't stand another minute of politeness. I can't take it." I steamed down the path with backpack jumping, just ready to break, thoughts tumbling over each other like agate in a rock hound's polishing bath, taking on a high, hard sheen. I rehearsed what I would say as I went, then threw it all out and started over in the space it took to walk from the road to the cabin.

"Where's Greg?" Harry asked me, innocent as a babe. He was sweeping the cabin floor. I felt helpless in the grip of my own need, but floor sweeping wasn't the kind of first aid I longed for. Where the hell was assertiveness training when you need it?

But I pulled it out of somewhere; necessity has a way of helping you speak your mind: "Harry, I'm going to have to ask you to leave. Greg's not coming today, and I have *got* to have some time alone."

"Oh, no problem," Harry said. "I know exactly what you mean. I'll just finish up here."

"No. Thanks. I'll finish," I said, biting off my words and holding out my hand for the broom. I didn't trust myself to full sentences.

I'll be damned, it worked. In moments I was alone—and not a second too soon.

I couldn't stop. When Greg was away I couldn't keep my hands off his saws. I was anxious to see progress even if I had to make it alone, and I would have liked this work for its speed if nothing else.

The neat angles where the roof overhang meets the building were

Trimming out the bay windows—measuring with scraps.

Greg's doing; the trim is precision cut, as neatly joined as the angles of a honeybee's octagonal comb. He showed me how to fit the trim to the outside of the windows so I could work while he was busy on another job; these were nowhere near as complex as the compound angles where trim met roof and cabin and adjacent trim, and I was anxious to jump in. First, you fit two scraps of cedar one-by-threes beside the windows, lined up with the upper edge of the opening, and nail them temporarily in place, one on each side. This gives you the exact measurement for the trim, from outer edge to edge. I cut the top piece just this length, slicing through the narrow board with Greg's trim saw. The bottom frame board fit just inside the lower measurement, taking its length from corner to corner, and the two side pieces are measured from the edge of the top board to the lower edge of the bottom board.

I was not as good at this as Greg; I had trouble figuring the width of the saw blade itself into my computations, throwing each cut off by a fraction — but when all the windows were framed in one-by-three-inch rough cedar I stepped back to look at them with pure pleasure. Each trimmed-out window suddenly looked professional — and finished; when I looked at my work I couldn't help beaming. The radio blared away by the deck; Mick Jagger wailed that he "can't *get* no sat-is-*fac*-tion." I could. I could frame out windows, and they looked good.

When I finished the windows I moved on to the one-by-four-inch trim boards on the cabin itself. Corner trim is done much the same way as the windows; all these measurements that I looked at with such apprehension are cut using tricks and shortcuts rather than the math that reads — to me — like ancient hieroglyphics; I could do most of them without ever needing my tape measure. After watching my carpenter cut the neat angles where these boards met the eaves on one corner of the cabin, I tackled the next one myself. As my dad used to say, it's all in knowing how — and knowing how is a matter of poking through the bag of tricks that separate the amateurs from the pros and pulling the right one out for the job at hand. That's why there were craftsmen's guilds in the Middle Ages — to keep those secrets (and the job security they offered) or to pass them on to apprentices. I was Greg's apprentice, and I liked being in on the secrets.

"You're not an amateur any more, Cathy," Greg told me one day. "You're a journeyman carpenter. You could get a job. In fact, I'd hire you myself." All lies, but it felt great.

It didn't occur to me that he might not be happy that I was using his expensive tools while he was away, not until I read Tracy Kidder's book, *House,* and saw myself in the home owner. She, too, used these precision tools, wanting to have her hand in, and the carpenters resented it; they pointed out that she might have asked their permission. But by this time I was tired of delays. Greg wasn't here to ask in any case; he had left to finish another job. I could do it, and I did. If I thought at all of Greg's concern for his tools, I didn't much care. I wanted to make things *happen*.

As we neared the end of construction, six weeks behind schedule (thanks in part to the necessity of using hammer and nails rather than nail gun, I reminded myself in order to keep calm), my patience level hovered somewhere around empty; I was running on fumes alone.

I hated the helpless, ready-to-cry feeling that sat just behind my eyes. It was pure held-in nerve, sharpened by exhaustion. "I want my *life* back"; there was that refrain again. But life — life as it was now, a wild jumble of building and writing, illustrations and deadlines — was backing up on me; the dam threatened to burst. I felt the pressure of unmet obligations at my back and I was almost over the edge; scratch me and I would have bled to death before your eyes.

Lights are
coming down
the drive.

9. Completion — or Thereabouts

There are a hundred decisions to be made on a day-to-day basis on any building project, balancing possibility against desire, vision against practicality, time against money. Could we afford running water? A quick check with the federal water district convinced me we could not; the meter alone would cost $850—$1,150 if you were across the road from the water line. We were. That expense was independent of laying pipe from the meter to the cabin— nearly 600 feet—and burying it deep enough to keep it from freezing and hooking up to an outdoor stock pump. Plumbing the cabin itself wasn't even considered. We could carry water down the hill for drinking and bathe at home.

Would there be electricity? At first, caught up in the idea of simplicity, I thought I'd do without—a kerosene lamp would do. An unseasonably hot spring reminded me; this is Missouri, not Michigan. If I planned to work here in July and August, I'd want a fan. It's not pleasant to work on a drawing when your arms stick to the paper; besides, even with all the windows I'd still need a source of light at my drawing board. Kerosene puts out prodigious amounts of heat; scotch the lamp.

Insurance, oddly enough, was the deciding factor. As we spent more and more money to put the foundations under this dream, it became obvious that we would want to protect it. But there was a catch; we couldn't get insurance if we stuck to the original plan of a tiny wood stove vented with double-wall pipe—and at that stage we hadn't yet decided not to go with wood. The stove still waited in my workroom at home for the correct stage in construction to install it. According to my insurance agent, we would need either a masonry chimney (too late for that, without a lot of reworking) or a primary heat source that wasn't wood.

Liquid propane gas was out. After seven years of farm life, surviving those periods when the gas truck couldn't get down the drive (a much better one than the unused tractor path we have here), the memories were too fresh. That left electric heat, with the attendant expense of putting in a pole, burying the cable, wiring the cabin.

Here in rural Missouri, electric service is parceled out in strange ways; the hill road is served by one company—it is their box by the road near Rachel's Meadow, where I considered building for practicality's sake. They are our electric supplier in town, a big company with home offices in Kansas City and a good service record. The north road is served by a rural electric co-op that I'd never dealt with.

There were too many options; trying to sort them out to make an intelligent decision made my brain ache. In order to utilize the electricity I already had on the east, I'd have to clear a path from there down along the north road to set the poles—and lose a section of the woods I had just bought the place for, fifteen feet wide and a quarter of a mile long. But after that expense of time, money, and trees, installation from the road to the cabin would be free, or virtually so. The co-op that serviced the homes just across the road from our dirt path, on the other hand, required a hefty membership fee (returnable after the first two years) and recommended the expensive process of burying the wire from road to cabin to minimize problems with blow-downs and brush cutting later. With this plan I wouldn't have to cut a single tree, and I decided to spend more of my declining financial resources to save the trees. I'd get better interest from my investment.

The day the electricity arrived, the place swarmed with workmen and equipment—pole setters, and the huge truck long enough to hold a telephone pole, plus the machine that buried the wire. The electrician rough-wired the cabin a day or two later, and we returned the rented generator with relief.

The inside of the unfinished cabin smelled of cedar, sun warmed and redolent of forest. The color was rich, a warm sorrel-colored room in the woods. We had turned the rough side of the boards out to the weather. The inner surface had been planed as smooth and glossy as though sanded, and I wished there were a way to leave it showing. I imagined a hundred little bookshelves lining the wall, tucked in between the two-by-fours where we set our cola cans and coffee cups—but the romance of that vision faded when strong morning light fingered its way between the rough boards and through a loose knothole. Winter would be cold; we'd have to finish the walls —building convention gets that way for a reason.

Insulation is nasty stuff; I hate to handle it. The tiny bits of fiberglass migrate between the fibers of my clothing and seem to infiltrate my very cells. But this time Harris and I would do it; we didn't need Daniel for places we could get to easily, and I had begun seriously to pinch my nickels where I could.

It was already a hot day in late spring when we jammed the long streamers of unfaced fiberglass between the studs and filled the smaller spaces with specially cut pieces, holding them in place with friction fit; the finished walls would keep them where they belonged permanently. Harris took bits of glass fluff and stuffed them loosely into the cracks around the doors and windows with the blade of a screwdriver; this cabin would be tight, snug as an insect's cocoon against the winter winds. When we finished we shrouded the room in heavy plastic, a moisture barrier that would stop any errant drafts.

Moisture infiltration from the inside out is not a big problem in a building without plumbing; an occasional cup of coffee and the moisture contained in my breath is not enough to seep through Drywall and damage the insulation. The plastic sheeting was more a matter of doing everything up right and proper than of meeting any real need.

I wanted rustic, planned for it — but to my surprise, rustic cost more than smooth. The wooden boards I had wanted as interior walls would have been another $400 or $500; drywall (Sheetrock, wallboard, whatever you choose to call it) is a pittance in comparison.

There's always a price to pay for penury; drywall is labor-intensive. It's a messy, nasty job that commands all my respect for the guys who do walls for a living. By the time we finished the cutting, nailing, patching, taping, mudding, sanding, and the endless sweeping of drywall dust, the project had eaten almost another full week and still needed two coats of paint to finish it. Again we had underestimated the amount of material that we would need; under this fine finish you would find a wild jumble of odd-shaped pieces of Sheetrock, some no larger than six inches wide, and all requiring taping, mudding or spackling, and sanding. I was beginning to lose my composure.

Harris helped finish up the walls while Greg was away on someone else's project. We sanded and smoothed and dusted, refilling the dimples and cracks with drywall mud where our first coats had shrunk and cracked, then sanded and dusted some more. The borrowed shop vac helped; the floor was covered with a fine white gypsum powder and we tracked it everywhere. So did the resident raccoons. We had dusted them for prints and they left evidence of their larceny everywhere. I liked knowing I'd have their footprints on file forever, encased within the walls and floors of my little retreat.

The painting had to wait for the trim work; windows were in place and trimmed on the outside of the cabin, but inside they looked surprised, unformed. The simple yellow pine boards that would give them a finished mien would be Greg's job; I wanted this to look good. Sixteenth-of-an-inch gaps that look fine outdoors would look like the Grand Canyon in here.

I had assumed that Harris and I would varnish the woodwork, too, a tedious but simpleminded job. But Greg had a sprayer and would lacquer everything at once, as soon as we had it ready. We put in another few days of sanding, this time of wood—no hard job until we got to the ceiling. The exposed rafters and the beautiful pine car siding above them would be lacquered to a low sheen, a warm glow to light the cabin on blue winter days. But meanwhile, every other board and all of the rafters had been stamped with the lumber company's logo. It was impervious to our efforts to erase or wash it away; someone should use this stuff to mark the center line of the freeway, if only it came in yellow. It had to be sanded off, standing at the top of the ladder with my arms over my head, beating down my fear of heights and eating sawdust. I don't envy the wood-boring insects that survive on this stuff; it tastes awful.

Greg put on two coats of lacquer on all of the woodwork in the cabin in approximately the same amount of time it took me to sand away one logo. I tried not to think about it.

I left one logo in a tight spot between the last rafter and the far wall where it was difficult to fit even the little palm-sized electric sander. I could have removed it by hand, but I like knowing it's there—like the raccoons' footprints, another reminder of a step in cabin building. An invisible step, unless you stand against the wall and crane your neck to see it, but it's there. Like the wooden ceiling itself, it's a part of the process.

Overhead
Sanding
gets old
in a
hurry.

I finished the baseboard and trim myself. Greg was off somewhere, and I was alone with his tools again. Normally, perhaps I wouldn't have used them; normally, I was not running a month behind with my life.

This was a new one for me, a miter saw that moved in its metal frame, calibrated to cut any angle you like and capable of a hair's breadth deviation on either side. It was a precision instrument, a bit daunting but—in Greg's hands, anyway—wonderfully accurate. And once I learned how to turn the damned thing on, I was out of the gate like a racehorse, mitering corners quickly. I had watched Greg do the first corners earlier, and he fit and cut and tried the boards and trimmed again along the odd angles of the bay window. If he needed to work this way, shaving scraps of wood over and over with the miter saw until the perfect fit and angle were found, why not me?

I was not the only one who wanted to see the baseboard in. Mike, the electrician, needed to know when he could finish his part of the job—he hadn't been paid for his work and wouldn't be until he was done. Until the baseboards were finished, he couldn't install the long electric heating units. I gave it my best shot, satisfied with my results. After all, I wanted to be able to see that I did part of the work; the rationalization helps to gloss over the small canyons between the boards.

I took photos of nearly everything, roll after roll of color film to record what we had done. They turned out to be practical reminders, as well. In our haste, we had covered one of the electrical boxes when we applied the drywall, and no one remembered exactly where it was. I hauled out the photographs to show Mike when he came back to finish the wiring, and he located the box in an instant.

Finally the walls were smooth and the woodwork and ceiling were lacquered. Two coats of creamy white paint would catch and hold the light inside, so electricity would be needed only at night.

But even here there were tricks. Greg showed me how to apply the masking tape around the freshly lacquered woodwork to make the painting go quickly and cleanly, holding the long strips out taut and laying them in place, then burnishing them down with the back of his fingernail. Harris and I could slop the paint on thickly to cover the mottled gray and white of the mudded drywall without worrying about cutting carefully around the woodwork and get by with only two coats. The job was faster than anything we had done since framing, and I loved it; I'm all for instant gratification. Removing the tape was like ripping the ribbons off a gift.

And suddenly the place looked like more than a rough shell of a cabin; it was elegant. It was a seashell, iridescent with light. The rays bounced off the pale golden ceiling and around the walls as though exploring their virgin domain like cats in a new environment.

The floor was the same story, a tenuous balancing of time against money with a happy ending. We had thought to use an inexpensive vinyl floor covering in my favorite tile pattern—easy to sweep, easy to lay—a quick fix to seal the chemical-treated underfloor away from the living area. But the pattern I liked was not, after all, inexpensive; it would have cost $1200 for my fourteen-by-sixteen square feet of space, an investment suitable for a mansion, not a cabin—and that was if we installed it ourselves. The next cheapest was $800. Floor covering too ugly to spend a dime on was nearly $400; what a decision! We scrapped the vinyl floor plan and cast about for alternatives.

At the lumberyard, owner Rob Maples showed me pine porch flooring; I was immediately hooked. A pinewood, tongue-and-groove floor would cost about $300—still much higher than I had imagined, but it seemed my imagination was beggared when it came to building. The bank balance was in a state of drought but my desire to see the cabin done was unquenchable; we went for the porch flooring and returned the smooth mahogany underlayment Greg had already bought.

I was relieved; using mahogany from tropical rain forests just to make my vinyl floor smooth was not my idea of good stewardship. I was relieved, too, to get rid of the stuff from the purely physical standpoint. Every morning when I arrived to work I'd haul it all out on the deck and out of our way; every evening, we carried it back under cover for protection. The stuff was only a quarter of an inch thick, but four-by-eight sheets weighed enough to make me glad to see it go, and good riddance.

The relatively inexpensive yellow pine porch flooring looked smooth and lovely at the lumberyard; just right for a cabin. Harris and I prepared the subfloor together, sweeping away the last of the debris and laying down a layer of tar paper to seal the drafts. The new hammer-style staple gun made short work of this; we bent along the seams—whack! whack!—and the tar-impregnated stuff was down in minutes. If it bubbled a bit here and there, no problem; the pine boards would flatten it. I couldn't resist that expanse, like an immense blackboard just begging to be written on, and finding a piece of chalk in Greg's toolbox, I scribbled "C.J. loves H.J." on the floor, grinning at my husband.

"Remember that's there when I'm cranky, okay?"

I imagined that Greg and I would get the tongue-and-groove flooring down quickly—perhaps a day's work. We managed it in two, instead, a nasty job that required a great deal of nail setting. Greg hammered them in, holding the boards permanently in place; I came behind, sliding along on my backside, banging each nail head just below flush with hammer and nail set.

These last are interesting little instruments of torture designed, I am sure, by the Marquis de Sade. They look a little like a chubby nail with a big, square head. The business end fits into the dimple in a finish nail's head—in

Tongue-and-groove yellow pine floor.

theory—and you drive the nail below the surface of the wood. In practice, it slipped off almost as often as it stayed on, causing me to set the fingers that held the tool instead of the nail. On other tries, the hammer glanced off the nail set's head and banged into my knuckles. Either way, the result was the same.

"Ouch. Ow. *Shit.*"

"Don't look at the nail set, Cathy," Greg said. "Keep your eye on where you want the nail to go." It was follow-through, a golfer's best friend, that was called for here.

And it seemed to work. I only hit my fingers every second or third board now, instead of every five or six nails. My hands were numb and swollen, and Greg offered to take over and do it all, but it seemed faster with both of us working.

I envied him, nailing in the boards, keeping at least three feet ahead of me across the width of the floor. The boards seemed to fit together much more easily than the cedar siding on the outside of the cabin; the tongues really did fit in their grooves. And whether it was long practice on the job he's chosen or just a fine-tuned hand-eye coordination, Greg, at least, wasn't turning the air as blue as I did. His swearing seemed to take place, instead, when he banged the edge of a board with the grid-headed framing hammer as he drove the nails home.

125

"Damn! There's another one."

The boards carried a neat checkerboard pattern, like a brand; they still do, here and there, even after we finished the floor.

Once the boards were down, the bumps and ridges became obvious; the yellow pine may have been lovely but it was definitely not smooth. It needed sanding if we weren't to spend the next twenty years picking splinters from bare feet—another day's delay, another expense to rent a floor sander, and more endless sweeping, this time of sawdust. The floor had to be completely dust free before I could put on the finish; I went through tack cloths like tissues in allergy season.

Now there is an interesting pattern on the floor; yellow pine has broad growth rings, a marked grain in which bands of wood dense enough to qualify as a hardwood alternate with much softer bands. The harder, darker strips resisted the sander; the softer ones yielded without a fight, so that the surface of the floor undulates gently like the small waves on a calm lake. I like the effect; it has a depth, a dimension I hadn't expected. It says what it is and with character.

The roof detail was a bit of joinery I couldn't resist, a traditional wooden cross of the sort tucked beneath the eaves of many of the cabins I had stayed in as a kid. Greg had left his power tools, and I experimented with cutting tightly-fitted rabbet joints until I could make the crossmembers neat and flat. The lower vertical I cut to a shallow point; fitting the angles of the ends of this bit of decorative fluffery to the roof-gable angles took five or six trips up and down the ladder to measure and re-measure—but when I was finished I surveyed it with satisfaction all out of proportion to the effect. This was no longer rough carpentry.

Building seven days a week and trying to keep up with my normal work

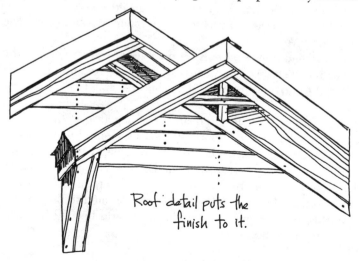

Roof detail puts the
finish to it.

schedule evenings and before starting in again the next day hadn't helped to maintain my equilibrium. The half-open window of time I had arranged in my work load had slammed shut. The building went so quickly at first — deck and walls the first week, rudimentary roof of pine boards and tar paper shortly after — but now it seemed a thousand obstructions were thrown up in my path.

I had liked the framing; it went fast. It was satisfying: visual progress, hour by hour. I went home to get Harris each evening to show him what we had done and was as amazed as he after even that short time away. The thousand details of finishing were more complex, more demanding. Insulation, drywall, trim, flooring — they seemed to take forever and were tedious in the extreme.

Greg's work was backing up on him as well. The schedule that fell apart had thrown both of us, and more and more often he left my job for someone less patient — or more desperate — than I was. Or more outspoken; I damned my reserve daily and wondered why I felt that it was not polite to say what *I* needed.

"I've got to peel out early today, Cathy," and so at three o'clock I stood there, frustrated, wishing I knew what to do and how to do it, wishing I could finish this thing alone; keeping busy with the things I knew.

"I hate to ask you, but would you mind if I finished up that job for Jack and then came back? It'll only take four days." It took eight.

"I've gotta go. I'll be here bright and early tomorrow, though — see you by eight." It was eleven by the time I heard his truck on the road, and I was wound so tight I would have spun off the edge of the universe if I'd let go my hold on my hammer.

I wanted to be alone in the walnut grove, alone in the finished cabin. I wanted my brain to work again, for words to come out of my pencil point onto my paper. I was hungry to start using the cabin as it was intended. I didn't want excuses, I didn't want apologies. I wanted him done and out of here. I couldn't imagine what it would have been like if he were not a friend as well as a carpenter; I'd have killed him.

Something shuts off deep inside a contractor's brain just before any building project is complete. Greg carried around the last board to finish the wonderful gazebo he had been working on for the first two weeks he was here. Some of the other jobs he had left to work on were also things that had been started but not quite finished. Now it was our turn. As he drifted away to other things, we reminded him that we still needed screens on the windows and the long shelf above the bay windows. We were approaching completion right in the worst of Missouri bug season, and although I enjoy camping — and accept the inconvenience of bugs — even my tent has screens. I wanted the cabin in usable condition. I wanted to sleep here.

"*Screens.* Ugh." He gave a mock shudder.

"Well, we have to have them," I reminded him. It got so when either of us saw him we'd say, "We need those screens, Greg." Harris's temper was getting short, and mine was no better.

I would have built the damn things myself, but my carpenter had already taken his saws off to another job. I was getting so desperate I considered investing another hundred dollars or so in a miter saw of my own so I could get the job done right. I sketched them out, planning my project, as usual, on paper. But the day before I had planned to shell out the money for a piece of equipment I might never use again, Greg showed up to build screens. It took him all of half a day.

"I didn't want to build them, Cathy. I don't know why."

"Well, I don't either; they look great."

And so they did, at last. They are nothing like my drawings; Greg had looked at the rough sketches, then gone off on his own. The corners are mitered rather than lapped, and there are no center bars to obstruct the view. But they do have boards that fit just inside the windows' frames holding them tightly even if he had not screwed them in place.

The screen door was no more difficult. We bought an inexpensive one from the lumberyard and with only a little fitting, cutting off an inch or two from top and bottom, it fit its space as if it, too, had been custom-made. We stayed overnight that evening, reveling in the place at last as it was meant to be used.

We waited awhile longer for the shelf, wondering if it would ever be done. I had had to go to Maine on a teaching workshop—agony, when my dream had been so recently realized; it was less than three weeks since the screens were in place, and already it felt like part of me. I hated leaving it.

I hated it more when our flight back home a week later was the worst I'd ever had, at night and with a raging thunderstorm. The pilot clammed up just outside of O'Hare, apparently concentrating all his skill on getting us the hell out of the sky. Even the flight attendants were anxious; they strapped in long before descent. We were anxious, too, and wondered who would get the cabin if we died trying to land; we hadn't included it in a will. Morbid thoughts have a way of coming to the fore in these conditions.

The flight that was supposed to get in at five thirty instead landed at one o'clock the next morning. We were exhausted but delighted to feel the hard concrete of Kansas City International floors under our feet. The cabin had to wait until the next afternoon, after sleep and recuperation.

And when we arrived, we were amused to see the shelf in place and Greg's key left under the mat. It was finished. We put things away on the new shelf, opened the windows, made out the folding Japanese futon, and napped in the sweet Missouri woods, still sleeping off our anxiety and exhaustion. We awoke to find we'd gone to heaven after all; it was a perfect June day.

PART III:
SYNTHESIS

June, at last.

10. The Cabin Finds Its Place

There is satisfaction in completion—in finishing a job and closing doors both literal and figurative. Until that door shuts with a nice, solid *click*, I feel unsettled as seeds on the wind.

It was that way with building the cabin. Until we were through—at least with the initial phase of getting the walls up, roof on, and window screens in place—and could bid Greg a cordial farewell, I felt a lack of closure. Something that needed doing wasn't done. It's like that when something has a beginning, a middle, and an end, no matter what it is; once launched, you're committed—to some degree—to finding the end of it.

The land, on the other hand, has no end, needs no closure. It is linear, not circular; discovery can continue as long as there is breath and the energy to put one foot in front of the other. Perhaps that's why the land itself is a source of peace in a way the cabin can never be. Whatever happens, it goes on.

Our being here has affected the walnut grove profoundly. Before we came, there were only random signs you could see if you looked hard enough for them; a cut stump in the path, the Boy Scouts' well-hidden trash hole filled with rusting tin cans, the latrine pit discreetly screened by the denser woods beyond the grove. Occasionally I found a spent shotgun shell, now faded with time and chewed by God knows what.

At a casual glance, the grove might never have seen another human before we built—if you discount the fact that weeds rather than understory fill the spaces between the trees. That seems to indicate that the normal sequence of events, the progression from open land to brush to young forest to climax conditions, has been artificially altered. Someone must have mowed here in the past, encouraging this lusty carpet of wildflowers to fill the spaces between the trees. And even that is pure speculation; if the walnuts were planted rather than occurring naturally, perhaps the one who planned ahead for a profit cleared the small competing trees. Or perhaps it's true that walnuts themselves discourage interlopers, infusing the soil with a chemical that sends a signal to other plant life: you're not welcome here. Given the jungle of head-high weeds that obscure their bases all summer, that explanation is harder to buy—these weeds aren't the least discouraged. The signs of human intervention here are hints and whispers, at best; I hazard a guess at my own risk and enjoy the apparent wildness of the place.

It's pretty hard to overlook a fourteen-by-sixteen-foot cabin standing tall on wooden pillars, with its observation deck wrapped around two sides; this thing is no whisper, it's a flat statement of fact. At first, red-gold with new cedar, the cabin was like a lamp set among the filtered green shadows, impossible to ignore. Even now it focuses the attention wonderfully, makes a visual and emotional impact as it slowly weathers into place. And it distracts me from the thing I first loved about this landscape, its seemingly untouched forest—or perhaps it enhances it. There is undeniable charm in this backwoods grove, and its locus is as much cabin as walnut trees. It's the pioneer outlook, improvement on nature—making my mark, taming the wilderness as my great-grandparents did on their way west. (Ed Abbey would have a fit.)

In my mind, the cabin started out both larger and smaller as we mulled over the possibilities; we settled on fourteen-by-sixteen feet as being just big enough. In fact, it is not; if we were to install the wood stove I'd have to forfeit nearly a quarter of my room for safety—these stoves require prodigious amounts of clearance. At that distance, opening and closing the cabin's door would bring it dangerously near to a heater fired to January levels. And if even that tiny stove were fully stoked for efficient burning, I'd need to open the windows of this small place in midwinter or count it a sauna.

In any case, the actual measurements are somewhat closer to fourteen and a half by just over sixteen; it's nearly sixteen by sixteen if you include the bay that juts two feet out onto the deck. It's that small square footage that most often draws me; the changing view is the magnet. The deck is usually full of feeding birds, crowding each other on the two long feeders that hang before the windows, on the boards beneath them, or on the newly covered platform feeder. The squirrels, cautious to the point of paranoia, flick their tails anxiously and retreat in a heartbeat if I move.

My chair is there in the bay, an ancient rocker of bent twigs and sprung oak splines woven like a basket to carry my body. The seat was shaped for optimum comfort by someone else's bottom, sagging just so by use and hap-

Twig rocker and footstool.

penstance. Shined by the caress of many hands, the arms of the rocker still bear their polished bark. With the little twig footstool that sits before it, the old chair welcomes me year-round. A small octagonal table at arm's reach completes the accoutrements, supplying a place for coffee, binoculars, and a book; its top is no more than a foot across.

This is not as antisocial as it sounds. Next to my rocker is a folding deck chair of Chinese origin, for husband or guest. It looked forbiddingly rigid, but a quick test-sit—plus a look at the ten-dollar price tag—earned its place. If we have more guests, an extra folding chair, my rickety desk chair, and the futon provide seating.

Decor is more by chance and need than by design, though I had planned from the first where my desk and the futon would go, the chairs in the bay, and the kitchen corner. I had drawn it out on graph paper again and again to make sure the necessities would fit. But the little building holds much more than I had originally imagined, a happy mixture of junk and hand-me-downs and treasures carried in from the woods.

These last I *had* planned for. I know myself and my habit of carrying home bits of fungus, skulls, finely designed weeds, lichen-encrusted bark, and whatever else catches my eye. I often pocket something I want to draw when time permits, so I designed two shelves, the sixteen-foot one that would span the width of the cabin above the bay and one to stretch over the

133

two low windows on the west, just where the rafters meet the walls. They were crowded as the bleachers at a homecoming game after only a year of occupancy, and the floor acts as additional storage. So does my desk. So does the deck rail outside. There seems always to be a need to tinker with the arrangements, moving things around to make more room, looking for space for more.

An antique kitchen cabinet just fits by the door, but it proved inadequate for our needs though every inch is stuffed full. Even the top provides storage and display space, with a set of enameled coffee cups and a pot and a big bouquet of dried winter weeds. A heavy wooden table holds a two-burner electric hot plate and a toaster oven, allowing me just room enough to make a sandwich or cut up a salad. The shelf beneath the table is crowded, too; here there are two large picnic baskets, one full of my carpenter's tools, the other of miscellany from cat food to weather stripping. Also tucked away on this shelf, when not in use, is my radio/tape player and a bowl of dried ear corn for the squirrels. On the floor below are a jumble of sneakers and slippers and my wooden shoes from Holland, Michigan, just right for a rainy-day trip to the creek.

A cream-colored rug with an oriental design in blue and ochre set a rather more elegant tone than I had originally planned; it was a gift from Patti. Now I luxuriate in its warmth on winter days and love the class it suggests; the blue just matches the color of the painted wooden window frames and the checkerboard stenciling around the room. We supplemented it with throw rugs as the floor began to radiate the winter chill in spite of the thick layer of insulation. Now, two rag rugs warm the floor beside the door and in the kitchen corner, one woven from the softly varied blues of old denim. A hooked wool rug keeps our feet snug before the bay windows; that jutting bit of floor, overlooked when we insulated, borders on arctic when the temperature drops. I sit in my chair with a cheap plaid afghan over my knees and another around my shoulders, cupping a hot mug in my hands until the heat comes up.

The old-fashioned cooler gave way to a tiny refrigerator beside the table when we discovered we were spending a dollar a day and more on ice. It didn't take long to pay for the electric model at that rate, and running it costs perhaps thirty dollars a year. The luxury of ice cubes in August is not to be underestimated; there is no air-conditioning to subdue the ovenlike heat. The old red metal cooler stayed with us, though; it's now a blanket chest where we keep spare bedding.

We made room for a small bookcase when it became obvious that the single shelves on each side of my desk were inadequate to a writer's needs, and after only a few months I already felt the itch for more. I had planned to haul my resource books back and forth, but as I work here in the uninterrupted quiet of the woods, instead I carry more and more books one way to the cabin. Books are piled everywhere, and I survey the long wall beside the desk imagining a sturdy shelf or two along its length.

The futon is low to the floor; it doesn't block the view from the rear windows. If I'm desperate for room I can fold it up so it protrudes little more than two feet out from the wall, but most often I leave it in lounge position and sit there surrounded by a pile of papers and books laid out in a semicircle for easy access. At night it's a simple matter to sweep everything into a pile, stack it on the floor, and make the futon down into a bed. We catch the breeze from the low windows and lie there, watching the sun rise over the ridge. I can observe raccoons at midnight without ever leaving my covers. With an insulated blanket and a heavy old bedspread, we're comfortable even at below-zero temperatures. A handmade Cherokee dream web, a gift from Wendy, hangs just over my pillow; the web catches good dreams and the hole in the center allows the nightmares to escape, or so the legend goes. It must work; I have only good dreams here.

Our final addition of furniture was a tiny, three-drawer chest of drawers to hold a change of clothes and our pajamas; everything else is hung from Shaker pegs along the trim boards or folding wooden racks on the walls — or from the rafters themselves. Where these come down within reach of the two-burner hot plate, pots and pans and utensils dangle from cup hooks. You could live here in Thoreauvian simplicity, if you didn't mind bathing in the pond.

No sooner did we have walls than the resident wildlife made to claim them. A line of tiny brown ants explored the siding of the north wall, coming up from the back corner, trailing along a crack between boards in the siding, climbing in a miniature conga line over the window and door and exiting, stage left, down the front corner. I had no idea what they wanted. I found no evidence of feeding or nest building; perhaps we were only in the way of their ancestral route and they let nothing stand in their way.

Under the soffit boards, some invisible spider constructed a fine, hammock-shaped web. The guy wires were impossibly delicate, but they did the job; each was hung with a full load of gnats, caught as though drying on a line. Or so I thought. Instead, when I blew on them they scattered in a panic and flew off a few inches, then landed again on the web. I took a perverse pleasure in watching them fly and land, fly and land each time I blew in their direction; I've no love for gnats. Their propensity for exploring my mouth and nasal passages and the corners of my eyes gives me leave to heckle them in return.

The earth under the cabin is dead and dry; photosynthesis halted in its greening tracks the day the deck was finished. No, that's not quite true.

Curious fingers of light reach between the cracks, and when spring returned I found a thousand sunflower sprouts, as spindly and pale as paper-cup bean plants started by a class of kindergartners.

When I looked beneath the cabin for a misplaced screw, I found instead a Carolina wren scratching in the soft, bare earth. It was the same flute-voiced singer that inspected the two birdhouses, looking to lease one for the summer season, but now it was silent and furtive and looked as though it didn't expect to be discovered grubbing there in seclusion.

An occasional field mouse checked into the housing possibilities between the floor joists, where the bats of exposed insulation offered good nesting material; I found the woolly shreds on the ground among the trees, as though someone had shorn a pink sheep, and shoved them back into place before they could be rained on. No sooner were there window screens than some nocturnal flying insect had laid eggs there, neatly filling the tiny squares like hen's eggs in a carton. The two front corners of the cabin bear the muddy footprints of a generation or two of raccoons, intent on my bird feeders, and the wood is scratched with the needlelike claws of the squirrels who share their fondness for sunflower seeds.

The birds, artificially attracted for what I hope is our common good, leave their marks on the cabin as well. The deck rail tells a story of tool use; where Greg devised a neat V to join two long boards, the birds widened his tight seam into a miniature crevasse. I watched them brace up seeds in the crack and hammer away at them to open their shells, chipping away at the wood as well.

We impact this place in a hundred ways; there seems no way to avoid the repercussions as our lives take root here among the trees. The driveway that was a grassy, unused tractor path a year ago, overgrown with weeds and sedges, is now a double-rutted dirt track. It bleeds good topsoil each time it rains.

Twenty feet or more from the deck, sociopathic birds have carried off their bounty to eat in peace—and with relatively little rivalry. Blue jays are famous for "food dispersal" tactics, discouraging competition at the feeder or simply stocking their private larders. A downy woodpecker flew in on an emergency mission, grabbed a seed, and tucked it hastily into a crevice in the bark halfway across the grove, then seemingly forgot it there. Everywhere these forays ended up there are new plants sprouting; the grove is becoming civilized.

The tree closest to the deck—the one with a hanging suet block—bore signs of heavy traffic after the long cold. Normally, trees are soft gray, adorned with the blue and green of lichen; this one was a raw-looking sienna, almost red-orange against winter's subtleties.

Busy summer feeder —
cowbirds, finches,
nuthatches, cardinals,
and more.

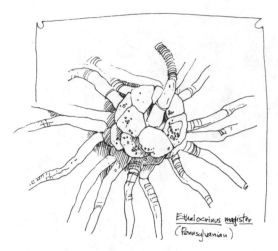

Ethelocrinus magister
(Pennsylvanian)

At the geology museum at the University of Missouri at Kansas City are some of the finest specimens of indigenous fossils in the country. Scientists from all over the world come here to see, among other things, the huge perfect crinoid, or sea-lily head, an *Ethelocrinus magister* nearly five inches across.

Brachiopods and corals and ammonoids; the fossils are impossibly clear, impossibly perfect. When I think of those I find in the limestone rocks in my creek, broken shell-like shapes tightly locked in a matrix of stone with only a corner showing, I am amazed at the perfection of the museum's collection.

It has to do with time. The first geologists to study this area over 100 years ago simply had more of it. They spent hours in the field, and when they found a treasure encased in stone like Excalibur, they didn't wait for the true king to extract it. They patiently went about the process of picking away everything that was not fossil, bit by minuscule bit, with dental picks and styluses. Like a sculptor finding an image locked in the stone, these careful scientists simply spent as long as it took to free the fossil form, chipping away at time with a toothpick.

The birds had done the same with their tiny needle claws, picking away lichen and moss and the slow accretion of dirt embedded in the bark until the clean pith layer shone through. If they had kept it up long enough they'd lay bare the heartwood.

But of course they did not. When I took down the suet block in the spring, the birds abandoned the tree; within three months it weathered as gray as the rest. In the fall the picking and chipping will resume, and the red-brown tree will shine again in a slow semaphore.

There are always things to fix or change or improve; it's the human condition, I suppose. I looked into installing a ceiling fan when an early June heat wave seemed to foretell a miserable summer but I couldn't bear the necessary exposed wiring. With the solid foam insulation sandwiched between ceiling boards and metal roof, there was no way to hide the conduits; we make do with fans on the floor and step gingerly over them until fall. I imagine Orion wheeling above a skylight and wonder how difficult it would be to install. (Not terribly; what's difficult is keeping it clean. The walnut trees drop prodigious amounts of sticky sap, which in turn holds the dust from the road. So far, the necessity for getting onto the roof to clean this inaccessible window has been enough to deter me.)

A more serious change became necessary when the first autumn rolled around. The field mice and raccoons had briefly forgotten the exposed insulation under the cabin after their initial explorations. When the winds chilled and the leaves began to fall, they rediscovered this cozy spot and began to burrow there, gnawing on the floor joists or the plywood underfloor. I could hear the irritating *scritch* of teeth against wood as I worked and again found it necessary to replace wads of pink insulation each day when I walked down the hill.

Greg had taken a permanent job in the city, so I called Charlie, who had worked on our house in town.

"Charlie, help! I'm being invaded. We need to box in the bottom of the cabin or do *something* to keep that insulation in place."

"Had you thought about latticework below the rim joists?" he asked me.

"Yeah, but it won't work. Anything determined enough to chew through my subfloor could tear that stuff up in a minute. I need something up against the floor joists themselves."

"I'll come out and have a look."

A few days later, he was on hands and knees surveying the cabin's underbelly. There was no room to swing a hammer underneath the joists; that's why I wasn't taking this on myself. To put up quarter-inch plywood we'd need a nail gun, something I didn't own. Charlie did.

Having electricity certainly helped. When Greg had tried to use his nail gun at the beginning of this project, it tossed the fasteners at the wood in a disconsolate, bored way as though aiming playing cards at a wastebasket. This time the nails bit crisply into the wood with a satisfying *chunk*!

Charlie had his regular crew with him, two men who didn't know me very well. One thought to frighten me when they squeezed under the cabin to reconnoiter.

"There's a snake skin under there, lady," one of them told me when he crawled back out.

"Oh, great! Would you get it for me when you go back?"

That was not the answer he had expected; I'm not the squeamish type. His eyes widened in surprise and he mumbled something about "just kidding, lady."

While they worked, I decided to take a walk; a look for fossils down the creek sounded much better than listening to them discuss Greg's workmanship and mine. I could hear every word from where I sat at my desk, and I wasn't in the mood to hear "This baby's really out of square." In fact, it is not; there's only a quarter of an inch or so off in one corner of the cabin.

One design flaw could have been easily fixed early on: there's not enough roof overhang at the front of the bay. When I compounded the mistake by putting a bench in front of the window, rain catapulted into the windowsill. Greg had slanted the lower sill somewhat and cut additional slanted stops, but it still needed more drainage. The problem was complicated by the fact that the lacquer wasn't thick enough there; the wood quickly discolored and warped.

I whittled on the warped wood to make the window close again, but the problem remains. Almost any precipitation splashes into that window, even without the bench; the three-inch overhang just doesn't provide sufficient protection. A hard rain, windblown from the east, fills the sill like a bathtub. Another four or five inches of overhang would have solved it, but it's always harder to fix after the fact—harder to know just what to do. We talk about awnings, or a roofline extension, or a cedar gutter, but so far I'm stymied.

A more worrisome problem is the foundation system itself. When we sunk the posts we expected to hit bedrock; the building is only seventy yards from the limestone slickrocks and a hundred feet or so from the rocky creek; how far down could it have been? But we never hit rock. And instead of making concrete pads to support the posts, letting them dry, then proceeding, we simply sunk the things and poured concrete around them. Fine for a fence post, but how long will it hold a cabin?

I didn't think about it at the time. The ground was dry and had been for two years. But when the rains finally came, the soil's water level rose almost to the surface. Would the earth under the cabin turn to porridge? Would the foundation posts mire down in a muddy quicksand, lowering the floor joists onto the dirt? I don't know. Nothing's happened yet. If it starts to sink—and all houses settle somewhat—perhaps I'll make limestone pillars to support it as my ancestors did their log cabins. Like the roof overhang, it would have been better to do it right when we built it.

There was much caulking and sealing to be done to ready the cabin for winter. As autumn came I enjoyed the work: running a transparent caulk along the tops of the outside window and door frames, sealing the siding's knotholes, weather-stripping the windows and around the old door. The final task was to cover all the windows with plastic film; I put it off till cold air whistled through the cracks, but once in place I scarcely noticed it. I felt like a woodchuck, making my cabin home safe from winter's storms.

I am disoriented as often as not when I come into the woods; nothing seems where it should be. The east-west road I left only moments before seems suddenly to shoot off at an acute angle; the sounds of traffic approach at a tangent.

It's an odd thing, this confusion I feel on entering the walnut grove. It's as if the cabin were in another reality, a parallel universe cocked just out of plumb with the everyday world. My pocket compass tells me where north —magnetic north—is located; I sketched its line on the railing of the observation deck to find that the creek, at least, runs a corollary to this mark, pointing northward to the road.

But so, it would seem, does the tiny dirt track, the indelible muddy mark of our passing. We followed the old tractor path to get here, arrowing our way at near right angles away from the road that scribes the northern boundary of our property. To me it seems as if dirt track and creek leave the gravel at roughly the same tangent, both heading south into our land. Both arrive at the mecca of walnut grove and cabin. But between the turning and arrival something clearly goes askew. Here at the entrance to the grove, dirt lane and creek are not parallel at all but convergent. They form a sharp angle to each other—leaving me, as always, perplexed, bemused. Where am I, anyway? And what happens as I sink into this place? I'm out of kilter, turned around, and my directions elude me. Harris feels this disorientation, too. Invariably he calls the back of the cabin the north elevation; it's nearly exactly west.

I thought this dislocation was unique to us—or some strange distortion in the earth's magnetic field that skewed our perceptions—until I read John Jerome's book, *Stone Work,* and was delighted to find someone else as confused as I was. "I keep expecting the points of the compass to fall back into place....with a thunderclap and a great psychic lurch, but it never happens," says Jerome. "Actually, there *is* a small lurch, every time I come driving up the hill. I've become fond of it; it's as if the whole place spins on its tumblers, a combination lock securing the borders against a deluded world that still thinks north is over that way." Me, too.

Perhaps it is magnetic after all; it's a force far more powerful than gravity. My tiny refrigerator magnet overcomes the other force with no difficulty, many times stronger than the pull of the poles. Geology fascinates me again; there is a directional orientation in volcanic magnetite, tiny crystalline needles that point toward the poles as they form in molten lava. Now these miniature magnets tell us of the movement of Earth's tectonic plates. Wrenched from their original configuration, the tiny magnets don't have the same azimuth or bearing as when they hardened into rock. My place may have moved out of alignment with true north, and I feel the pull along the long veins of my arms.

But there was never any question about the cabin's orientation in the walnut grove. Function demanded the big windows across the front face south for solar gain; my sometime profession as an artist necessitated the adjacent wall with my desk and drawing board should have north light and plenty of it.

So much for practicality. The cabin with its bay of antique French windows faces nearly due east. It was the view I craved; form may follow function in the architect's office, but here orientation is determined by sheer beauty. East is the creek, the tiny waterfall, and the huge limestone slump blocks with its mammal den behind it. East is the old tractor road, embroidered with the tracks of deer and coyote. East is the rough stone wall thrown up without plan or skill by some previous owner, a rubbly palisade that catches the dying rays of the winter sun; in summer it is invisible behind a curtain of trees. East is sunrise, reaching insistent light fingers across the cabin to snatch sleep from our eyes, catching us at our morning coffee, making us feel yeasty and warm like bread rising in the oven. The studio window faces south southwest, and in the afternoons the sun casts a blinding light on my watercolor paper; practicality be damned, I face the spot where we first saw the deer.

I like the cabin's position in the larger scheme of things, as well: hidden in a little valley, tucked against the flank of the west hill as though for protection. This scheme, at least, works well—we hear the wind rattle the tops of the trees, watch them wave and bend, but the cause of this particular effect reaches us only rarely. We are at the bottom of the well of trees, and the winds that touch us here have been gentled to breezes. The hills by the road and the pond show on my topographical map at 950 feet above sea level; the cabin is some 60 to 70 feet lower.

The day departs slowly in the hollow, its light extinguished so gradually that I have time to get used to its leaving. By four-thirty on a winter day the cabin itself has slid into shadow, as have the lower two-thirds of the slender walnut trees beyond the French windows; the tops of the trees are still gilded with sunset.

Violet shadows crawl up the eastern hill beyond the cabin slowly as the hours pass; only the crest of the hill and the trees that surmount it remain washed in butterscotch light. The darkened walnuts in the grove are etched against this bright glow in angular, rhythmic strokes, spelling out the distance between the two hills.

If we had built in Rachel's Meadow high on the east hill instead, the days would be longer. But when they were gone, they'd be done, finished. There'd be no time to adjust to their going. It's better this way; I need time to come to terms with the fact that it's time to leave, time to reenter life outside the grove, the life of town and noise and interruption. Dr. Eugenie Clark wrote of "the rapture of the deep," nitrogen narcosis, a condition affecting deep-sea divers that tempts them to stay below until oxygen runs out; once that happens, they're finished. Like an emerging diver, I leave the valley slowly—when finally I can tear myself away—to avoid getting the bends as I reenter real life. As I walk up the hill to my car, I pass outcroppings of limestone and shale that mark recurring encroachments of the prehistoric inland sea. I surface with a shock.

Weathering in.

11. Weathering In

The cabin began the weathering process the day it was raised. The warm sienna glow of new cedar silvered in the sun and the rain. The deck, at first so stridently yellow-green, the colors of pine and preservatives, became a subtle gray within the first few months. The days shortened and cooled and the snow began to fall, accelerating the transformation as the cabin mellowed and seasoned.

The piles of construction debris and the cache of wood scraps beneath the deck were gone at last. When it became obvious that the wood stove would not go in — not this first year, anyway — the stack of moldy kindling looked more like litter. Charlie hauled it away when he sealed the underside of the floor. I had spent the last few months removing all the other signs of building — the nails and errant scraps, the cigarette butts and pop can pulls — I wanted nothing to remind me that this was new and unfamiliar.

The birds and animals considered the cabin as much theirs as ours. At first they appeared to resent it when we arrived and scolded irritably. As autumn passed into winter and we began to stock the feeders in earnest, we became more acceptable. The platform feeder was a popular place, busy from dawn until nightfall — and beyond, when the raccoons were about.

The strange winter storm began with two days of freezing rain that coated everything with ice. Trees, weeds, grass — everything was dressed in a quarter of an inch of the frozen stuff, causing small branches to bow double under its weight and weakened ones to come crashing to earth. The roadway was littered with dead limbs, the coating of ice broken away in glittering shards as though someone had thrown crystal glasses into the hearth in celebration.

I hadn't been able to get to the cabin for two days. When the storm began I drove out through the rain and ice to fill the seed feeders and check the suet holders; with the birds' main diet of weed seeds locked in ice, I

145

knew they would be hungry. My offerings are meant only as a supplement, never as the sole source of nutrition of my guests—for that I leave the meadows unmowed and the walnut grove waist high in weeds. These mixed sunflower family members and thistle seeds meet the birds' nutritional requirements, 100 percent of minimum daily requirements without my treats—except when ice covers every seed head and branch.

The promised four to six inches of additional snow had barely begun to accumulate when I decided I needed the cabin as much as the birds needed me. I drove out on only slightly slippery roads and walked in over the rapidly accumulating layer of ice and snow, each step as audible on grass as on gravel.

The birds were waiting as though they expected my arrival. The platform feeder had seed still on it, but like everything else, it was impounded in ice. All the other feeders were empty. Two long tubes of black sunflower seeds had disappeared into tiny gizzards. Suet feeders waved in the wind, innocent of a shred of food. Even the frugal peanut feeder was empty—not only empty but knocked to the ground and bent crazily out of shape. Something had been aggressively foraging, as though desperate.

It didn't take the birds long to come flocking back as I refilled each feeder. Now as I stood inspecting the creek eighty yards away, I could see them shoving and bickering with not a shred of manners among them. There was a gaggle of chickadees and nuthatches already on the platform feeder. A hairy woodpecker, dapper in a black-and-white tweed, hurried to inspect the suet. A male ladderback woodpecker moved in on the hairy, and there was a brief disagreement as to ownership of these fresh provisions.

This ice storm was irresistible; its crystalline shapes flashed prisms like signal lights. The grass crunched underfoot like popcorn; it was surprisingly easy to walk on. The morning's paper had shown a policeman crawling back uphill from an automobile accident, unable to keep his footing. I had imagined the same here north of the river and would have crawled all the way to the cabin, if necessary, to get here.

The ice told all the secrets, holding nothing back. I could hear each least breath of wind in a chorus of soft crackles and a bird's featherweight as it landed on a limb; the nearly inaudible whisper of fracturing ice gave it away.

Just the right combination of temperature and precipitation must occur to breed an ice storm. Rain falling through warmer air temperatures strikes the colder earth and hardens on everything it touches like a coat of enamel. A few degrees warmer and the rain wouldn't freeze; a few degrees colder and it would fall as sleet or snow. This day, it appeared the ground was still too warm to hold the ice; even the big limestone slickrock by the creek crossing was merely wet, not icy. With this new slow-falling snow on top of the ice, the world looked odd; the fat, ice-lacquered grass blades thickened further with whiteness.

Overnight the temperature nose-dived, huddling in the bottom of my thermometer as though for warmth. The weather system had immobilized much of the country's midsection, an immense, unseen, and implacable glacier of air. A front like this brings home our utter helplessness in the face of nature. We can't even fully measure its width and depth and degree; when I arrived at the cabin, puffing and blowing inside my layers of clothing, I went first to my amateur weather station.

The temperature for this twenty-second day of December was minus fifteen at two o'clock in the afternoon, legacy of a glacial front that dipped all the way to Texas on the maps. The weatherman said it was the strongest high pressure front ever recorded here; I believed it. My barometer was unequal to the task. The arrow pointed a quarter of an inch past the last measurement of which it is capable. It would have said almost 1,060 millibars—if it hadn't given it up at 1,050.

When I am too long out in cold this extreme—even wrapped in so many layers that I feel immobile—my eyes water and my nose sets up an immediate running. A headache lobotomizes the frozen place between my brows; I suspect my brain cells of freezing one by one until my gray matter is the consistency of a banana daiquiri.

I can hear the bones in my face creak against one another in the cold. The large plates of my skull are knit together with tiny interlocking fingers of bone; under normal conditions these are as brittle as my frozen eyelashes and contracted in the cold. With each step there is a faint crackle coming from the neighborhood of my forehead as though the bones had pulled just slightly apart and grated, one against the other. No wonder I get a headache.

Flesh can freeze in minutes at these temperatures; the wind chill drove the apparent temperature to a howling fifty below zero. To go out without a hat is insanity—this thin, greedy chill can suck 80 percent of your body heat out through your uncovered head. Strange white extremities—a frost-colored nose or stiff, pale fingers—are alarm signals; the blood has been driven from the cells and replaced with freezing water.

It takes the cabin well over an hour to attain a degree of comfort, with both heaters blasting away at nearly full throttle, a degree that still requires my coat and hat and afghans across my lap. I can't write or draw until my fingers become supple, but no matter. The enforced wait allows the luxury of a cup or two of hot tea and time with a good book. I enjoy the rigors of winter.

The tiny downy woodpecker just beyond the deck clung to the dead branch like a shelf fungus, its claws dug in, stiff tail feathers braced to make a tripod. It was asleep—or dead—eyes closed, motionless. It was a male; its patch of scarlet shone like a spot of blood on the back of its skull.

Woodpeckers are finely designed to their task, their heavy skulls

tiny downy woodpecker (*Picoides pubescens*) —

this one is a male, with a red spot on the back of his neck

equipped with shock absorbers to keep them from banging their miniature brains out. Now this one was still, his long tongue wound back into its cavity like fishing line in a reel: it seemed so odd to see a bird in stasis, and only a few feet from me, that I was bemused as well. I couldn't stop looking at it, waiting for it to move, change position, cock an eye, drop a white wad of excrement — anything but that strange stillness. I couldn't move until the bird did — but at last the tiny creature opened an eye, cocked its head at me, and shifted position as though to get more comfortable.

I had never lived close enough to wildness to catch a bird catnapping; now the birds and I nap together in this wooded solitude. Downies, hairies, red-bellied woodpeckers — all prop themselves for sleep in the same way — and today a tiny chickadee rested its tail against my window screen, propping itself up on the frame.

In winter, when I carry my drinking water in gallon glass jugs down that long, snowy drive or through the woods, I pack my dirty dishes *out* as well. There is no chance of carrying enough of these heavy jugs over uncertain footing to maintain a semblance of civilization. I rough it. I could melt enough snow for the amenities — washing, dishes — but the load seems lighter this way. As yet I haven't resorted to the questionable convenience of paper plates and cups, but if I did, those too must be packed out; I don't burn my trash here but carry it home to add to the mess at the local landfill.

There's an obscure ethic at work here, a desire to leave as little mark as possible — never mind the cabin. A burning trash heap would mean I owned this land and could do with it as I would. Once-a-month check writing notwithstanding, ownership still eludes me. It's a state of mind, and I remain convinced I'm here on borrowed time. Not that I think someone will come and evict me from my cabin, interrupt my work, and unplug my computer, not unless I stop writing those checks. It's just too good to believe. Sometimes when I awaken here I don't know where I am — it's taking time to sink into my unconscious.

Winter passes slowly. A deep quiet descends, unbroken by visitors' voices or the sound of cars. No one arrives unexpectedly; no one interrupts my work. Even Harris prefers the even, constant warmth of home for the most part, and I am alone here.

Alone, but never lonely. There is too much to see and feel and explore, too much to absorb. In summer there is a whirl of activity — human and otherwise. Nature spins by before my eyes and I feel as though I am watching a merry-go-round, trying to hold just one child in focus and failing as that child is snatched away and replaced by another and another. Changes come too fast to track. Too many flowers bloom in the meadow, too many birds pass through the treetops, too many butterflies tumble with apparent aimlessness among the weeds. It is — as they used to say — an embarrassment of riches, and I can't keep it all in my mind. What begins in order ends up in disarray. It's a lovely embarrassment, if a confusing one.

But in winter things slow down. There is time to see and time to absorb the truth of what it is I see. One day is, if not just like another, at least similar enough to allow a fine, bone-deep absorption. Ice has frozen time as well as water, and the hours move as deliberately as sand in a fine-throated hourglass.

There are those who say that winter is colorless, a black-and-white photo negative that damps the soul with monotonous sameness. They're wrong. Rough-leaf dogwood is a pickup-sticks game of fine red lines against the cold blue shadows; the color reflects back into the snow and warms it with a blush. Lion-colored broom sedge bristles through the snow, and in the meadow the mixed grasses are pale and golden as pulled taffy. When the

Male
Cardinal—
Cardinalis
cardinalis

snow stands deep against the limestone rocks and on the banks of Shack Creek, the mosses and lichen soak it up greedily, thirsty after the long drought; they are moist and richly hued. There is no green like the acid green of moss; the pervasive winter damp keeps it at its most vivid.

Two red cardinals and their mates appeared at the edge of the clearing, "chipping" loudly. Each time the cardinals came, scarlet grace notes penned on the chill calligraphy of winter, I stopped, transfixed, trying to read their meaning in the trees. There were so many—I hadn't known they formed feeding flocks; in town a gathering of two or three would be a crowd.

The two males posturing at the sunflower seeds were only the advance guard. As I waited inside the big French windows, more came to join them, alerted by their arrival at the platform feeder. The gaudy males that waited their turn in the trees stood out against the blue-shadowed hill; their more modest mates and young were harder to see. I strained to number them each time I saw this winter flock: "two, four, five, God! No, there's another at the feeder, and a female in the tree, and *whoops,* a whole bunch of them feeding out of sight by the deck. There are six more down by the creek; no, eight…."

Birds stand out against the more subdued palette of winter as though painted on a rice-paper scroll by an Oriental master. Blue jays streak through the woods, loud as ever; with the cardinals and woodpeckers they splash color everywhere. Purple finches the color of raspberry jam visit my feeder, vying for space with pine siskins and winter-subtle goldfinches. Even the faint blush of color beneath a chickadee's wing seems rare as rubies—but it's a Croesus's treasure of color. There are dozens of these cheeky little birds in the winter woods; they've abandoned their territorial concerns to band together with tufted titmice, nuthatches, and brown creepers.

A small movement outside the window caught my eye as I sat at my desk to work. A bee had found its way into the long, tubular bird feeder and flew up and down as though confused. I stepped outside to rescue it and found that the unseasonably warm weather of a January thaw had roused a number of these hungry insects.

The bee was not trapped, after all. It flew in and out of the feeder ports at will (once it rediscovered them), bumbling over the sunflower seeds at each opening in search of—something. Others were on the deck beneath the feeder, where birds had tossed the pale golden seeds that somehow failed to pass inspection and the discarded, woody hulls of sunflower.

Bemused, I knelt for a better look. Three honeybees sorted through the debris, feeling their way among the hulls and seeds; what could they want here? Now and then one rose and hovered, then returned immediately to the task.

The summery sound of their buzzing was all around; now there were six or seven going through this same sorting business on the platform feeder beyond the deck. There were more on the ground below, taking inventory among the seeds. The fifty-five-degree weather mimicked spring, but there was no pollen or nectar to be had. Not even the silver maples had opened russet-colored flowers, no harbinger of spring bloomed in the woods. It was the seeds themselves these bees were after—but why? Perhaps there were remnants of pollen on these dusty seeds—or maybe the seed dust itself was manna.

My pocket microscope revealed nothing, though I was on hands and knees, focusing on seeds and hulls and chips of corn on the sunny deck. A bee landed beside me and grabbed a seed, gave it a quick once-over, and moved on to the next, working its way down the seed-filled crack between the boards of my deck. The microscope is only 30X power—too weak, I suppose, to discern pollen grains among the dust.

I drove the feeder birds to distraction, crawling around under their food source; I heard the startled whir of wings above my head and their disgruntled chirps. I must have made quite a sight, backside in the air, nose to my microscope, up to my elbows in bird droppings and seeds; fortunately there was no one to amuse but the birds—and as Queen Victoria said, "We are *not* amused." They were annoyed, instead.

Eventually, so were the hungry bees.

There were maybe thirty of them at the platform now (it's hard to count busily feeding bees). Like earthquake volunteers burrowing through rubble to rescue survivors, each bee dug a miniature hole in the seed pile. But each moved only three or four grains before moving a few inches and beginning over again, frantically picking up a seed and passing it down those three rows of legs before kicking it away with hairy hind feet. One even tried the drill down the regular rows of kernels still left on an ear of corn, with no more visible results than the seed sorters. Or rather, the only results were the ones they were probably after. Those hairy legs were covered with a yellow-gray powder—but pollen or seed dust, I couldn't tell.

I wouldn't have been surprised to see them make for the suet block I had put up this morning. It was a new kind, raisin flavored; the ingredients listed both these sweet little fruits and sugar, as well as peanut butter. I sniffed it as I stuffed it into the feeder and was tempted to take a bite myself —it smelled that good. The only thing that stopped me was the binder that held it all together: beef suet. And thinking back on my English grandmother's rich Christmas treat of steamed suet pudding that we all fought over, the cholesterol-laden fat of the suet was not much of a deterrent. The bees, however, had no such family tradition. They ignored the raisin-rich block for their endless seed sorting.

A female red-bellied woodpecker landed on the platform among the foraging bees; knowing her fondness for insects, I watched to see if she'd make a bee run. But no; she simply sat beside the feeding bees as if at a smorgasbord, each species choosing a favorite tidbit from my offerings.

This was odd enough in itself, I suppose. I've been told woodpeckers don't frequent feeders, but no one told the birds. Latest advice has it that they will visit suet feeders, or maybe a hanging peanut feeder, but certainly not a low-class mixed bag of seeds and corn chop on a platform. The woodpeckers here don't care. If they're hungry they'll eat whatever I offer, side by side with chickadees, titmice, goldfinches—and bees.

Most of the usual crew of birds avoided the feeder, put off by the heavy traffic and the continuous buzzing. But the female red-bellied woodpecker was replaced by the more aggressive male, who seemed very much aware of all this free protein. At first I thought he was simply unnerved by all this buzzing and flitting, looking this way and that as the bees flew too close for comfort. That was not the case, or so it seemed. Instead, he stabbed at the air with that sharp bill, trying to catch a meal on the wing. The landing platform cleared of feeding insects while the woodpecker was present.

A quick call to a beekeeper that evening confirmed my hypothesis; it was the remnant pollen that clings to the seeds these bees were after; close inspection revealed that pollen baskets on the hind legs bore parsimonious loads of grayish dust instead of the fat golden baggage I was looking for.

The beekeeper thanked me for my call; I had alerted her to the activity in the hives, and she would put out soybean flour for the hungry insects. "They love that stuff. It's the pollen in the flour." But by the time I remembered a promised bucket of soybean flour for these bees, they had found a richer source of nutrients and ignored my feeder as they had since late January.

Empirical evidence is great stuff. It applies to a lot beyond the art of carpentry—and woodpeckers. It's said that gray and fox squirrels don't share territory, that the more aggressive fox squirrels displace the smaller grays, and it had seemed to be true. In the city we had gray squirrels; in the country, the larger, red-brown foxes were much in evidence. Our local animal rehabilitation center says you should never release grays into fox-squirrel territory and vice versa.

At the cabin the squirrels refuse to follow the rules; both kinds visit the feeders, though not together—not amicably, at any rate. There seemed at first to be a rudimentary schedule; fox squirrels early and late, grays in the afternoon, though feeding time nearly overlapped. Both obviously live near-

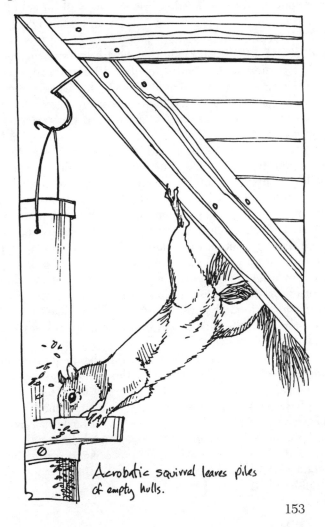

Acrobatic squirrel leaves piles of empty hulls.

153

by; I could see their lounging platforms in the walnut trees and watch them crawl out of their den holes in the dead snags each morning. The grays and foxes follow parallel tracks through the trees—parallel but not convergent.

One hapless gray was hungry at just the wrong time and showed up early for brunch. He scrabbled among the seeds that had fallen to the deck beneath the hanging feeder, and now he seemed to notice where all this raining manna came from. He looked up to discover the source, and I swear I saw the light dawn in his dark shiny eyes. He quickly shinned up the corner of the cabin as though it were tree bark and tried to reach the feeder. It was just that much too far; he looked like one of the Flying Wallendas in training, trying to get the hang of letting go of the trapeze. Stretched to his full length, impossibly cantilevered across the air, still he couldn't quite reach the feeder; his tiny paws reached out like hands, shaking with frustration. "I can *do* it," he seemed to be saying. "I *know* I can."

And he did. Finally he made the short leap from the secure footing of the cabin's corner to the feeder itself and hung there, upside down and swinging. He wasted not a moment. Gaining his balance, he climbed down the length of the tube, his back feet stuck in the upper holes for purchase and his sharp little teeth making short work of sunflower seed hulls at the bottom porthole.

After a bit of this, he tired of his upside-down position and wrapped himself around the feeder like a furry snake, moving up and down the tube and feeding at first one hole, then another. I was amazed at his dexterity; I could have watched him for hours. The birds, on the other hand, were irritated beyond measure. They owned that feeder and they wanted the squirrel to know it. They dive-bombed the oblivious animal, trying to dislodge him from their territory, but he was adamant; he wasn't going anywhere.

Then the fox squirrel came on the scene. This larger squirrel dined, oblivious for a few minutes at the far end of the deck, then noticed the source of the birds' agitation: his arch rival. Quicker than I could follow he leaped off the feeder and across the deck, bristling like a chow dog. The gray saw him—or heard the ruckus—at the same time and was gone in less time than it takes to tell.

But a month or two later, the gray had had enough. He came first to visit the hanging feeder; I had moved it so the bottom was within range of the tiniest squirrel as it hung only inches from the rail. The little gray lay on his stomach, leisurely as a kid watching television, and dined on the fallen seeds within easy reach. Then, he pulled himself a bit farther along with his elbows and ate some more. If he ran out of spilled seeds he simply reached up with one paw and pulled more out of the cookie jar to scatter on the railing. It was a comical sight. And soon there was a mound of empty hulls fully three inches tall beside the little squirrel.

I made him nervous; shortly he bounded away up the path toward the latrine, disgruntled. I promptly forgot my visitor as I returned to my work, but moments later the squirrel sounds resumed. This time it was the fox squirrel, fat as a puffball on my offerings. And apparently the little gray heard him too and returned to protect his diminishing hoard. A quick blur, a scrabble of tiny claws, and the gray jumped the larger fox squirrel, like Sugar Ray Leonard on Mike Tyson.

It was all show. The skirmish was over in a heartbeat, and they both disappeared into the weeds. The feeder was momentarily deserted except for the titmice and chickadees and sun-colored goldfinch.

This rivalry continued with a kind of uneasy truce as the squirrels returned to eat. One made use of the hanging feeder, one the platform; then with a quick pas de deux and a skirmish, they would trade places—until I stepped outside. The fox squirrel hightailed it up the tree nearest the deck and the gray took off in the other direction up a towering walnut, skittering to the top of a skinny limb and dancing out over thin air. It landed with an impossibly loud *whump* and hit the ground running; I can't imagine how. It must have fallen thirty feet. Perhaps squirrels are like cats, equipped with an internal gyroscope that enables them to right themselves in midair—given enough time; cats that fall short distances may be badly hurt, while those that plummet eight stories or more may land on their feet with little more than a broken claw or two, if they're lucky. At any rate, it was all over in an eye blink, and the little gray disappeared into the trees beyond the creek; I wouldn't feel right until I saw it eating from my feeder again.

I tempt the squirrels to the platform with big ears of golden field corn, which they devour on the spot or string halfway across the walnut grove to their chosen tree. These directional arrows are much more effective than Hansel's bread crumbs; the big red cobs lead straight from the feeder to the

wet squirrel
on the deck

shagbark hickory. The trail has lasted for months, unaffected by snows or rain; we pick up the bare, red cobs to start the fire in our outdoor fireplace.

Even the dry corncobs must be of some interest to these cheeky rodents; the one I picked up under the shagbark hickory this morning had a hole gnawed halfway through it. Perhaps if the squirrels were hungry *enough*, this trail, too, would eventually be eaten. It wouldn't surprise me; I remember the delicate taste of the pithy center of an ear of sweet corn in high summer. How different can this be?

Whatever the truth of squirrel territoriality, the walnut grove is definitely squirrel country. Even on rainy days they leave the shelter of their den holes to visit my deck. Protected by the small overhang by the winter feeder, I found a small gray squirrel carrying its own umbrella, a wet tail arched up over its back as protection from the cold, relentless rain. It seemed to work just fine, even if the fur was so wet it parted neatly along the surprisingly scrawny, bony tail; the rest of the animal looked perfectly comfortable as it picked up the dropped sunflower seeds and cracked them, one by one, to get at the rich, oily nut meat. The larger red fox squirrel must have been bivouacked in its hole in the black locust tree; there was no sign of the animal all the long, rainy afternoon.

A flicker set up a loud, mechanical whirring, like a small engine trying to start. I was pleased, at last, to see these big birds in the grove, wings shafting sunlight as their powerful, looping flight carried them from tree to tree.

I didn't know what I was getting into. This innocent exchange marked the opening guns of a short, mean firefight. The flicker was not content with the standing dead trees and limbs on my place; it had designs on my brand-new, bugless cabin. I found the first evidence—a big hole in the cabin's south side—and remembered that my friend Patti had warned me about woodpecker damage. At their place in the Ozarks, they'd tried almost everything to discourage the birds: rubber snakes, fake owls, noisemakers, wind socks to wave in the breeze with the brisk whisper of ripstop nylon.

"You'll be sorry," she told me when I described our red cedar plans. "They'll eat your cabin down to a pile of sawdust. We've got woodpeckers big as chickens at our place."

I scoffed and said I was sure I could handle it.

And now I stood surveying the damage—the first attack took out a three-inch hole in my cabin wall. Picking up the pink fluffs of hard-won insulation where it had blown like dandelion seed across the grove, I began to get the picture. It was war. It was a territorial dispute, and this—staked out and built upon, bearing the marks of my own blood, carrying its weight of dreams—was my territory.

I heard the relentless drumming as I worked and sneaked silently out to the deck railing, leaning far out beyond the edge of the cabin to see the shameless culprit hard at work—nest building in the wall of *my* nest.

"Hey! Get the hell *outta* here!"

The bird flew off, wings whirring, and I congratulated myself on vanquishing it. But moments later we repeated the scenario.

"*Hey!*" The whir of noisy wings as the rascal escaped to the woods, faking panic.

I nailed a metal plate over the hole, an old advertising sign shaped like a duck—perhaps this would discourage the big flicker. And it did. It abandoned this hole and started another, to the left and just under the eaves. (Patti laughed and said it was because woodpeckers aren't spooked by ducks —I needed owl-shaped plates instead.)

But I had two plates, and before the flicker could gain entry to my fiberglass insulation, I aborted this hole at conception. Now what? A metal-sided cabin?

A friend told me about the virtues of tree tanglefoot; just spread it on a board and nail it beneath the hole—the flicker will hate the feel on its toes and disappear to more hospitable climes. But before it was necessary to get out the big ladder to reach the hole—typically, nearly twelve feet above the ground—the damage stopped. I didn't see the flicker again—until I walked through the woods in search of early mushrooms. There was a pile of gold and black feathers near the barred owl's tree, and I took a guilty satisfaction in the sight.

A week later, there was evidence of a new hole, but I covered it with a metal tobacco can lid and hoped for the best—and perhaps that's what happened. Another pile of flicker feathers near the owl's tree seemed to indicate that this night hunter had developed a taste for these largest of local woodpeckers.

Patti said more power to the epicurean owl. Once the big woodpeckers at her cabin made entry, the squirrels and bats were quick to co-opt the condo. She had a zoo in residence; that's a bit too much togetherness with wildlife for me.

Spring came one day as though someone had thrown a switch. There were signs and ciphers, to be sure: advance notice. Scouts reconnoitered the territory, like the big flickers looking for a good neighborhood to nest in. Crocuses were up at home, grasslike, deceptively tender; a few small, wild flocks of optimistic geese plied the rough, gray skies in February. I should have taken the hint.

But today, March 3, spring arrived independent of the calendar — announced, loud and clear, by the silver herald voices of spring peepers. I had work to do; my desk was piled with it, and I knew I should head straight for the cabin—but I couldn't. Those silvery voices were magnetic, drawing me closer. I wanted to find their source and crossed the dam to the weedy meadow beyond.

New heralds added their voices to the tiny amphibians' loud huzzah; as I topped the hill I heard the geese, high and exultant, and stood at attention until they were gone. This was one of the largest flocks yet, snows and blues and Canadas all booked for passage together.

I was well past my usual direct path to the cabin; the woods beyond called nearly as loud as the peepers in my neighbor's little slough just beyond the fence. The barrier of wild blackberries that might normally discourage such irresponsible behavior, snagging my jeans, holding me back—pointing me toward the more accessible path—was powerless as smoke. My clothes were old and far past the time when it mattered if they showed another rip; before long they bristled like a blowfish, studded with dry, dead thorns.

I accepted the impersonal invitation of the peepers; it seemed early, much too early for this much activity, but a sable-dark mourning cloak butterfly didn't think so. It made its erratic way between the trees as though through the bars of a cage: a jailbreak from winter. I would have followed, but a tiny splash of bright red caught my eye. A black-spotted beetle, huge as ladybugs go, emerged from hibernation literally at my feet. Even the insects were delighted with the weather.

In the shed, a white-footed mouse had taken up residence in a soft white nest fashioned from the remains of a roll of paper towels. She was as startled as I; she skittered out between the slats in the back of the rustic cabinet and up the wall as though it were flat-out level.

It was ridiculous. You just don't see that much wildlife, all in a single walk from road to cabin. It was as if the cinematographer had edited tape to follow a set script: "Let's have as much action as possible, okay? Never mind what's likely, just keep it moving."

But a day or two later the scenario was confirmed; mating and homemaking were definitely on the agenda. The white-footed mouse was much put out by my intrusion; she didn't trust me to leave her family be and moved her nest—lock, stock, and shredded paper—from the little cabinet to a spot I could not find. There was nothing left but the empty cardboard roll and a few discarded hulls of sunflower seeds.

Sex is in the air in spring, a single theme that plays itself out wherever you look. The chickadees had lost interest in hanging out in loose feeding flocks and paired off to chase wildly through the brush. The downy woodpeckers that once noticed one another only when they were feeder competition now zipped through the treetops in tight aerial formation.

The peepers, of course, had nothing on their minuscule minds but mating. That's all they talked about, up there in the slough. The best singer mates most often, and we had a whole chorus of tiny Pavarottis vying for the attention of the choosy females that riveted their attention to a single instinctual drive.

And now a pair of bluebirds looped and sailed through the walnut grove, half singing, half chattering to one another. I was transfixed by the blue of their wings, as achingly pure as a note of music; I had called them sky-colored, and they are—but a much more intense hue, as if the color had been concentrated, distilled—an eighty-proof blue that takes my breath away like good Scotch whisky.

12. *The Other Side of the Hourglass*

Bobwhites called softly into the evening, turning down the covers of night. When I walked up to the pond to watch the fireflies reflected times two in the water, I put up a covey that had bedded down, roseate fashion, like the petals of a flower—all facing away from the center. They took off as they roosted, in all directions, as though a bomb had detonated in their midst, startling me almost as though one had. It had taken me a while to recognize their call; these seemed to have forgotten the full repertoire: "bob-*white*?" and asked only the last, over and over. "White...white...white?" As soon as they exploded underfoot, I remembered what it was I had been hearing.

Donny had told me we had a covey on our place; his dogs had mapped its whereabouts. My neighbor trains springer spaniels for hunting. He allows them to run free for a while when he gets home from work, and they head first for our place. The elegant red-and-white animals wear bells on their collars so he can track them audibly as they hustle through the weeds, jingling like the Budweiser Clydesdales.

One night when Harris and I drove up the tractor path to the road, a young female bobwhite crossed the dirt road alone, stopped beside the road, and watched us pass as though polite. I stared into that black onyx eye for fully a minute before the bird bobbed its head twice and dashed off into the weeds. A few weeks later this same bird or another just like her led her tiny progeny across the road, and I slowed down to let them pass. The chicks were fully fledged, running in a wavering conga line after their mother until I drove up level with them. Then tiny wings lifted off and they all sailed into the brush, purposeful but not panicked.

Fireflies seem to come first to the pond and its meadow. Long before the first phosphorescent bug pierced the darkness of the cabin's immediate environs, these intermittent stars lit the air just above the pond and reflected there in quick, green flashes. When they finally appeared in the grove—a different family of fireflies, perhaps—the effect was magic. We lay in bed at night and watched them shine their tiny lamps in our windows, creeping up and down the screens as though looking for something besides one another.

You don't realize, in town, how much candlepower these little bugs put out. There is too much competition from streetlights and town glare and the windows of our houses. But on a summer night the cabin is lit by the cool phosphorescence as fairy flashes reflect off our pale walls, are caught, and magnified in the gloss of the ceiling's lacquer. I could almost hear Titania laugh just outside, knowing the radiance kept us awake in a way that car lights never could.

Luna Moth
found near the
creek.

And like Titania herself, a luna moth hangs by my cabin's lighted window on summer nights, long "tails" slightly turned, graceful as pale green scarves. The caterpillar of *Actias luna* pupates in a thin, silken cocoon; I found one wearing natural camouflage and incorporating a leaf, nearly invisible among the other leaves on the ground. We are fortunate here in Missouri; this huge moth—perhaps four inches across—is common in our deciduous woods. According to my Audubon field guide, they are now considered an endangered species, victims of pollutants and pesticides. Near my cabin they fall victim only to the flying squirrels and little brown bats, which consider them a delicacy; I see them far more often than any of the other Saturniidae, the giant silkworm moths.

In winter the intimate stars feel close enough to touch. They tangle in the bare branches of the trees and hang there like ornaments. Unlike the cold, remote stars of a summer's night, these invite me to sweep an arm overhead to pull them down to me.

The yellow-crowned night heron of the darkened pond is built like the picture in your mind when you hear the word "heron"—at least when he extends his neck. When it is retracted, it doesn't fold back on the shoulders like the larger great blue heron's but disappears into the plumage (or perhaps into skin as loose as a cat's), giving the appearance of a much shorter-necked bird. I watched as the heron slowly stalked its prey, tilting its head as though listening. It gave nothing away, made no indication that it had zeroed in on anything in particular. It was a surprise when suddenly its neck telescoped to capture its prey; the fish apparently believed it was a safe distance from the hunter as it swam within range. It was not.

The silver of the small fish flashed once, then twice; then it disappeared down the heron's gullet without a trace.

We are used to the sounds of raccoons rattling up against the quiet of the night; we leave them our dinner scraps against all our better judgment, just for the guilty intimacy. It's just as well we only eat here once or twice a week—we contribute to their delinquency and create a sometime dependence; it's bad enough they raid the bird feeder each night.

For the most part our relationship is benign. I watch them; they watch me. If I must go outside in the small hours on being awakened by their rowdyism, they run up the nearest tree as though pursued by demons and hang there twenty feet above my head, eyes shining green in my flashlight's beam. The mother raccoon brings her young; I swear she practices their training runs on us, knowing we are harmless to her kits. One night our deck was the site of a gathering, with coons of various sizes bobbing and craning to see everything there was to see like first-graders at the dinosaur exhibit. There must have been seven of the little bandits out there, as curious about me as I was about them—as long as I knew my place. It was fine when I stayed

163

inside the big bay windows to watch; I was allowed to pull my chair up close or to kneel right by the screen to peer out at raccoon's eye level—the youngsters practically touched noses with me. I could even turn on the deck light for a better look. Once I ventured outside, they were gone. The female must have had a silent signal for her young—I didn't hear so much as a squeak, but the little ones got the picture immediately. They tore out, diving under the deck or making for the nearby creek, their fat little bodies careening through the weeds.

We *expect* relationship. We've read about Rascal, the endearing raccoon that lived with humans; we've grown up on nature films. We are touched by wildness; we want to touch wildness in return, whether a raccoon baby or a young squirrel or a red-gold deer.

I haven't escaped the expectation. Last summer when it was necessary to care for a young caged raccoon before setting it free in Wendy's woods, I was delighted with the opportunity to watch and sketch and take my photos. The little animal was adorable; the sweet chirring sounds it made as though trying to communicate with me had their own poignancy—the kit had imprinted on humans, and I wondered if it would be able to survive in the wild.

I was afraid to open the cage to replenish its water for fear it would escape prematurely here so close to the traffic of town, so I handed it an ice cube; this was perfect. The little coon reached through the bars of the cage to grasp the melting ice and licked it like ice cream. We spent a large part of the day together; I sat nearby and watched it nap the daylight hours away. And when it was time to take the youngster out to the woods and set it free, I missed it acutely after only a day's acquaintance.

It's the inevitable legacy of my youth, tomboy child of a hunter and fisherman who occasionally brought home a young wild animal that had been abandoned or its mother killed—the latter scenario far more likely, since wild young are seldom really left to their own devices; the mother is almost always nearby, trying not to draw attention to her babies. We raised crows and squirrels and owls in the days before such things required federal and state permits, and I still miss the easy innocence of relationship. It's just as well; we possessed neither the scientific knowledge nor the feral common sense to do the job right. Our wild charges had a just slightly better chance of surviving our ministrations than they did alone—and motherless—in the woods.

Tonight the moon was full. It sketched black shadows on the floor of the grove, a tangled macramé of lines and shapes moving in the winter wind. I was awakened by a familiar sound; I'm a light sleeper, and the instant the raccoon's feet touched the step leading to the deck I was aware of it. It shambled along, inspecting our barbecue grill, feeling its way along the old trunk that holds the charcoal and the birdseed, trying the hasp. The big coon tightroped across the deck railing toward the turn that would take him to the front of the cabin, where his massive form was as visible in the moonlight as though it were full day.

He climbed the window frame hand over hand as though it were a tree trunk and pulled himself, upside down, along the upper edge. I imagined a rock climber's chalk bag hanging at his waist to keep his handlike paws from becoming sweaty—but there was little enough chance of that. It was well below freezing. The raccoon's breath was visible in the cold, coming in frosty gusts. The big animal hung on with those nearly prehensile back feet and swung out to grab at the bottom of the feeder, missed, and tried again. This time he was successful and pulled it to him impatiently. He hung there, upside down, gulping greedily. The feeder's ports are metal; it's a wonder his tongue didn't stick there as mine once did as I concentrated too hard on installing a television antenna one frigid January day—a ridiculous position to find oneself in. But the animal seemed to have gauged the situation well; he wasn't deterred for an instant.

The show was too good to interrupt; we gave the coon a 5.9 and left him to his dinner. We watched, laughing, until at last he tired of being our entertainment—or perhaps he, too, was concentrating on his task until our gales of laughter became impossible to ignore. At any rate, suddenly he let go of the feeder, rappeled down the window, and waddled off into the woods without finishing his repast.

The thought of damage didn't occur to us until morning. When the sun rose weakly, pushing its way through the heavy frost, we could see that the coon's weight had ripped the screen wire, leaving an eighteen-inch gash that widened with each subsequent raid. The windowsill filled up with discarded sunflower seed shells as the birds perched there to eat; the squirrels, too, found this a handy place to perch.

The gap would keep till warmer weather. There are few insects about in midwinter, and we wouldn't be opening the window for a while to need the screen's protection. But one night an amorous male of some sort sprayed the window with his musk, and we were glad for the coming of spring. At the first opportunity we removed the old frame and replaced the wire with strong new metal screening.

We washed the windows to let in the view and moved the feeder to the corner of the cabin, just out of easy line of sight of the big windows but far enough from them that the wildlife couldn't climb the screen; it was a tradeoff I could live with. There are muddy coon tracks up the cedar trim at the corner, but here there was no real harm done: they are signs of other life in the grove. Now when I want to watch the traffic jam at the feeder, I move it to its original hook and try to remember to put it back when I leave. My memory is quickly jogged if I forget; the first night I left it hanging before the window, the new screen was bent and scratched and there was the beginning of a tiny tear along the side.

I saw the odd, dark shape from a few feet off and noticed Bob's immediate interest. I went closer to see what my neighbor's dog inspected with such attention and found a dead raccoon in the grove. It wasn't here the day before; I was sure of it.

The storm that caused the pond's spillway to overflow and made a new creek across our drive was the remnant of a larger, deadlier weather system that devastated a 100-mile swath of neighboring Kansas. The twister was a half-mile wide and stayed on the ground for mile after terrifying mile, knocking off counties like dominoes. Perhaps it was a dying fragment of this storm that dislodged the coon from its perch in the walnut tree.

It lay in an impossible position, its spine twisted in an S, front paws in one direction, back paws the other. Perhaps it had broken its neck in the fall. Its fur was matted with mud; the animal must have been foraging out in the storm. Now its fur stood out stiff and spiky, still wet from the night's rain.

I overcame my natural reluctance—and dread of death—to seize the opportunity this happenstance closeness offered. There was something touching, childlike about the forepaws. Relaxed in death, they looked as though they could never have grasped and probed and explored. I knew different. This raccoon or one just like it was the window-screen vandal, eating delicately from the feeder it held in those fine handlike paws. Now these forepaws lay in forced repose, beyond vulnerability and use.

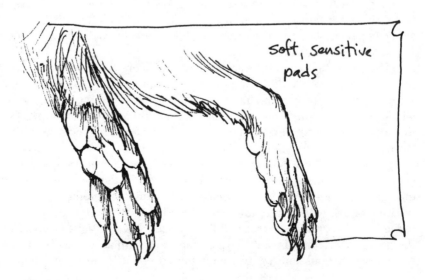

soft, sensitive pads

I dug a grave for the big animal; in a few days it would begin to stink, even in the cold, and as I dug my mood turned black as this alluvial soil. The grass around the corpse was trodden down in a fifty-foot circle. The rose-shaped tracks of dogs were everywhere; no boot tracks, I noted with relief. My "no hunting" signs went unheeded by the illiterate dogs, but I was glad not to have to deal with the trespass of their owners.

The avid, bloodthirsty howls of the neighbor's coonhounds ricocheted around the valley, full throated and eerie. My father would have smiled with pleasure, reminded of our ragtag beagles at full bay; I hear the breeding that fine-tunes these hounds, suiting them so perfectly for their bloody task, and I hate it. I shivered; my hackles rose as though a genetic memory stirred and ancient dogs splintered the air with their yammering.

It's tough to dig a grave in saturated soil; ask any sexton. The heavy mud clings to your shovel, making it hard to lift, hard to wield. The ground was woven with walnut roots, and half of my digging was the sharp jabs that slice through these ropey supports. My sneakers were old, the soles worn thin and poorly suited to digging; my foot was quickly sore as I bore down on the thin metal shoulder of the shovel and my mood did not improve. I heard those damned dogs baying off up the hill and didn't know whether I wished they would shut up or come back for another try. My fingers itched to bang skulls with a shovel.

Foolish, friendly Bob, my neighbor's young black labrador retriever, kept me company at my grim task; I was tempted to tar his black hide with the same brush I mentally used on the marauding night pack, but he was just too anxious to please. He sat nearby, or sniffed inquisitively, ineffectually, at the corpse, or inspected the tracks of his fellows, and I couldn't stay mad at him. He cocked his silly head at me as if to say "I can't believe this happened. *I'd* never do anything like that." He lies, as they say, like a dog, and we both know it.

It must have happened in the night; we had planned to stay over, but the storm kept us away. Now I was just as glad we hadn't. If I had heard the small-hour mayhem or watched the raccoon plummet into the pack of dogs, I would have been hysterical. My father's gun is long gone; I don't miss it— but I don't imagine that my shouts would have been sufficient to break the bone-deep hunting instinct.

The hole was dug and I fetched my drawing tools; I hate to waste an opportunity for study. The creature's position was disturbing; its wet, mud-caked fur was hard to capture on paper. I drew the childlike paws carefully, remembering the almost human grasp of the young raccoon on his ice cubes; the animal lacks only an opposing thumb to make its hands as dexterous as mine.

There were few signs of injury; there was only a single tooth mark on the back, no gunshot wounds; little blood. But when I turned the animal over, I recoiled in disgust.

The guts had exploded out of the body cavity on impact, no doubt what killed this hapless coon. I hurried to drag the animal into his grave. I had lost all desire to draw the details; the glossy ropes of gut had no appeal. If this *was* the raccoon I had watched at midnight raids for the last year, I would miss it greatly. And I wondered if it lost its life because it knew to come here for food.

The chocolate brown soil of Rachel's Meadow and the varieties of plant life affect the types of wildlife found here; birds love this insect smorgasbord. This secluded place with its rich, populous soil should be fine woodcock habitat. But last year at this time we were busy building the cabin; by evening I was home, exhausted, soaking away my stiffness in a hot bath. I missed their mating rituals. I never saw their spiraling flight to catch a mate, never heard their comical voices.

It's easy to recognize a woodcock's mating song if you know what to listen for; it helps if you can at least take an educated guess. That tenor croaking up on the hill; that was it. Not frogs—though similar, it was too far from water to be the resident frogs. *That* song was woodcocks. What else could it have been?

Dinner was smoking on the grill and I was hungry as a werewolf this full-moon night, but I had to go, had to get *up* there.

Harris and I had gone to the high meadow one evening the week before to look for woodcocks; Jim Wilson, of the Missouri Department of Conservation, told me the birds had begun displaying. I had forgotten that Jefferson City, where he is, was enough south of here to give the birds an early start.

It was rough going through the darkened woods; I took a sapling slap to the face; Harris slipped on the loose rocks and sat down, hard. He was sore for two days, and I looked as though I had been struck with a riding crop. Our small injuries were for nothing; the hill was deserted.

This time I went alone; I couldn't resist that pied-piper sound in the meadow; I'd follow it through hell.

But hell it decidedly was not. The air was tender with spring, the woods redolent with it. Bob, the dog, kept me company, and I feared his youthful bumbling would scare the birds away. There's no discouraging Bob, though. His good-natured friendliness is impossible to shake; always has been. If he wants to jump up, he jumps. If he wants to go with me, he goes. No protestations get through that thick head. No sharp "Go *home*, Bob" makes the least bit of difference. Like the "Far Side" cartoon, I give Bob a severe dressing down, with orders worthy of a drill sergeant: "*Down,* Bob. Go home. Get on out of here, Bob. Go! Bob, *no!*" And he hears only his name—"Bob. Bob. Bob." I swear he thinks we're going steady; he's always there, faithful as Lenny in *Of Mice and Men* and near as stupid.

To my surprise, this night he was quiet. We gained the meadow together, and rather than scaring off the birds as I had feared, he retired to the far edge of the woods to wait.

There was that sound again—the froglike "peent," followed by that strange chippering. And suddenly I saw it, flying higher and in much wider circles than I had expected. The stubby-winged bird was far above me against the darkening sky, but I knew it was a woodcock. Each time those short wings fluttered, I heard the chippering sound of wind in its primary feathers. Up and up it went, then went into a power dive, following the ancient choreography of mating.

It pulled out of the dive, then to my excitement flew just above my head across the meadow to a new display ground. I could see that darning-needle bill with its sensitive, nearly prehensile tip, silhouetted against a skyful of broken clouds. The bird probes for earthworms here in the rich dark ground, feeling them with that bill tip as surely as I would with my finger—and with considerably more enthusiasm.

The effect of this spectacular display was riveting, as if I'd been impaled by that long bill. I couldn't move; I could barely breathe. The bird dove again and again and buzzed me each time as though adding a new bit of business to the ancient ritual, ad-libbing his swooping lateral flight less than five feet above my head. I could see every detail of the feathers in the fading light.

And then I realized that this was not the only woodcock on the hill. There were at least two other birds spiraling and buzzing and chippering for prospective mates; where were the females during all these virile aerobatics?

The light was growing dimmer by the minute; I hated to walk out on the play before the final curtain. But hunger and the thought of that savory barbecue charred beyond recognition forced me to give it up for the night and feel my way back down the hill and across the creek in the gathering dark. The full moon lit my path, strobing intermittently through the bare, black branches.

The fullness of the moon extended the play's run, perhaps. When I went out before going to bed hours later, I still heard the buzzing of woodcocks in the meadow—and one, to my surprise, plying the air just above the cabin.

There is another movement in the night symphony, set to the intermittent calls of the owl and the high keening of crickets. It's a sound that rings sweet in memory, that calls up a half-formed thought I can't put down on paper, a sound you either love or hate: that of the whippoorwills. These nocturnal members of the goatsucker clan divide up the generous territory of

American
Woodcock
(_Philohela_ _minor_) whistling and chippering
overhead.

my woods among them, claiming it with their song. One night we listened as a type-A bird seemed to have downed amphetamines; its call was nearly twice as fast as the more laid-back birds near the cabin. Another was so close we heard an intake of breath like a hiccup before each call, as if drunk: "_Hic_! Whip-poor-_will_. _Hic_! Whip-poor-_will_." I called my sister in Nevada to let her hear the sound; our family always made a pilgrimage on spring nights, supplicants to the song of the whippoorwill.

It's a sound that lulls me to sleep, makes me smile into the darkness; who cares if it's a bit repetitious? Like a heartbeat to an unborn child, this constant is comfort and home to me. Not everyone agrees with me. If you let it get under your skin, you're lost. Begin to count the repetitions and I guarantee you'll be mad by midnight; one fellow was driven babbling to his liquor cabinet after counting over 2,000 reiterations of the whippoorwill's mating song.

These weak-footed birds don't really perch; they stay close to or on the ground, singing their nocturnes for anyone who will listen. You can't much help it; they're loud. When you say a whippoorwill has a big mouth, you're referring to more than the obvious physical characteristic shared by all goatsuckers—although there is that. Caprimulgidae family members fly, mouth agape, to gather in all the insects they can muster for their meals.

Another family member took to the sky above the cabin as spring brought the return of flying insects, slicing the air with long, pointed wings bent like a brace of scimitars. A flash of white in the twilight marked this as a common nighthawk—neither strictly nocturnal nor a hawk, as it turns out. The woodcocklike *peent* echoed overhead, seconds before the bird folded its wings and dived in a mating display. My field guide says this spectacular aerial maneuver produces a musical hum; I wondered where the author was standing. This bird booms, blasts, honks, whomps—reverberates—it was as though there were a novice tuba player overhead, trying out a new horn. I suppose to the tuba player's mother it might sound like a musical hum; I never fail to jump out of my skin.

We imagine the night to be quiet, restful—uneventful. In the woods it is anything but. The deer wander by in the dark, their eyes huge and glowing in my flashlight's beam. If I come too near they erupt into the darkness, snorting and whistling in alarm. The cottontails bound off with bobbing, candlelike tails. By midsummer, snowy tree crickets and katydids racket away endlessly. If I want to sleep, I stay in town. If, instead, I enjoy this dark habitat, I know where to find it—the cabin calls like a nighthawk, and I answer every chance I get.

13. Violation

The woods are deep and thick. I can't see another house from the cabin; I built the thing as far from other human habitation as possible. In the winter, from the south end of the grove, I can just make out lights on the hill and the headlamps of cars on the north road nearly 600 feet away. Sounds play hell with my carefully crafted notion of isolation. The idea of wilderness, however small, is a visual one only, nearly unbroken from spring to fall; it's blasted by the time first light rouses the neighbors, if not before. As everywhere in this country (in the world!) the sounds of jet traffic are unavoidable —here, only twenty some miles from Kansas City International Airport, the cabin seems to lie directly under an air corridor east.

As the sky changes from star-pierced blackness that becomes paler and paler as though dye were slowly diluted with clear water, I can hear the whine of cars on the back-country gravel artery of our road and on the blacktop half a mile away. Some mornings I swear I can hear the sleepy morning traffic on the state highway another mile or two up the blacktop.

I'm cursed with acute hearing; Harris calls me "hawk ears." Sounds good, and most of the time it is—when I want to hear a birdcall in the woods, when I'm listening for the footsteps of deer. But at the cabin I'd just as soon not hear the lawn mowers on the cul-de-sac on the east hill or the chainsaws in the woods. I hear voices that sound as if they are just beyond my fence line and imagine someone about to cross the clearing; I realize instead that it's the neighbors up the hill, working in their garden a quarter of a mile away.

The phone is a benign tyrant with a lousy sense of timing. Installed so Harris could reach me in an emergency, instead it rings ten times a day while I am trying to write. If I'm in the middle of a tricky watercolor wash, one guaranteed to go wrong if you abandon it for a second, the ring demands attention—*now*. Plan a break as a reward for an afternoon's work, take a soda to the bench by the creek, and the phone will call plaintively after me.

It's always those calls that seem to ring forever. I decide I can't make it back to the phone before whoever is calling gives up, settle down to enjoy my break, and it rings again and again and again. Sometimes the caller is so determined I actually make it back, out of breath and panting, trying to sound as if I hadn't just sprinted thirty yards.

I get the same kinds of calls you do; friends, business, siding salesmen, window-replacement offers. Someone wants to sell me a packet of color portraits for only twenty-five dollars. Someone else wants to know if Eugene is there. It renders the idea of a retreat, a place to work undisturbed, somewhat moot at times.

The phone was a novelty when we first installed it. Harris had begun to miss me after weeks of cabin building and was delighted to have contact reestablished. If I climbed to the top of the ladder to sand the logos off the ceiling boards or handed up load after load of scrap to Greg in the truck, Harris would choose just that time to call. I nearly ripped the thing from the wall the first day; contact was established at least six times. I still think about taking it off the hook, disconnecting the wires, silencing the ring. Instead, I'll probably do what I did at home: buy an answering machine and take one more step toward an unplanned-for civilization.

Some sounds are more ominous. We had barely begun building the cabin when one day I heard the sounds of gunfire. Close—too close; I thought I heard a bullet whiz through the trees overhead. I yelled down the creek, as loud as I could: "Hey! We're down here! Be careful where you aim."

When the firing didn't stop, I drove up toward Wendy's to see if I could tell where it was coming from; I knew it had to have been from the cul-de-sac of mobile homes on the hill, but sound is deceiving in the valley. It bounces off the limestone ridges, ricocheting around until we can't begin to tell where it originates.

It was the hill, a new neighbor right next door to Wendy. When I arrived, the man was aiming directly down the hill toward the creek, in the general direction of the cabin, firing a twenty-two pistol into the woods.

"Uh, excuse me," I said as I walked up to him from behind, trying not to startle him. "How far does that thing shoot?"

"Pretty far—but not nearly as far as the .357 Magnum I was using a while ago. That thing can shoot a mile or more. Why?"

Why. Why indeed; I struggled to control my voice. My dad taught me gun safety early on; never, never shoot downhill into woods you don't know; never shoot toward habitation; always target practice into a solid earth wall that will stop your bullets. This guy had just violated all three.

"We're just up the creek, building a cabin; you nearly blew our heads off."

"Oh, my God—I didn't know anybody was down there. I'm sorry."

"People walk in those woods all the time, you know. Kids play there. People hunt." I laid it on thick; I wanted to impress on him the seriousness of what he might have done, and he was shaken when I left. He just hadn't thought.

Scant comfort if it's your head that's blown off. A slug from a Magnum could not only have easily traveled the half mile to the cabin, it would have blasted right through the wall as though it were paper. When I called my friend, the chief of police, to ask him about relative range of these firearms, he told me that a bullet fired at a forty-degree angle from a .357 can travel a mile and a half, and, to my surprise, so can a .22. My "no hunting" signs are next to worthless when just one guy isn't thinking. Our isolation, such an advantage normally, put us squarely into terra incognita—he didn't know we were there. And what about the rest of the gun-bearing citizens on the hill? Down the creek? Across the road? Gunfire never fails to make me jump.

In the country, the celebration of Independence Day begins at least two weeks before the day itself. Sometime during the previous month, bright yellow-and-white-striped tents sprout along the highway, meant to convey a sense of fun and excitement. Disgruntled instead, I grouse about the coming artillery barrage, building a schizophrenic half anger, half anxiety. At first there are only brief firefights, a skirmish or two of firecrackers, the quick crackle of lit gunpowder. I invariably forget it is fireworks and look toward the woods as though I could penetrate their heavy cover, wondering if someone is not thinking. As the day itself approaches, the noise is like occupying the next hill over from Gettysburg. The barrage is nearly constant; star shells split the night and any thought of peace is quelled. It's a long time until cease-fire.

When dark falls on the Fourth itself, I simply stay away. The first year we owned the cabin we spent the night listening to the boom and crack of high-powered firecrackers and the explosions that announce the occasional chrysanthemum of light in the sky; sleep was impossible. After two years of drought, fireworks and bottle rockets that would have been banned in town rained down on tinder-dry woods. In the country, anything goes: Fourth of July revelers recognize no legal bans—or are subject to none—as though the right to bear firecrackers were protected by the Constitution. And it's not just in the country. When we returned home we found a spent rocket on our deck that had burned a hole in the wood a quarter of an inch deep before it died. It wasn't an easy choice; I wanted to be there to douse the cabin if need be, but home and pets come first. If something takes incoming on the

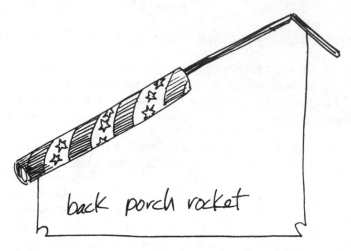

back porch rocket

Fourth, burning to the ground as an old friend's home did in the city, better it should be the retreat than the primary residence, no matter how much I love it.

Hunting season is the same—only longer and more dangerous. The opening morning of deer season saw the crackle of gunfire even before the light strengthened into day. Hunters must have the best chance that first day when the deer are not expecting to be shot at—or perhaps it was only that it was a Saturday. At any rate, I was awakened at the thin, gray corner of daybreak by nearby cannonades, and I rose to pace and curse. Our place backs up on two sides to woods I don't own: the long, back dimension to the south and a narrow arm to the west. Hunters seemed to be stationed along every inch.

I had checked our own woods time and again for deer stands. A nearby neighbor told me he had found a stand in a tree on his land, destroyed it, and come back to find it replaced as though it had every right to be there. If I still owned my shotgun I'd have been tempted to remove an illegal stand by blasting it to Swiss cheese.

Not that deer stands are themselves illegal. It's perfectly kosher to set up a stand above a deer trail, sit high where the animals seldom look, and blast away at them. Kosher, but disquieting; I keep expecting equity. It's being on posted land that would have made a stand illegal, and I had every intention of making my feelings known if I found one.

During our open house, the kids found plenty to do in the creek; construction engineering must be inborn, the desire to dam up flowing water as instinctive as breathing. When everyone had gone home I inspected the waterfall and its deep pool to see just what they had built for me—one of the boys told me they overheard me discussing a footbridge with Greg and took over the project themselves.

It was quite a feat; no wonder they had been nowhere in evidence, quiet except for an occasional heavy splash and a burst of laughter. The waterfall's catch pool, now a small, impounded body of water, was effectively cut off from the rest of the stream by a twelve-inch-high dam, straight as a yardstick —"we built you a dam and a bridge at the same time," the boys told me. The pool no longer had free egress into the creek, though it reasserted its downstream imperative through leaks and trickles.

I couldn't help but be impressed. The huge rock that had been ripped away from the face of the falls by tons of water in flood, propped up like a dictionary between stacks of rocky bookends, had been liberated and now lay flat on the creek bed. The gravel bar below the pool was nearly featureless—the rocks that were folded there like raisins in rice pudding had gone to make up the dam. The deep pool itself was the recipient of an astounding number of rocks of all shapes and sizes, tossed there by the younger children just to see the splash.

"Wow," I told Judy, the last of our departing guests. "Come look. You're not going to believe this!"

"No wonder I hadn't seen a kid in hours," she said as she surveyed the dam. "The corps of engineers couldn't have built a better one."

The next day I tackled a creek restoration project of my own. "Something there is that doesn't love a wall." Robert Frost said that. I think it must apply to the wet wall of a dam, as well, if my sudden need to rear-

the dam/bridge

range this tiny barricade was any indication. I couldn't wait to free the big pool, breach the dam, monkey-wrench the newly built bridge, and return things to a semblance of naturalness. My fingers itched to get into the creek, up to my knees like a kid, and find where each stone had come from.

It was a gigantic jigsaw puzzle. The dark-stained rocks were from the submerged area near the crossing; the moss-furred ones, from the grassy overhang where they remained wet most of the year. The clean light gray stones must have come from above the falls, and the red-brown ones were the undersides of darker, more naturally colored rocks. I flipped them over in place and they disappeared into happy anonymity.

Some I couldn't place at all; they were just too nondescript. They weren't without a good use, though; the new bench by the creek, I noticed, was in some danger of being undercut by high water. The bank nearby seemed six inches closer than when we sank the pilings and set them in concrete. So these homeless stones became not riffraff but riprap, holding the dirt in place against the next small flood.

The big dictionary stone that sat diagonally upright after last fall's high water was more of a challenge. I lifted it as we had the cabin's first wall, and soon I had it propped at approximately the angle I was used to, propped and supported by a jumble of smaller rocks. I'm not as artful as Mother Nature; the thing looked a bit awkward, a bit raw. But after the first high water I couldn't tell the difference between my work and the water's.

High water would have taken care of everything, all by itself. I knew that. Each time the creek runs bank full down to the Missouri River, I look to see what has changed. There's no way I could begin to be so carelessly, so artlessly a stonemason. When the creek itself moves its rocks a bit farther downstream, they are seated with a bed of midsized stones and mortared with a loose accretion of gravel; the variety of size and shape can't be duplicated, not by a Japanese garden master.

But I couldn't wait for high water; this was a do-it-yourself project. The concept of time — natural time, endless, moving, flowing time — was as dammed in my mind as the creek, and I had to initiate change on my own. And so I spent an hour or two getting as muddy and hilarious as the boys had. There was muck to my elbows and grit under my fingernails, but each new rivulet that flowed free — muddy at first, but then clear and cold — felt right, felt good. I startled away a huge bullfrog tadpole, which disappeared into the still-opaque pool upstream; I strained to see it again to discover if it had begun to grow its vestigial legs. I watched for crayfish shells here, where they were before the dam; the raccoons visit to hunt them each night. I stepped into a side pool that was much deeper than it appeared, and water rose over the tops of my Wellingtons and into my socks. I wiped my hands on my backside; my jeans were cool and wet and smelled of creek water.

178

But the effort pleased me. I sat on the bench with a cup of coffee and looked out over the pool and the little waterfall, hopping back up a time or two to adjust a too-uniform placement of stepping-stones or to tuck a smaller rock beside a large one in imitation of my tutor. I felt better. Like a dog that must rearrange its bed to suit itself after another has intruded, I felt the need to reestablish my claim.

Not that I wasn't glad to have my visitors, not that I didn't enjoy the easy camaraderie; I did. But now the place was mine again, mine and the creek's, and I surveyed my work with pleasure.

I hoped no one came to visit for a while, not one of the proud young dam builders anyway. How could I explain away my craving to demolish their efforts and as speedily as possible?

As Judy said, I wouldn't remember where the rocks were after the next high water, but Andy and Eddie and Billy Joe will remember their afternoon and evening in the creek for a long time. Just so they didn't see that I erased them so quickly.

Invited guests are one thing; trespassers quite another. I am territorial as a mockingbird; this is *my* place, and I am uncomfortable with evidence of trespass.

Out here in the country trespass is not to be taken too lightly. Vandalism and theft are all too common. When they were younger, the boys in the housing development up the road were infamous for their exploits, stocking up on other people's goods. So far, all that has disappeared from our place has been a bit of lumber from a pile beside the deck, saved to build steps. It was a benign disappearance—the pieces looked like scrap, and I could use stone instead. My bird feeders and outdoor furniture have stayed safely on the deck; the cabin itself has been untouched.

Patti's cabin has been vandalized and broken into more than once, this last time with a spectacular degree of sheer stupidity. The would-be thieves wrecked the doorjamb but failed to make entry, never noticing that the adjacent window was already open. Ann tells me her Colorado retreat has been broken into four times. Most recently, the thieves made off with all her furniture; "not worth much," she said, "but it all fit. It worked. It was my own."

I feel that way about the odd collection of junk and hand-me-downs and make-dos that fill our cabin. I *like* them. They fit. I don't want my nest taken over by a cowbird, my useless treasures stolen. I don't even want them touched by a stranger. They have my scent on them.

It's an uncomfortable tightrope to walk, this iffy question of right-of-way, considering my own tendency to wander. I'm uncomfortable with strangers here; I'll admit it. When I come up the woods path to find an outsider fishing from the dam, my first inclination is to fade back into the woods, take a different tack—become invisible.

I know that if you look quick—and at the right time—you can see the cabin from the road. The tunnel of trees provides a brief window. We are *not* invisible here, though if I could have pulled it off, I would have been.

We're close. There's only that one split second when you can spot us from the road as you barrel by in your car—a thin crescent of time made more noticeable by our lights at night. One evening after the veil of leaves had begun to fall, I was unnerved by a car that must have made that connection, seen us, stopped, and backed up for a better look. I could not make out the car's occupants; it was twilight and too far in any case as I stood on the deck peering into the half-light. But I knew they were peering back at me; I

A few tracks on the drive.

could feel myself silhouetted against the cabin door, against that warm incandescence.

I don't own the air. I'm no stranger to curiosity. I empathize with these unseen lookers, but I was glad when they drove on. I want to watch, not be watched.

Sometimes these reminders of the outside world strike much deeper and hit a vein of buried fear you didn't know existed. Last summer I hurried to the cabin, hungry for the peace it afforded, and found the road nearly blocked with sheriffs' patrol cars; I had passed an ambulance on my way out from town and heard the sirens from my backyard.

Had there been an accident? Was someone hurt? Was something wrong at Donny's? The questions careened through my mind at speeds too fast to track, but I knew I couldn't simply turn down the dirt path to the cabin without asking them. With a shot of instant paranoia infusing my veins, I wondered if I'd be allowed to, anyway.

A gray car sat empty near the drive. There were at least five patrol cars parked at sudden-stop, cop-show angles along the road; two were by the pond, and I was terrified that someone had drowned there. Mr. Jackson had told me the winter before that he had stopped neighborhood boys who had ridden their bikes across the frozen surface, not knowing if the ice was thick enough to hold them or not. Now, in full summer, the coolness must be inviting.

I was almost afraid to ask.

"What happened, officer? This is my place; is it all right for me to go in?"

"Sure, ma'am; someone was shot here."

I couldn't think of anything to say for a moment. "On *my* place?"

"Yes, ma'am. Here by the road, about fifteen minutes ago. The guy ran into the woods, that direction," he told me, pointing toward the cabin. "I can't tell you any more than that."

"But was he killed?" I had to know.

"Not yet, ma'am."

Oh, my God. I felt as though all the blood had drained from my body. I stumbled back to the car and started it up, pulled down the drive, and tried to act normal. There wasn't a chance. My heart was beating as though I had run a long way and was badly out of shape, a painful thumping that wouldn't subside. I tried to sit and couldn't. I tried to work and failed.

I gave it up and walked back to the road, this time through the woods to the road where Donny stood. He had seen the whole thing; he had been the one to call the sheriff.

"What happened?"

"I don't know, really," he said. "The guy was being kidnapped, locked in the trunk of his car; he'd already been shot about six times and tied up. He got loose, kicked his way out of the trunk, and somehow ran off into your woods. The other guys were still after him, shooting. They shot him four or five more times."

It sounded like the Old West. It sounded like Beirut. It most definitely did not sound like my peaceful gravel road, my woods, my sanctuary.

"I yelled that I was calling the police," Donny said. "The men that had been chasing him jumped back into the other car that had been following the gray one and peeled out, throwing gravel half a mile. I was afraid to go in after this guy; I knew he'd been shot but I didn't know if he was armed. I just called the sheriff."

It hadn't taken long for them to arrive. The ambulance got here first, but the paramedics are instructed not to take a chance if someone may shoot. They couldn't go in after the man until the sheriff came.

Amazingly, he dragged himself up out of the woods, shot in the head and the arm and the abdomen, and walked out by himself. In the end, they say he had been shot a total of five times; fewer than the barrage Donny had heard but more than I could imagine a body sustaining and still being able to walk. His shoe lay beside the road, and his blood stained the pale limestone gravel.

It was drugs. It always is, it seems, though the story is garbled and as many layered as an onion. The man lived, amazingly; the story was that he had been called to his would-be killer's house ostensibly so he could be repaid $5,000 owed him — $5,000 advanced for dope or as a loan, the story varies here. At any rate, the second man had planned a rather violent default on his loan; he had others there to help him shoot the victim and rid themselves of his body, planning to dump him someplace in the country. But they botched the job, even after shooting their victim and binding him with duct tape.

It wasn't known for some time if the man would live or if he would be able to tell police what had happened; he was unconscious for a while after his ordeal and his Herculean effort.

The sheriff and his men stayed at my place the rest of the day, looking for evidence. They returned the next day and combed through the woods and weeds. The victim's gun (or the shooter's) was never found; it may still be there. The sheriff told me if I found anything suspicious, anything out of the ordinary, to let it be; just call. I had no desire to find anything at all, and I avoided the path for months after my first morbid foray.

The peace was shattered, shot with as many holes as the victim himself. The presence of the sheriff and his men made the woods seem ominous. I jumped at every sound, running to the door of the cabin to see if someone were shooting; I locked the screen door behind me as though its fine nylon mesh might deter a shell. I looked for bullet holes in my walls and was amazed not to find any there. I wondered if the perpetrators—still, some of them, at large—might return to look for their gun.

The story emerged slowly over the next few weeks; the shooter was a young man I knew slightly; he had lived a few blocks from me in town for a time, and it was hard to picture him involved in this sad affair. Rumors flew; I never did make sense of it. But eventually all those involved were caught and brought to trial. The man I knew may serve thirty years in the state penitentiary; the victim, who lost an eye in the attack, returned to thank Donny and his family for saving his life.

And the cabin returned to a kind of peace. No longer an idyllic one, no safe Camelot; touched by the ugliness of a drug deal gone sour and of attempted murder. I no longer hear guns in the woods, except during hunting season; I no longer lock the screen. And I no longer imagine the place inviolable. It's just as well. After the shooting, I felt vulnerable, paranoid; it's made me more cautious.

The memory is fading, but the image is always present, on some level; it doesn't take much to bring it to the fore. I watch for tracks each time I come; strange footprints are alarming. This winter I was so taken aback by a footprint I didn't recognize in the mud of a January thaw that I wondered for days whose it might have been. I tried to find evidence of where the boot's wearer had been, tracking like an amateur Olaus Murie.

Amateur it was, too—the footprint was my own. My insulated boots, seldom worn, have an unusual tread, one that I don't see often enough to remember. I was mortified when I realized I had tracked myself for a week, wondering who this stranger was who had made himself so at home.

Game trail leads
back into deep, cool
shadows.

184

14. A Fine Equilibrium

I look for balance, tightroping between the desire to make as little impact as possible and the need to be here, walking the paths every day to learn what's happening in the woods and meadows and up by the pond. The difficulty rests chiefly in how I choose to look at my part in the scheme of the woods, my own niche in the ecosystem. If I am an outlander, bent—as my ancestors were—on settling, taming, then my marks are damaging and I make myself unhappy when I see them. If, instead, I feel as much a part of all of this as the deer and the herons and the ubiquitous raccoons, the marks I make are as natural as theirs. My cabin is simply a larger nest, my muddy driveway no more than a game path in the woods. It's a difficult tightrope to walk, and my balance is none too steady.

My paths are inevitable, of course; to get from here to there I find myself using the same traces as I did the day before, the week before, and hope it doesn't reflect a certain sameness in my thinking. As Thoreau noted after leaving Walden, "It is remarkable how easily and insensibly we fall into a particular route, and make a beaten track for ourselves. I had not lived there a week before my feet wore a path from my door to the pond-side; and though it is five or six years since I trod it, it is still quite distinct....The surface of the earth is soft and impressible by the feet of men; and so with the paths the mind travels."

The paths to creek and woods are beaten flat by my own feet, but they're not my paths alone; squirrels and woodchucks and skunks use them as game trails; deer tracks are impressed in the mud. Birds hunt along these paths, listening for worms and grubs beneath the soil, and butterflies travel

185

here from nectar to nectar. Spiders fish for insects, hanging their steel-strong nets across the way, waiting for certain prey. "The path of least resistance" is a common with all life; we followed game trails to find our way here in the first place. I accept the perplexity and keep them open for our mutual benefit, roaring through the woods in deep summer with Harris's weed whacker. When my neighbor comes with his big brush hog and tractor to clear the drive and the path around the walnut grove, the foot-wide path becomes a sixteen-foot swath. In this disturbed area, the brown-eyed Susans that filled the spaces between the trees that first summer carpet the path with gold, encouraged by the sudden lack of competition. Ragweed takes hold as though delighted, waiting impatiently for autumn and allergy season; poison ivy is its most enthusiastic rival.

I try to beat down my desire to rearrange. Planting nonindigenous flowers or plants would defeat my purpose: to learn what is here and why. But I couldn't quite resist "fixing" the existing landscape when it came to planting a pair of white dogwoods near the cabin's deck. These are indeed indigenous—to the Missouri of a hundred miles or so south at any rate—and I stretched the truth in favor of the dogwoods' incandescent glow in the April woods. We pamper these young beauties, carrying water to them from the drying summer creek, mulching them, pruning overhanging branches.

No sense fighting it for the most part; I'm not interested in landscaping but in the land itself. It's too lusty an environment for city plants in any case, too full of variables. The petunias that Patti gave us were spindly and sparsely flowered within a month. The pot of mixed geraniums, bug-eaten and yellow, dropped most of their leaves by midsummer in spite of diligent care.

Even the dogwoods are cause for a good ribbing. At our open house our friend Bill took one look at the young trees and said, "Sure, that's what I'd do in the middle of a forest: take one look at the woods and say 'what this place needs is a few more *trees*.'"

The cabin works as I had hoped it would, allowing me to watch unobserved the life of the walnut grove—or actually attracting that life. The feeders and the mineral block are artificial lures, it's true, but the chance to sketch and observe wildlife close up is too good to pass up. The skinks and moths and spiders need no invitation; they accept our little edifice as just another tree in the forest, weaving their webs or being caught in them, searching among the siding for prey. A day or two after the window screens were up, an opportunistic moth laid her eggs in the tiny wire interstices as though in a carton from the grocer's, a few eggs short of a dozen in a double row down the screen.

One day my hackles rose in prickly waves; I had the sensation of being watched as I sat at my drawing board. Not fifteen yards from me, a doe stood regarding me with her cautious gaze. These were mixed feelings indeed; the deer was eating the branches of the dogwood tree I had nursed so carefully through the drought. But she fixed me with questioning eyes as though asking if her presence was not, after all, what I had come for.

It was. She browsed quietly on the young tree for fully five minutes before she moved across the clearing to the mineral block—the first time I had ever seen evidence of use, besides the salt-loving butterflies that congregated there. She left her delicate, cloven tracks impressed deep into the salt-softened soil.

The rivalry of the squirrels is a never-ending source of amusement. One, relaxed beyond the usual anxious chittering after a good altercation with a smaller animal, rested his chin on his paws and napped, suspended between a Y of twigs by the feeder. Before I could find a blank page in my sketchbook, he heard me and disappeared.

One night triplet raccoons invaded the bird feeder and we listened, laughing under the covers, to the mammalian equivalent of a fuss among siblings. At first the youngsters chattered quietly, chirring and peeping to one another; then, as one reached for something another wanted, there was a quick skirmish. Pandemonium erupted until ownership was established, then the sweet chirrings resumed as though nothing had happened.

A young skink found the cabin and environs to his liking. I was surprised to discover him climbing the sheer face of the new cabin wall as though it

Triplets at the feeder.

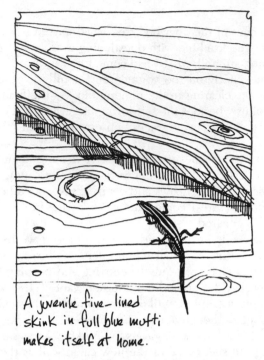

A juvenile five-lined
skink in full blue mufti
makes itself at home.

were Yosemite's Half Dome, but those long toes found plenty of purchase on the rough-sawn cedar without need for ropes or crampons.

The immature five-lined skink *(Eumeces fasciatus)* sports a bright blue tail that acts as warning or signal to protect young from a hungry adult male —and it seems to work. The bright-tailed juveniles are allowed to wear their colors, staying on the aggressive adults' territory with no harm done; perhaps the blue color is the equivalent of a white flag.

This yellow-striped whiz kid has the run of the place, dancing straight up the cedar-clad walls as though they were its natural habitat. I would have expected to find these parti-colored creatures in the nearby woods; an adult skink near the creek skittered anxiously off across the rocks before it made for the roots of an overhanging oak. It was much more somberly dressed than the juvenile. The subtle tans and deep browns made the little reptile nearly invisible when it stopped on the bark; only when it resumed its bow-legged, swaying gait did I see where it went.

It takes time and lots of it, to see all there is to see. Patience is no longer a virtue but a necessity. The birds and mammals, reptiles and amphibians here are not interested in entertaining us; at best, they tolerate us with a kind of wary disdain. They accept us only briefly.

Wildlife photographers put in hours of fieldwork—a lifetime of hours— to catch those scenes that appear so effortlessly happenstance, investing thousands of dollars in telephoto lenses and camera equipment, and still I expect to see the whiskers on my local woodchuck with my unassisted eye. And once in a while I do, though certainly not with the regularity that I see birds at my feeder. Mammals are far more secretive, far more wary, and streak for cover when we appear. Many are nocturnal; I'm not. About the time the resident raccoons come on watch, I'm heading for my covers.

More often than not the sound of their footsteps on the deck sounds reveille. As they become more used to us and the sure thing of the birdseed, they make our place a nightly stopover. They appear almost as soon as we turn out the lights.

One night we had raccoon wars on the deck and under the cabin until nearly 2:00 A.M. as the territorial creatures fought over a handful of seeds. There was a constant caterwauling, punctuated by hisses, grunts, growls, and chirrs, and the whole was set to the percussion of thumps and bumps as raccoon bodies careened into the foundation posts or banged against the underside of my floor. The voices sounded to be a variety of ages, from young kits to testy adults; I suspected a mother raccoon had her young ones out for fast-food when the big male came on the scene, and the mother let him know what she thought of his intrusion—over a period of hours.

I could never prove my hypothesis. Each time I'd crawl out of bed and switch on the deck light or shine my flashlight into the bushes, there would be an unbroken silence. There was not a sign of a coon up the surrounding walnut trees. Nothing sat hunched under the cabin floor. Nothing skittered off down the path. It was as though this brouhaha were noise only, slam-dancing against the small hours of the night.

But one young raccoon has apparently accepted our presence. One evening we sat by the outdoor fireplace, savoring the unseasonably cool weather; if it were always like this in June, Missouri would be a mecca for tourists. The coon seemed to enjoy it as much as we, beating his fellows to the birdseed. We were talking quietly when a head appeared above the edge of the deck. Black eyes looked at us without a trace of fear. Only a natural caution lit their depths, and the young animal came right on, scaling the feeder post like a lineman. He hoisted himself over the edge of the platform, squeezed through the opening of the roofed feeder, and snaked around to the open side, sitting not five feet from us.

"Look," Harris said, unbelieving.

"I *saw* it; he's getting bold, isn't he?"

And apparently our low-voiced conversation was no more threatening than it had been when he was under the deck; the animal went on about his business, glancing at us occasionally to make sure we hadn't moved. He lost his composure only when we made the mistake of addressing him directly: "How ya doin', fella?" Harris asked.

It was as though the raccoon couldn't believe he had been spoken to. He raised up to his full length, standing on hind legs like a fat meerkat, and looked piercingly at us over the deck railing for a full twenty seconds.

And that was that. We had apparently broken protocol, been unspeakably rude, and he skated down the pole and off under the deck again, to wait for us to vacate his turf. Not, I might add, particularly patiently; we listened to his ungracious chirrs and bumps for another ten minutes until we took the hint and went to bed, leaving him to the territory of night.

Not all the resident raccoons respect the arbitrary boundaries of light and dark. Like youngsters everywhere, the growing raccoon kits seem to need to test their frontiers and learn their limitations. One late afternoon as I made to leave the walnut grove to the original inhabitants for a time, I stepped out to hear a clunk and quick scuffle just by the trash can. I assumed it was the gray squirrel, back for a last feeder run, and I looked for it up the tree less than two feet from the back of the cabin.

It was, instead, a pair of young raccoons. They skittered up the tree and perched just overhead in the U-shaped crotch, staring at me as though they'd never seen such a thing.

"Didn't your mother tell you raccoons are nocturnal?"

And again, these kits didn't care to be addressed. The larger of the two climbed up one side of the trunk, the other took the high road, and they

Young raccoons up a tree in broad daylight — no one has told them they are nocturnal.

paused at the next cross-branch to regard me solemnly, apparently wondering what breach of etiquette I was capable of next. When I remembered my sketchbook and popped inside to get it, they hightailed it on up the tree and plastered themselves tight as a bandage against an upper branch, only daring to stick a nose over the edge to ascertain my position. I went into town to pick up Harris for a night at the cabin and the kits were still there when we returned; they didn't abandon the high ground until we turned out the lights and went to bed.

Sometimes these encounters are startling in the extreme. I've never gotten used to the idea of sharing wild space with an animal as large as a deer. A male deer can weigh up to 300 pounds and more; one record Missouri buck tipped the scales at 369. A full-grown doe may weigh nearly as much as a buck (though usually they are considerably lighter). But big as they are, they're elusive. Most days they leave only footprints to mark their passage, assuring me they have passed this way; they trail up the hill through the woods or beside the creek, not twenty feet from the cabin. Once in a while an adult watches me guardedly; unlike the dogwood-eating doe, they seldom stay to see what I'm about but turn tail and disappear—with equanimity or hysteria, it depends on something I cannot see.

But a few weeks ago I took a slow walk up through the woods to check on the progress of the blackberries. It hadn't rained in weeks, and I imagined the fruits would have dried to brown, hard knots as they did last summer; it was hot, and I was tired, only half awake. I moved as though in a dream, taking my time as I pushed my way through the wall of heat and humidity.

I heard a sharp whistle and a rustling at the edge of the woods, just where the path emerges into the meadow; I thought in those few seconds that there must be a large bird in the trees above me. But suddenly the rustle became a thunder of tiny hooves, and a fawn barreled toward me down the path.

It couldn't have been more than six or seven weeks old, still big of ear and eye (wild-eyed, too, now, in panic) and wearing a honey-colored coat still spotted with childhood's marks. It came on a dead run, and I realized that if I didn't move it would run right through me—this was a familiar path to the frightened little creature; I had seen its dainty tracks only minutes before. I stepped aside like a matador and it bolted past, eye whites glaring in alarm, drilling new heart-shaped holes into the damp earth with those flashing hooves. It turned aside into the woods twenty yards farther down the hill; my heartbeats were as loud in my ears as its hooves had been, and I wished I had reached out to touch it.

I heard another whistle in the woods where it had gone, then the stamping of hooves in the meadow above me. I turned to hurry on up the hill but too late. The doe had disappeared into the trees south of the track, whistling and snorting to her fawn as she bounded off, calling it to her. I was sorry to have been the cause of the wild fright I'd seen in the fawn's eyes, hoping they would find one another in the woods but pleased nonetheless by the encounter.

A buck deer had fallen by the creek—victim of a hunter's bullet or of old age; his bones were strung like ivory beads in the grass, his skull still proud with its rack of antlers. It must have died in the autumn, then, for them to be still in place on the skull—normally a buck loses his antlers after the autumn rut when hormones return to normal. They've served their purpose as excellent dueling tools and won't be replaced till next fall. It's this that separates antlers from horns; the latter stay put.

It's unusual to find antlers in the woods; they're a nutrient-rich source of minerals. Small rodents gnaw them to nothing, and these are indeed cross-hatched with the tiniest of teeth marks along their length; something got the good from them.

I picked up the pieces—as many as I could hold in my two arms—and staggered back to the cabin with a load of bones: tibias, vertebras, jawbones, ribs, and skull. I had no idea why. The trek, through the heat and chest-high brush, up and down the rugged hills that surround my place, was ridiculously difficult. A hundred times I told myself to put down my prize and come back for it later with a bag or day pack—and a hundred times I refused. Too likely to forget where I laid these shining white relics, too easy to get turned around among these limestone bluffs; besides, the creek forks and twists like Wyoming meanders. I wasn't that familiar with landmarks—not just yet. I held on, juggling bits and pieces, sweating and swearing, until at last I made the cabin and dropped my load on the deck. All, that is, but the skull. I guarded that delicate beauty as though it were a flower.

The skull looks down from the shelf over my bed. I look for it, first thing, when I wake in the night and smile into the darkness; I like the intimacy with wildness it implies. The thing glows white in the moonlight that pours in the window as if it had a candlepower of its own, a sentience beyond understanding.

My itch to colonize doesn't seem to be fading; once you learn how to build, it's hard to put the knowledge in cold storage. There's undeniable satisfaction in seeing something you only imagined suddenly standing before you as concrete fact—satisfaction and an appetite for encore.

I've gotten the desire for a house on the hill pretty well in hand; *living* this close to my retreat would defeat its purpose. Financial considerations helped. A house—as we had found out in the beginning—would cost many times what the cabin did, and if we had tried to build *that* this year instead of last, the money simply wouldn't have been there.

But a dock or a fishing pier out into the pond would be lovely, and another pond, this one in Rachel's Meadow—with an island in it, perhaps. An observation deck where the house might have gone could overlook the pond—or, as a friend suggests, a gazebo.

I'd love a place to put things away for the winter, something more protected and less unsightly than shoving them under the deck. A little shed, then, kept small and simple this time. How big would it need to be to hold a cart and the twig furniture and Harris's old lawn mower—and the folding chairs and birdseed and barbecue equipment? The thing grows in my mind as the cabin did, a Trump Tower of sheds.

The creek's crossing is difficult, especially in winter when the stones are locked in a polished armor of ice. In high water it's impossible, forcing me to change my tack toward the cabin, to walk in from another direction altogether. This thoroughly salutary experience prevents boredom and keeps me from taking the place for granted; I see much that is new when I am forced to take another path. It's another good reason *not* to build a footbridge.

But how about a roofed picnic table and benches on the flat spot by the creek, like the ones at the campsites in nearby Wallace State Park? It would be a great place to observe, to work and sketch under cover from the rain and sun.

I read of Edwin Way Teale's room in the woods made of brush, where he sat to observe the wildlife, and eye my brush piles with a certain greedy purposefulness. If they survive the voracious appetite of the outdoor fireplace, I know just where I'd put such a rough edifice to best advantage.

We buckled under our own interior pressure and built a permanent bench overlooking the pond, just between the big oak tree and the red cedar, where we sit to watch the carp move silently through the water. Beside the creek, an old wooden porch swing—sans chains to swing it from —rests on treated wooden pilings that turn it, too, into a bench, just where we used to sit on our folding chairs to admire the changing water. We constructed a step out of the outhouse to replace a rocking length of six-by-six; the step became, instead, a small stoop, then a miniature deck, which then still needed a step to reach the ground. But even that was not enough; a second step, this one of the stones from the creek, bridges the space between that step and the path that falls more steeply away from the door than I had calculated. The new construction ties that tall outbuilding nicely to the earth, grounding it comfortably, but it never fails to make me laugh; it looks as though I should put a small chair and a hibachi there and wait my turn for the john.

It begins to feel like I am building a compound here; it's Hyannis Port, not rural Missouri. Rather than the single, low-impact shed-sized cabin, alone in the woods, I imagine accoutrements—or build them, concrete and visible. Charming ones, to be sure, but still—more signs of my trespass here, pushing back the wilderness with a handsaw and a hammer.

There is an end to it, however. There are things I find I cannot touch. The meadows go unmowed, and the fruit-laden brambles stake out their turf more aggressively each year. The wildflower carpet in the midst of the walnut grove stays, waist high and weedy; perhaps one year it will bloom with gold as it did the first time I saw it. There are dead limbs in most of the walnuts, threatening mayhem with every stiff breeze; we waited on the deck for dinner guests one evening when one of these broke loose, hit the cabin's metal roof with a crash, and fell heavily to the deck just inches away from us. Half an hour later and someone could have been hurt. But I see the woodpecker holes Swiss-cheesed into the dead wood and watch the variety of Picidae-family members and their beneficiaries—the chickadees, screech owls, and squirrels, which find their ready-made nesting holes to their liking —and leave them be.

The cabin is an adjunct to the land that surrounds it, a part of this place for as long as board joins board—one woman's contribution to the informal family history of underground architecture. And once it was finished, I could step off the plateau of the finite back into the infinite, the timeless, boundary-less flow of woods and water. I liked it better. The time spent ensnarled in the day-to-day concerns of building, concerns that devoured the hours, was time-out; I missed too much. It was our first spring here; morels and Dutchman's-breeches in a tiny limestone glade by the creek, the building of nests, and the winding tracks of fawns passed without my notice. The experience was a good one—overall. I learned and enjoyed the learning, and the payoff was big-time: a building made of peace.

A flood the second spring brought home the vulnerability of our constructions. The heaviest rain—nine inches in neighboring Lawson, just upstream—hit the drainage basin of the Fishing River, filling and spreading till it resembled the Mississippi. Harris and I stared dry-mouthed at the angry brown water near our house in town and instantly forgot about our errand.

"The cabin!"

"If the river is this high, what about our creek?" I asked no one in particular. "What about the pond?"

"We'd better get out there."

But to our relief, it had withstood the storm. The creek was bank-full and roaring; the pond was turbid and running over its spillway. The driveway ran brown, turning the space between the cabin and the creek into a broad, shallow river; water flowed under the floor joists and threatened to back up against the foundation pilings.

It's not entirely fanciful to wonder about the cabin's fate. The dam just up the hill had failed before, and my explorations in this second spring, when the leaves were off and the details were easily visible, had revealed two things. An Osage orange tree had been ripped from its upright position near the creek and lay pointing downstream like an arrow. And across the creek a huge gravel bar rose like a beached whale, its summit nearly level with the cabin's floor.

Both were old; the Osage orange is long dead, and the gravel bar sprouts trees well beyond the adolescent stage; perhaps the force that created these somewhat ominous portents swept them downstream when the dam broke, releasing tons of implacable water. Perhaps the woods and new ponds, the yards and fences upstream will dam further floods, dissipating their force and keeping the tiny wet-weather creek to its banks, as it has been each time there was a threat of high water. Our neighbors, those who have lived here longest, told us the creek never floods. But still....

The cabin has developed an identity of its own, a shifting sensibility that just escapes the chameleon. You'd think that four walls and a roof, nails and windows and foundation posts would be as concrete as anything you could imagine—like Popeye, it "am what it am"—but it's not so simple. In building inspector's parlance, the cabin is an outbuilding, a shed—it has no plumbing to bump it into dwelling category, and it does just fine without it. I carry in a gallon of water at a time for drinking and wash my hair in creek water.

To my insurance man, on the other hand, it *is* a dwelling, a "second home." If I call it a studio, it becomes a business and must be insured under a different set of criteria. My neighbor's little girl says "I like your little house." My friend Ann Zwinger calls it my "elegant, eloquent space in the woods." It is all of these and more. It's Base Camp One, shelter from the storm; an observer's blind, a writer's retreat, an artist's studio; home away from home; a naturalist's cabin; delight.